175 best
babycakes®
cake pops
recipes

175 best babycakes® cake pops recipes

Kathy Moore & Roxanne Wyss

Robert
ROSE

For complete cataloguing information, see page 230.

Disclaimer
The recipes in this book have been carefully tested by our kitchen and our tasters. To the best of our knowledge, they are safe and nutritious for ordinary use and users. For those people with food or other allergies, or who have special food requirements or health issues, please read the suggested contents of each recipe carefully and determine whether or not they may create a problem for you. All recipes are used at the risk of the consumer. Consumers should always consult the Babycakes manual for recommended procedures and cooking times.

We cannot be responsible for any hazards, loss or damage that may occur as a result of any recipe use.

For those with special needs, allergies, requirements or health problems, in the event of any doubt, please contact your medical adviser prior to the use of any recipe.

Design and production: Daniella Zanchetta/PageWave Graphics Inc.
Editor: Sue Sumeraj
Recipe editor: Jennifer MacKenzie
Copy editor: Kelly Jones
Proofreader: Sheila Wawanash
Indexer: Gillian Watts
Techniques photographer: David Shaughnessy
Techniques stylist: Anne Fisher
Techniques hand model: Shannon Knopke
Recipe photographer: Colin Erricson
Recipe associate photographer: Matt Johannsson
Recipe food stylist: Kathryn Robertson
Recipe prop stylist: Charlene Erricson

Cover image: White Cake Pops (page 24), decorated

We acknowledge the financial support of the Government of Canada through the Book Publishing Industry Development Program (BPIDP) for our publishing activities.

Published by Robert Rose Inc.
120 Eglinton Avenue East, Suite 800, Toronto, Ontario, Canada M4P 1E2
Tel: (416) 322-6552 Fax: (416) 322-6936
www.robertrose.ca

Printed and bound in Canada

1 2 3 4 5 6 7 8 9 TCP 20 19 18 17 16 15 14 13 12

Contents

Acknowledgments 6

About the Electrified Cooks 7

Introduction 8

Part 1: Getting Started

How to Use the Babycakes Cake Pop Maker 11

The Cake Pops Pantry 16

Favorite Tools of the Trade 19

Cake Pops Magic 20

Basic Cake Pop Recipes and Decorations 23

Decorating Tips 48

Part 2: Cakes and Sweets

Cake Pop Favorites 50

Sweet Treats and Desserts 64

Coatings and Fillings 76

Part 3: Doughnuts, Ebelskivers and Muffins

Doughnuts 88

Ebelskivers 100

Biscuits, Muffins and Breakfast Bites 111

Part 4: Special Times and Special Flavors

Appetizers and Savory Nibbles 126

Dips and Fondues 140

Great Balls of Fire 148

Booze Pops 158

Gluten-Free and Vegan Treats 170

Show-Stopping Treats for Parties and Gifts 186

Cake Pops Problem Solver 226

Resources 229

Index 231

Acknowledgments

WE REALLY believe "it takes a village," and that is especially true when writing a cookbook. We are so grateful for the community of wonderful people who helped create this book.

First, thanks to our families. Writing a book takes a tremendous amount of time, and the testing generates many trips to the store and leaves stacks of dishes. We are grateful for our families and appreciate their love and endless support.

Roxanne thanks her husband, Bob Bateman, and their daughter, Grace, for all their love and support. They continue to make her life so sweet, and she thanks God every day for blessing her with them. She also thanks her mom and dad, whose lives have always been a loving inspiration!

Kathy thanks her husband, David, and daughters, Laura and Amanda, for sharing such love and making her days sparkle with laughter, hopes and dreams.

Thanks to Bob Dees, publisher of Robert Rose, for believing in this book and assembling the most wonderful, professional team, including Sue Sumeraj, our editor; Jennifer MacKenzie, our recipe editor; Marian Jarkovich, director of sales and marketing; Martine Quibell, our publicity manager; and so many others. Our thanks also to Daniella Zanchetta and the whole creative team at PageWave Graphics and Colin Erricson Photography for their design and photographs.

We so appreciate the Lisa Ekus Group, including Lisa Ekus; Sally Ekus, our agent; and the entire hard-working, talented group. We are grateful for your support and friendship.

Truly this book would not be possible without Babycakes appliances from Select Brands. We are incredibly grateful to have been part of the team for so many years. Thanks to Bill Endres, Eric Endres, Wes Endres and the entire committed, friendly, professional team that designs, manufactures, markets, sells, ships and supports the Select Brands line of appliances! You are all awesome.

A special thanks to the Select Brands team in Asia working daily on Babycakes product development and quality, including the A&S/Select Brands Office, Steve Bezant, Granton Li and Xiaosong Rao.

We want to thank our colleagues, friends and neighbors who support us each day and rally around us when deadlines approach. Thanks to Barbara Bins and Julie Bondank for their inspiration and support; they are wonderful artists, helping hands and friends. We are so grateful for Sheri Worrel — so much more than a friend and truly a blessing. Her creativity is contagious, giving us a vision we never thought possible! Special thanks to colleagues and friends Karen Adler and Judith Fertig for paving the way and extending a hand of encouragement to us!

Our most cherished support system is each other. The joy and laughter we share in our friendship blesses our daily journey.

About the Electrified Cooks™

WE ARE Kathy Moore and Roxanne Wyss, and we are the Electrified Cooks. We both studied food in college, and we come from a test kitchen background and are home economists. We first worked together in the test kitchen of a small appliance company soon after college. We tested appliances, wrote recipes and answered consumers' questions for years — and we loved it.

We loved it so much that we joined forces and have worked together ever since. We have been consulting with food and appliance companies for many years, bringing our test kitchen skills, our knowledge of food trends and our real-world food experiences to all that we do. Whether it is teaching classes, developing recipes or blogging, we love everything about cooking, and we want to share the most relevant, factual information with you. We want to empower you to be able to go home and cook something wonderful. We want to provide you with the best tips and how-to information so that cooking is easy and successful for you.

Our focus has always been on the home cook and answering the everyday challenge of "What's for supper?" This, plus our specialization in small appliances, led us to Select Brands. We have worked with the president and owner of Select Brands, William Endres, for many, many years. The Select Brands team is a special one, and we are fortunate to work with them. When the Babycakes concept came to us for initial testing and recipe development, it was a natural fit. The fact that we keep using the Babycakes cake pop maker and still love to serve the freshly made cake pops, doughnuts, muffins and appetizers we bake in it is a testament to its value.

We really are very close friends. We love working together and sharing the joy and laughter of the journey. At the same time, we have different tastes. So, when we say that one of us enjoys vanilla and the other chocolate, it's true.

Introduction

WELCOME TO the exciting world of the Babycakes cake pop maker. We were captivated the minute we saw this exciting new appliance, just as we were with the Babycakes cupcake maker. Cake pops are so very fun to make and serve!

As food consultants, we have had the privilege of working with Select Brands for many years, testing appliances and writing recipes. We are part of the team, so it was natural for us to test the Babycakes cake pop maker and write the recipes for the manual that comes with the product. Just as for the Select Brands Babycakes cupcake maker, enthusiasm took over and we kept using the appliance. We made cake pops for our friends and neighbors. We loved using it, and we adored all of the show-stopping gifts, centerpieces and party favors we could create with those little cake gems on a stick. Then we discovered ebelskivers, doughnuts, savory appetizers and more. We had so many recipes and fun ideas to share that we just had to collect them into this book.

Cake Pops Vs. Cake Pops

Much of the inspiration for this book came from Bakerella (aka Angie Dudley). Her blog and subsequent book, *Cake Pops*, are famous, and her talent is extraordinary. She paved the way for many sweets on a stick, and we want to thank her for opening our eyes to the world of cake pops.

As with any culinary journey, flavors and methods evolve. The Bakerella cake pops were soon made by many home cooks and bakeries across the continent — a sweet and tasty trend. Generally, Bakerella cake pops might be considered a confection, for they are a candy-like combination of baked cake that is crumbled and mixed with frosting, then shaped into balls. They are scrumptious, rich and sweet.

The Babycakes cake pop maker makes delightfully different cake pops. The appliance enables cooks to bake little gems of cake batter in rounds. They can also be decorated and even filled. They are not quite as sweet as their predecessors, but they are just as delicious.

Which type of cake pop is better? That question may become a classic culinary debate, just like the chocolate versus vanilla debate. There is no one right answer; it depends on whom you ask.

The Babycakes Rotating Cake Pop Maker

The line of Babycakes appliances from Select Brands keeps growing, and one of the latest additions is the Babycakes Rotating Cake Pop Maker. The rotating cake pop maker sits up off the counter and has a rotating mechanism very similar to that of a commercial waffle maker. It heats from both the top and bottom, and you can rotate the appliance so that the treats are turned upside down midway through cooking. This allows the tops of the treats to rest directly down on a heating surface, so the baking may be a little faster and the browning a little more even.

In comparison, the Babycakes Cake Pop Maker also heats from both the top and bottom, but it does not rotate. It was the unit we used to test and write the recipes in this book, but all of the recipes can be baked in either appliance with great results.

Whichever cake pop maker you're using, make sure to read the user manual packed with the appliance before getting started.

Baking in the Rotating Cake Pop Maker

If you're using the Babycakes Rotating Cake Pop Maker, the procedure for baking your treats may be slightly different from the baking instructions for the original Babycakes Cake Pop Maker, as outlined in the recipes in this book. First, you need to know whether the baked goods you're making can be rotated while baking:

- **Treats that can be rotated:** Cake pops, doughnuts, ebelskivers, biscuits, muffins, bread bites
- **Treats that should not be rotated:** Tortilla scoopers, wonton cups, meatballs

For treats that can be rotated, fill the wells as directed on page 11. Close the lid and bake for 1 to 2 minutes. Rotate the cake pop maker and bake for 2 to 3 minutes. Rotate the cake pop maker back to the original position to open and remove the baked treats.

For treats that should not be rotated, follow the instructions given in the original recipe and bake for the entire time in the upright position.

Tips for the Rotating Cake Pop Maker

- Always make sure the drip pan is in place in the cake pop maker before you start baking.
- Use a timer to remind you when to rotate the appliance and when to stop baking.

Baking Sweets and Savory Bites

The Babycakes cake pop maker is perfect for preparing many different types of treats. Plain cake pops, glazed cake pops, filled cake pops, cake pops dipped in candy melts — all are fun and scrumptious. Or serve cake pops with your favorite dessert sauce or fruit topping for an incredible dessert at your next dinner party.

Mornings will never be the same. Now you can quickly serve freshly baked warm muffins instead of dry cold cereal. And have you tried ebelskivers (pronounced *abel-skeevers*)? These Danish pancakes are truly fantastic, but enjoy them with caution: they can be addictive. Then there's the doughnut holes — just the right size for snacking.

The Babycakes cake pop maker also makes preparing appetizers a cinch. And they bake so quickly that you can easily keep the buffet table stocked with hot, fresh appetizers throughout a party.

We know you'll have a blast baking and decorating these tasty morsels for your family, as gifts and for all your parties and special occasions. Enjoy!

Part 1

Getting Started

How to Use the Babycakes Cake Pop Maker

THE BABYCAKES cake pop maker is so easy to use, but here are some tips that will help you get started.

Preheating

It is not necessary to preheat the Babycakes cake pop maker — just start baking, or bake batch after batch. Either way, it works great.

Using Baking Spray

A quick spritz with nonstick baking spray helps prevent sticking when you're baking cake pops. Spray the wells before baking the first batch, then as needed between batches. Do not use baking spray when the recipe instructs you to brush the wells with butter or oil, or when preparing higher-fat foods, such as meatballs.

Mixing the Batter

We used a handheld electric mixer to test all of the recipes in this book. Only a small amount of batter is needed to make cake pops, so you really don't need to use a large mixer. Because speed, power and beater design vary from mixer to mixer, the speeds listed in the recipes are guidelines only; you may need to adjust the speed on your mixer to get the best results.

Filling the Wells

The easiest way to fill the wells with batter or another mixture is with a pastry bag. (We prefer disposable pastry bags, but you may choose to use reusable pastry bags; just be sure to wash and dry them completely before reusing.) There is no need for a tip — just fill the bag and then clip the pointed end off. Or use a sealable food storage bag and clip off the corner. Fill each well with about 1 tbsp (15 mL) of batter, until the rounded well is almost full. If you don't use enough batter, the top of each cake pop will be a little less rounded than you might like. If you overfill the well, the cake pop will have a small ridge or rings around the center.

If you are using a cake mix, you may have to experiment, because each brand bakes a little differently and some may produce cake pops that are not as rounded.

With a little practice, you will learn to fill each well quickly and easily, letting the batter flow into each well. Press very lightly on the top end of the bag and ease off the pressure when moving to a new well. In between batches, bend the tip of the bag over and set it upright in a glass. (See the step-by-step photographs on photo page A for a visual guide to filling the wells.)

Another way to fill the wells is to use a very small scoop that holds about 1 tbsp (15 mL) of batter. Small scoops can be purchased at kitchen stores and specialty shops. We sometimes use a scoop when batters are chunky with nuts or fruits — or we simply cut a bigger hole in a sealable bag.

In general, fill all 12 wells of the Babycakes cake pop maker for each batch. But if the last bit of batter only fills 3 or 4 wells, that is fine.

The number of cake pops you get from a recipe will be affected by how much batter you add to each well. When measurements are so small, adding even an extra $\frac{1}{2}$ to 1 tsp (2 to 5 mL) of batter to a few cake pops can make a big difference and could reduce the total number of cake pops you get by three or more. The yield listed in each recipe is an estimate based on our tests.

Baking

Once the wells are filled, close the lid of the Babycakes cake pop maker. Set a timer and bake for about 4 minutes, then check for doneness. Most cake pops bake in 4 to 6 minutes, but even slight variations in the amount of batter in each well will affect the baking time. Cake pops are done when a tester inserted in the center comes out clean. Underbaked cake pops can become a little misshapen as they cool.

For other creations, such as appetizers, details on how to check for doneness are provided in each recipe.

Thermostats and the overall performance of all appliances vary slightly from unit to unit and model to model. This is especially noticeable with short baking times, as with cake pop makers. The baking times in each recipe are based on our tests and typical units, but your appliance may bake a little hotter or a little cooler. If the cake pops are a little darker or lighter than you prefer after the listed baking time, adjust the time slightly up or down. After a use or two, you will be better able to predict the ideal baking time for your unit.

Removing the Cake Pops from the Wells

The fork tool that is packed with the Babycakes cake pop maker is designed to lift cake pops or other morsels out of the maker. If you misplace yours or want another, you can order one from the Babycakes website (www.thebabycakesshop.com). Use the fork tool to remove the cake pops or other treats from the wells and set them on a wire rack to cool completely. Hot cake pops are delicate, so be sure to lift gently. Insert the fork tool near the bottom of the cake pop, working gently to avoid tearing the cake pop or scratching the nonstick finish on the cake pop maker.

Chilling the Cake Pops

If you will be attaching sticks, coating the cake pops with melted candy melts and/or decorating them, it is easiest to work with chilled cake pops. Transfer the fully cooled cake pops to a baking sheet and place them in the freezer for about 15 minutes or until they are well chilled. Keep in mind that you will not be able to insert sticks if the cake pops are frozen solid.

Once you have attached the sticks (see page 27 for step-by-step instructions), return the cake pops to the freezer for at least 15 minutes to let the sticks set (once the sticks are set, if you're not planning to decorate the cake pops right away, transfer them to an airtight container for longer freezer storage). When the sticks are secure, you can coat and decorate the cake pops as desired.

Coating and Decorating Cake Pops

You can create beautiful, fun, creative treats by coating your cake pops with melted candy melts and decorating them with swirls, sprinkles and much, much more! We've provided step-by-step instructions for many simple decorating techniques on pages 27–47, and inspiring recipes for more elaborate designs in Show-Stopping Treats for Parties and Gifts (pages 186–225).

Glazing Cake Pops and Other Treats

Many of the recipes in this book call for cake pops, doughnuts or muffins to be glazed. Because glaze cannot be used to attach a stick securely, it's best to enjoy these treats as miniature morsels that you can simply pop into your mouth.

There are several ways to glaze a baked morsel. For a treat that's coated in glaze, place the glaze in a deep bowl and use the fork tool to dip the morsel in the glaze, covering the surface completely, then place it on a wire rack set over a sheet of foil or waxed paper to dry. (Or just dip it halfway, for a different look.) Dipping works best with thinner glazes. Another option is to drizzle or pipe the glaze over the top of a baked morsel. For

easy drizzling or piping, fill a sealable food storage bag with glaze, then snip off the corner. Drizzling and piping work best with thicker glazes. If necessary, stir a little confectioners' (icing) sugar into the prepared glaze until it is the consistency you need.

How much glaze you'll need for a batch of cake pops, doughnuts or muffins depends on a number of factors: how thick or thin the glaze is; how hot it is; whether you're dipping, drizzling or piping; and how patient you are about letting the excess drip back into the cup.

Treats for Every Occasion

The Babycakes cake pop maker can do so much more than just make cake pops! It's also fabulous for making doughnuts, ebelskivers, muffins and savory appetizers. Here are a few hints that will help you achieve the best results when making each of these treats.

Cake Pops

Choose any of the easy recipes in this book or use any of your favorite cake mixes or recipes. One exception: angel food cakes and chiffon cakes are best baked in a conventional oven and not in the Babycakes cake pop maker. A cake mix will make a lot of cake pops, so you may prefer to use recipes with smaller yields, such as the ones developed for this book.

When using a cake mix, we have found that the results vary by brand. Some brands bake into firmer, more rounded cake pops than other brands. Experiment with different brands of cake mix to achieve the best results.

Doughnuts

No need to stop at your local doughnut shop when freshly baked doughnut "holes" are just moments away. Many of our doughnuts are delicious either glazed (see page 13) or coated with confectioners' (icing) sugar or cinnamon sugar. To coat doughnuts with sugar, place 1 to 1½ cups (250 to 375 mL) sugar in a paper bag. As you remove the doughnuts from the cake pop maker, add them to the bag and toss gently to coat. Make sure to coat them while they're still very hot.

Ebelskivers

These Danish pancakes are delightful in miniature form. Ebelskivers are traditionally rounded in shape, and are turned as they bake. Likewise, some of our ebelskivers made in the Babycakes cake pop maker need to be turned once while they are baking for more even browning. To do so, carefully place the fork tool between each partially baked ebelskiver and the edge of the well, gently turn the ebelskiver over, then continue baking as directed in the recipe.

Some ebelskivers are quite light and rely on beaten egg whites. Beat the egg whites until stiff peaks form when you lift the beaters. To fold the beaten egg whites into the batter, use a spatula and very gently cut vertically down into the batter, near the back of the bowl, then move the spatula across the bottom of the bowl and pull it vertically up to the surface. Turn the bowl about a quarter-turn after each stroke. Continue to fold gently until the egg whites are incorporated, but do not overmix.

Muffins

What could be easier for breakfast on the go than these miniature muffin bites? Mixing muffins is one of the most basic of cooking techniques. You begin by combining the dry ingredients — flour, salt, baking powder and/or baking soda. In another bowl, you whisk eggs with the liquid ingredients and melted butter or oil. Then you pour the liquid mixture into the flour mixture and stir the mixtures together with a spoon until the flour is just moistened and incorporated. (Overmixing can cause muffins to become tough, with airy tunnels and peaking centers.)

Appetizers

The Babycakes cake pop maker is perfect for a variety of appetizers, including tortilla scoopers and wonton cups, miniature rolls and meatballs. When baking meatballs, always use very lean ground beef, such as ground round or sirloin, to reduce the amount of fat that collects in the wells. For optimum performance and to minimize fat, turn the unit off between batches, let it cool completely, wipe away any collected fat with a paper towel, then bake the next batch.

Storing Your Baked Goods
Cake Pops

Store cake pops in a single layer in an airtight container at room temperature for up to 3 days. If they're on sticks, place them on their sides in the container. Cake pops can also be stored in an airtight container in the freezer for up to 1 month. Cake pops are best stored uncoated and undecorated.

Coating and decorating frozen cake pops works really well. However, it does cool off the candy melts more quickly, so you'll need to reheat them often.

Doughnuts

Doughnuts are best when freshly baked, and many people enjoy serving them still warm. If you must store them, they can be sealed in an airtight container at room temperature for up to 3 days. If you store doughnuts coated in sugar, keep in mind that the sugar will gradually dissolve over time. Sprinkle with additional sugar just before serving.

Ebelskivers

These fresh pancakes are best served warm. Let them cool just slightly, so no one burns their mouth, then serve.

Muffins

Muffins are best when freshly baked, but can be stored in an airtight container at room temperature for up to 3 days or in the freezer for up to 3 months. Let them cool completely first, then place them in the container, separating layers with parchment or waxed paper.

How to Clean the Babycakes Cake Pop Maker

Generally, cleanup is simple. Just unplug the appliance and let it cool completely. Wipe the surfaces with a damp cloth, then use a dry paper towel to absorb any residual oils.

But what about those extreme instances when a damp cloth can't get the appliance clean? First, be sure to unplug the appliance. Then, while the unit is still warm, wet a kitchen towel or paper towel and place it across the inner surface of the appliance. Close the unit and let it steam for about 5 minutes or until the towel is just cool enough to touch. The sugars and any other residuals will then wipe off very easily. Always use caution, and never place the towel in the appliance if it is plugged in.

The plates of the appliance do not come out, and there is nothing to take apart. Do not use soap or abrasive cleansers on it.

The Cake Pops Pantry

WE ARE foodies, and we always keep a few basic supplies handy to make baking more convenient. Always remember to measure carefully; baking requires accurate measuring. Here are a few tips on the ingredients we use and recommend.

Baking Supplies

Flour

We use all-purpose flour in most recipes. In the gluten-free recipes, we use gluten-free all-purpose baking mix. It's important to measure flour properly, especially with such small quantities. Spoon the flour from the canister or flour sack into a dry measuring cup and level it off with a knife or straight edge. Do not dip the measuring cup into the flour — it will compact the flour and you will end up with more flour than called for in the recipe. Don't tap the measuring cup or pack it down. There is no need to sift the flour.

Sugar

Granulated sugar adds not only a sweet flavor but also tenderness to baked goods. None of the recipes in this book were tested using artificial sweeteners.

Brown sugar is always measured packed into the measuring cup. You can use either light or dark brown sugar in any of the recipes, but dark brown sugar has a slightly richer flavor. Most people choose the brown sugar they are most familiar with. Given a choice, Roxanne chooses dark brown sugar, while Kathy favors light.

There is no need to sift confectioners' (icing) sugar in most of these recipes. In fact, we have found that you rarely need to sift confectioners' sugar anymore. If you feel it is necessary to sift confectioners' sugar, sift it after measuring.

Eggs

All of the recipes in this book use large eggs. Extra-large eggs or smaller eggs will give different results. You'll get the best results if you bring eggs to room temperature before baking with them.

Butter

We used real, unsalted butter for our recipes; they were not tested with margarine. Many recipes call for softened butter, which means it should be set out at room temperature for about 30 minutes before baking. If you forget to do this, slice the butter into slabs, place them on a microwave-safe glass plate and microwave on Medium-Low (30%) for 10 to 15 seconds for ¼ cup (60 mL) butter, or for 20 to 25 seconds for ½ cup (125 mL) butter, until it just starts to soften. Let butter stand for about 10 minutes, then proceed with the recipe. Do not microwave the butter until it melts unless the recipe specifically says to melt it.

Lower-fat butter and imitation spreads have different moisture and fat contents, and using them may affect the flavor, texture and baking time of your baked goods.

Buttermilk

Many cake recipes begin with buttermilk. Not only does it add a wonderful tang, but its acidity plays a special role with the leavening.

In a pinch and don't have buttermilk? Pour 1 tbsp (15 mL) white vinegar or lemon juice into a 1-cup (250 mL) measure and add enough milk to reach the 1-cup (250 mL) line. Let stand for 5 to 10 minutes, until it thickens, then proceed with the recipe.

Dried buttermilk powder is also readily available and, when reconstituted according to package instructions, can be used in place of fresh buttermilk. Keep a can handy in the pantry.

Sour Cream and Cream Cheese

The recipes in this book were tested with regular, full-fat dairy products. Lower-fat cream cheese and lower-fat sour cream deliver slightly different flavors, and — more importantly — their formulas may affect the composition of the baked goods.

Vanilla

Pure vanilla extract offers the best, purest flavor. Imitation vanilla may cost less, but the flavor is not as intense.

Decorating Supplies
Candy Melts

Candy melts (also called candy wafers) are ideal for coating cake pops. They are readily available at cake and candy decorating shops or hobby or craft stores, come in a wide array of colors and melt easily when heated. Common brands include Peters, Make'n Mold, Merckens and Wilton. The texture and flavor of candy melts vary by brand. Some brands are thinner and will melt more easily than others; experiment to determine which brand you prefer.

Because cake pops take time to make and decorate, we often make them as good as they can be by using premium candy melts or those made with real chocolates and flavors, available at cake or candy decorating stores. Be sure to check prices; you can sometimes save money by purchasing candy melts in bulk where available.

In general, 1 cup (250 mL) of melted candy melts will cover about 24 cake pops. But it depends somewhat on a number of factors: the brand of candy melts you use; whether you're coating once or making a more decorative pattern; and how patient you are with letting the excess drip back into the cup.

Store candy melts in an airtight container in a cool, dry place — but not in the refrigerator — for up to 18 months.

Colors and Coloring

Candy melts now come in just about every color of the rainbow and in different shades, though some are only available seasonally, such as black and certain shades of green for Halloween. Some types have sprinkles or color bursts already inside. Keep in mind that exact colors vary by brand — even the white candy melts of one brand may not match the white candy melts of another. Be sure to buy plenty of the color you want.

If you can't find the color you want, you can combine colors to customize the look of your cake pops; for example, adding white candy melts to pink candy melts results in a pale rose color. If you're really stuck and want to color white candy melts yourself, be sure to use candy coloring (a special oil-based coloring that blends easily with candy melts), and not typical food coloring. Candy coloring is readily available at cake and candy decorating shops.

Flavors

Many candy melts are vanilla-flavored, but you will also find milk chocolate, dark chocolate, mint chocolate and peanut butter flavors, just to name a few. You can also flavor your own candy melts, using candy flavoring from a cake or candy decorating shop. Candy flavorings are very concentrated, so add just a drop at a time, taste and add additional drops as needed.

Melting Candy Melts

Melt small amounts of candy melts in a 2-cup (500 mL) glass measuring cup or small microwave-safe glass bowl. Microwave on High in 30-second intervals, stirring after each, until melted and smooth. Do not overheat, or the liquid will harden. Add more candy melts and reheat as needed, keeping the liquid deep enough to immerse a cake pop.

Some people prefer to use a double boiler to melt candy melts and that is fine. You may also use a small appliance specifically designed for melting chocolates — just follow the manufacturer's directions. Always be sure to heat them gently so they don't harden.

Thinning Candy Melts

When it comes to painting fine details onto a cake pop, it's much easier if the melted candy melts have been thinned out. We use Paramount Crystals, a product made of palm kernel oil with lecithin. It is designed for thinning chocolates and is available at cake or candy decorating shops. Add 2 to 3 tsp (10 to 15 mL) of the flakes to the candy melts and melt as usual. Or, if you prefer, stir 1 to 2 tbsp (15 to 30 mL) shortening into the melted candy melts. Either way, add a little at a time, as you don't want the candy melts to get *too* thin, and too much shortening will create an oily taste.

Almond Bark

Almond bark is a popular and convenient alternative to candy melts, and most grocery stores carry it. It is available in both vanilla and chocolate flavors. Follow the package directions for melting. If it's too thick, thin it with 1 to 2 tbsp (15 to 30 mL) shortening. If you wish to color or flavor almond bark, be sure to use the oil-based colors and flavorings sold specifically for candies.

Sprinkles

Cake decorating and craft stores have all types and colors of sprinkles, sanding sugar, sugar pearls, edible glitter, jimmies and more, and any of these can be used to decorate cake pops. Other possibilities include finely crushed cookies, nuts, coconut or candies. Shake the sprinkles over the cake pops while the candy coating is still wet. Or dip the cake pop into a bowl of sprinkles — this is especially effective if you want to coat just the top of the cake pop.

Favorite Tools of the Trade

- **Fork tool.** Included with the Babycakes cake pop maker and sold by Select Brands at www. thebabycakesshop.com, the fork tool is indispensible. We use it to gently lift baked morsels out of the cake pop maker and to dip cake pops, doughnuts and muffins in glaze.

- **Cake pop sticks.** Sticks for the cake pops are readily available at cake decorating and craft stores. They might be called treat sticks, lollipop sticks or cookie sticks. They are also available online at www.thebabycakesshop.com. Any food-safe sticks are great for cake pops. You may select the length and weight of stick that you prefer.

- **Pastry bags.** We use these all the time to fill the wells and for decorating. We prefer disposable pastry bags, which we purchase in a roll of 100 for a reasonable price at our local bakery supply store. Another option is to use a sealable food storage bag with a corner clipped off.

- **Squeeze bottles.** Cake decorating shops sell inexpensive squeeze bottles that are perfect for so many techniques. Fill one with melted candy melts, fit it with a fine writing tip and use it to pipe fine lines, swirls or details, or fill it with a prepared filling (such as frosting or pudding) to inject into a cake pop. The bottles sold for cake and candy decorating are especially flexible. (Those made of thicker plastic or meant for condiments such as ketchup or mustard are difficult to use for cake decorating.)

- **Toothpicks.** A toothpick is the perfect tool for adding a drop of candy melts as a fine detail on a cake pop, or as glue when you're adding candies or other decorations. We also use toothpicks to catch drips and to make fine lines when we want to add texture.

- **Paintbrushes.** Choose inexpensive, food-safe paintbrushes and keep them handy. Fine brushes are great for painting on eyes, lips or other details. Slightly larger brushes are ideal for painting fur or adding texture. To add edible glitter or sprinkles in a specific area, coat the cake pop and let it dry. Use a paintbrush to paint a line, a pattern or an area lightly with water, moistening it lightly but evenly, then immediately sprinkle the moistened area with the glitter or sprinkles.

- **Tweezers.** Keep a pair of tweezers in the kitchen for all of the detail work, such as picking up a tiny candy, placing a seed in just the right spot or arranging sprinkles to look like hair.

Cake Pop Magic

Having Fun!

Cake pops are packed with fun, and our recipes, decorating instructions and tips will make it easy for you to create smiles and lasting memories.

The most common questions we hear are about the time it takes to decorate cake pops and the skill level required. "I am not an artist," so many people have said to us. Well, we aren't either, so don't let that stop you. If we can do it, you can do it! To make it even easier for you, we've provided step-by-step instructions for many of the most basic decorating techniques on pages 27–47.

Often you need only go so far as to coat your cake pops in a bright color or in chocolate. Find the perfect container to hold them, or tie them with a ribbon to make a bouquet, and you have a thoughtful gift or a dazzling centerpiece. But if you want to kick it up a notch, we've provided many creative ideas in Show-Stopping Treats for Parties and Gifts (pages 186–225). Use these designs as inspiration for your own masterpieces!

Making cake pops takes a little time, but what stunning dessert or gift from the kitchen doesn't? It is easy to save time and make great-looking cake pops if you follow these tips:

- Plan ahead and make sure you have the supplies you need. How do you want to decorate your cake pops? What color of candy melt will you be using? Do you have enough sticks, plenty of candy melts, the right color of sprinkles? Running out of a critical item right in the middle of decorating is frustrating.

- Stock up when candy melts and other decorating supplies go on sale. Some items are seasonal, so you may wish to purchase them when you see them. For example, pastel-colored candy corn may be perfect for ears on a bunny or petals on a flower, but it's only available in the spring.

- Be open to new ideas and supplies. Check out the displays at craft and cake decorating stores for the latest products and inspirations.

- Cake pops need to chill between steps, so it may be easiest to bake them one day and decorate the next.

- Work ahead. If your party is on Saturday, you can coat and decorate on Friday — or even on Thursday — and the cake pops will still taste fresh and wonderful.

- Keep cake pops, baked and on sticks, in an airtight container in the freezer, ready to dip and give away at a moment's notice.

Cake Pop Stands

Coated and decorated cake pops must stand upright until dry, without touching each other. Specially designed cake pop stands are available, such as the one included with the Babycakes cake pop maker. You may want to order extra from Select Brands (www.thebabycakesshop.com), as having more than one stand makes the decorating process much easier and faster.

Styrofoam also works well for holding cake pops and is readily available at craft stores. Choose sheets or blocks about 2 inches (5 cm) thick and cover them with paper or foil so you won't get flecks of Styrofoam all over your work area. (If you are serving the cake pops on the Styrofoam or giving them as a gift, be sure to use decorative paper or foil.) Place the cake pops about 2 inches (5 cm) apart, and space them evenly over the Styrofoam to distribute their weight.

A 2-inch (5 cm) thick wooden board is ideal if you want to make a lot of cake pops or plan to make them often. Drill the board with small holes about 2 inches (5 cm) apart. Be sure to use an appropriate drill bit size so the cake pop sticks will be held securely. You can even paint the board if you wish to use it for a display.

Lollipop stand trees also work well and might make the perfect display for your party. Look for them at craft or hobby stores. Or, if you are especially crafty, you can make your own by following online instructions. Again, be sure to space out the cake pops to distribute the weight evenly.

Once they're dry, the decorated cake pops can be arranged in your favorite container.

Creative Displays

How you package and display your cake pops adds so much to the magic. Your display can be as tiny as a test tube in a wire holder or votive candleholder, or as large as a multi-tiered arrangement. Here are a few starting ideas on containers you can use for displays or gifts:

- Vases
- Baskets
- Bowls
- Decorative tins
- Coffee mugs and teacups
- Small pitchers
- Sugar bowls or creamers
- Flowerpots
- Candleholders
- Gift boxes and cubes
- Decorative plastic or galvanized pails
- Topiary stands

Visit a craft or decorating store for more ideas. The choice of colors, sizes and shapes is nearly endless.

Are you hosting or attending a formal event? Look for a china or silver container. You may discover a vintage or used piece at a local flea market, thrift store or garage sale. Give it a polish and it will look gorgeous. Alternatively, look for a glass container or spray-paint a flowerpot or box with metallic paint to match the color theme or ambience of the event.

Use a piece of cut Styrofoam, fitted snugly into the bottom of the container, to help keep your cake pops steady. If the container is light in weight, cover the Styrofoam with a layer of glass beads or polished pebbles, which can be purchased in craft stores. Marbles from the toy store or even hard candies or jelly beans might provide just the look and weight needed for the display.

Remember that all containers and weights must be clean so that the food doesn't become contaminated. Check the label to be sure that there aren't dangerous chemicals in the paint or finish of your container or supplies. When using containers not specifically designed for food, such as candleholders and flowerpots, make sure the food does not come in contact with the container.

You can use Styrofoam rings to create a multi-tiered display. Select rings in increasing diameters and practice how they stack before going further. Once you are pleased with the size and number of rings, wrap each ring separately in wide decorative ribbon. Stack the rings and glue them or use dowel rods to secure them. Use craft picks, tissue paper, ribbons and silk flowers to fill in around the cake pops for a fuller appearance.

You can incorporate a tall cake pop display into a table with other desserts, such as Babycakes cupcakes. Cake pops also make perfect decorations for cakes or cupcakes. It's a win-win: the cake pops make for a pretty accent for the cake, and the cake serves as a stand for the cake pops.

To Wrap or Not to Wrap?

A cake pop wrapped in plastic or cellophane makes a great individual gift or party favor. Use treat bags that are 3 by 4 inches (7.5 by 10 cm), or cut a 7-inch (18 cm) square of cellophane and use it to cover the top of the cake pop, then fasten it around the base with a ribbon.

Cake pops coated in candy melts will stay moist for 3 or 4 days and don't require additional wrapping or covering. When we make a cake pop display, we usually leave the individual cake pops unwrapped so it is easy for people to take a sweet treat. (We may cover the top of a display loosely with plastic to keep the dust off, then remove the plastic just before the party.)

It is important to keep cake pops cool. If you must transport them outside on a hot day, try to keep them out of the sun and get them back into an air-conditioned space quickly.

Basic Cake Pop Recipes and Decorations

White Cake Pops 24
    Filling the Wells 25
Old-Fashioned Chocolate Cake Pops 26
    Attaching the Sticks. 27
Princess Cake Pops 28
    Coating Cake Pops 29
Golden Yellow Cake Pops. 30
    Decorating with Sprinkles. 31
Everyday Yellow Cake Pops 32
    Adding Decorative Swirls 33
White Velvet Cake Pops 34
    Adding a Sparkly Spiral. 35
Easy Red Velvet Cake Pops. 36
    Triple-Dipping 37
Classic Red Velvet Cake Pops. 38
    Marbleizing 39
Lemon Cake Pops 40
    Adding Decorations 41
Strawberry Cake Pops 42
    Creating Rose Buds. 43
Orange Cream Cake Pops 44
    Making Simple Faces with Curly Hair 45
Almond Cream Cake Pops 46
    Making Simple Faces with Straight Hair. 47

White Cake Pops

Makes 21 to 23 cake pops

It's always exciting to receive a wedding invitation. Of course, everyone looks forward to the sacred ceremony, but equally anticipated is the cake. Now, with these cake pops, you can enjoy bite-size wedding cake anytime you like.

Tips

Need a stand for your cake pops? Styrofoam wrapped in ribbon makes a quick and easy display base. Or hide a piece of Styrofoam in the bottom of a vase, basket, bowl, cup or box, for a pretty container.

Do you have a Babycakes Rotating Cake Pop Maker? If so, see page 8 for information on using it.

1 cup	all-purpose flour	250 mL
1 tsp	baking powder	5 mL
Pinch	salt	Pinch
1	large egg, at room temperature	1
½ tsp	vanilla extract	2 mL
⅛ tsp	almond extract (optional)	0.5 mL
½ cup	granulated sugar	125 mL
½ cup	heavy or whipping (35%) cream	125 mL
	Nonstick baking spray	

1. In a small bowl, whisk together flour, baking powder and salt. Set aside.

2. In a medium bowl, using an electric mixer on low speed, beat egg. Beat in vanilla and almond extract (if using) until blended. Beat in sugar until blended. Add cream and beat until blended. Beat in flour mixture until smooth.

3. Spray cake pop wells with nonstick baking spray. Fill each well with about 1 tbsp (15 mL) batter (see page 25). Bake for 4 to 6 minutes or until a tester inserted in the center comes out clean. Transfer cake pops to a wire rack to cool. Repeat with the remaining batter.

4. If desired, attach sticks to cake pops (see page 27).

See the step-by-step photographs on photo page A. ▶

Tips

Another way to fill the wells is to use a very small scoop that holds about 1 tbsp (15 mL) of batter. Small scoops can be purchased at kitchen stores and specialty shops. We sometimes use a scoop when batters are chunky with nuts or fruits — or we simply cut a bigger hole in a sealable bag.

In general, fill all 12 wells of the Babycakes cake pop maker for each batch. But if the last bit of batter only fills 3 or 4 wells, that is fine.

Filling the Wells

1. Fold the top edge of a pastry bag down to make a collar.

2. Using a glass to hold the pastry bag upright, fill the bag with batter.

3. Alternatively, use a sealable plastic food bag.

4. Clip the point off the pastry bag or plastic food bag.

5. Press very lightly on the top end of the bag, letting the batter flow into each well. Stop pressing when moving to a new well.

6. Between batches, bend the tip of the bag up and set the bag upright in the glass.

Old-Fashioned Chocolate Cake Pops

Makes 38 to 40 cake pops

Remember the chocolate cake Grandma used to make? This recipe recreates those fond memories.

Tips

Prepare instant coffee according to package directions and substitute it for the hot brewed coffee.

No buttermilk on hand? Stir 1 tsp (5 mL) lemon juice or white vinegar into ⅓ cup (75 mL) milk. Let stand for 5 to 10 minutes or until thickened. Proceed with the recipe.

⅓ cup	unsweetened cocoa powder	75 mL
⅓ cup	hot strong brewed coffee	75 mL
1 cup	all-purpose flour	250 mL
¾ tsp	baking soda	3 mL
¼ tsp	baking powder	1 mL
¼ tsp	salt	1 mL
⅓ cup	unsalted butter, softened	75 mL
¾ cup	granulated sugar	175 mL
1	large egg, at room temperature	1
1	large egg yolk, at room temperature	1
⅓ cup	buttermilk	75 mL
1 tsp	vanilla extract	5 mL
	Nonstick baking spray	

1. In a small bowl, whisk together cocoa and coffee. Set aside.

2. In another small bowl, whisk together flour, baking soda, baking powder and salt. Set aside.

3. In a medium bowl, using an electric mixer on medium speed, beat butter until creamy, about 45 seconds. Add sugar and beat for 2 minutes. Add egg, then egg yolk, beating well after each addition.

4. Whisk buttermilk and vanilla into cocoa mixture.

5. Add flour mixture to butter mixture alternately with cocoa mixture, making three additions of flour and two of cocoa and beating on low speed until combined.

6. Spray cake pop wells with nonstick baking spray. Fill each well with about 1 tbsp (15 mL) batter (see page 25). Bake for 4 to 6 minutes or until a tester inserted in the center comes out clean. Transfer cake pops to a wire rack to cool. Repeat with the remaining batter.

7. If desired, attach sticks to cake pops (see page 27).

See the step-by-step photographs on photo page B. ▶

Tip

Some people prefer to use a double boiler to melt candy melts and that is fine. You may also use a small appliance specifically designed for melting chocolates — just follow the manufacturer's directions. Always be sure to heat them gently so they don't harden.

Attaching the Sticks

1. To easily remove the cake pops from the wells, use the fork tool, gently inserting the tips between the edge of the well and the cake and lifting gently from beneath the cake pop.

2. Transfer the cake pops to a wire rack to cool.

3. Place the cooled cake pops in the freezer for about 15 minutes or just until chilled but not frozen solid.

4. Place ½ cup (125 mL) of candy melts in a 2-cup (500 mL) glass measuring cup or small microwave-safe glass bowl. Microwave in 30-second intervals, stirring after each, until melted and smooth. Microwave just until melted; do not overheat.

5. Dip the end of a stick in the melted candy melts.

6. Gently push the stick into a chilled cake pop. Be sure to push the stick far enough in — the tip should be about halfway or three-quarters of the way through the cake pop. Place the cake pops back on the baking sheet and return to the freezer for at least 15 minutes to let the sticks set. Once the sticks are set, the cake pops can be transferred to an airtight container and stored in the freezer for up to 1 month.

Princess Cake Pops

The delicate flavor of these cake pops will remind you of angel food cake — they're soft, subtle and oh so good.

Tips

If a more intense pink color is desired, add a few drops of red food coloring while beating.

Can't find strawberry instant pudding? Substitute French vanilla instant pudding and add 1 tsp (5 mL) strawberry extract.

Store the remaining pudding mix in a sealable bag in the cupboard for up to 3 months.

1¼ cups	white cake mix	300 mL
3½ tbsp	strawberry instant pudding mix (half of a 3.4-oz/96 g box)	52 mL
1	large egg, at room temperature	1
⅓ cup	milk	75 mL
1 tbsp	unsalted butter, melted	15 mL
	Nonstick baking spray	

1. In a medium bowl, using an electric mixer on low speed, beat cake mix, pudding, egg, milk and melted butter for 30 seconds or until moistened. Beat on medium speed for 2 minutes.

2. Spray cake pop wells with nonstick baking spray. Fill each well with about 1 tbsp (15 mL) batter (see page 25). Bake for 4 to 6 minutes or until a tester inserted in the center comes out clean. Transfer cake pops to a wire rack to cool. Repeat with the remaining batter.

3. If desired, attach sticks to cake pops (see page 27).

See the step-by-step photographs on photo page C. ▶

Tips

In general, 1 cup (250 mL) of melted candy melts will cover about 24 cake pops. But it depends somewhat on the brand of candy melts, and on how patient you are with letting the excess drip back into the cup.

Candy melts thicken as they cool, so dip the cake pops immediately. Reheat the melts as needed to keep the liquid thin and smooth. If it thickens too much, it will not coat the cake pops evenly.

Coating Cake Pops

1. Add 1 cup (250 mL) of candy melts to those left in the cup or bowl from when you attached the stick. (To disguise drips, be sure to use the same color of candy melts as you used to secure the sticks.)

2. Microwave the candy melts on High in 30-second intervals, stirring after each, until melted and smooth.

3. Gently dip the cake pop into the melted candy coating, using a straight-up-and-down motion.

4. Hold the coated cake pop over the cup so the excess coating can drip back into the cup.

5. Gently tap the stick against your fingers, over the cup, letting the excess coating drip off.

6. Set the cake pop in a cake pop stand to dry.

Golden Yellow Cake Pops

Makes 34 to 36 cake pops

These golden, buttery morsels are both rich and moist.

Tips

Cover and refrigerate leftover egg whites for up to 3 days. For longer storage, freeze them for up to 6 months. (Be sure to label and date each container.) When you're ready to use them, let egg whites thaw in the refrigerator and use 2 tbsp (30 mL) for 1 egg white.

Do you have a Babycakes Rotating Cake Pop Maker? If so, see page 8 for information on using it.

1½ cups	all-purpose flour	375 mL
2 tsp	baking powder	10 mL
¼ tsp	salt	1 mL
¾ cup	granulated sugar	175 mL
6 tbsp	unsalted butter, softened	90 mL
1	large egg, at room temperature	1
1	large egg yolk, at room temperature	1
1 tsp	vanilla extract	5 mL
½ cup	milk	125 mL

1. In a small bowl, whisk together flour, baking powder and salt. Set aside.

2. In a medium bowl, using an electric mixer on medium-high speed, beat sugar and butter for 1 to 2 minutes or until fluffy. Add egg, then egg yolk, beating well after each addition. Beat in vanilla. Add flour mixture alternately with milk, making three additions of flour and two of milk and beating on low speed until smooth.

3. Spray cake pop wells with nonstick baking spray. Fill each well with about 1 tbsp (15 mL) batter (see page 25). Bake for 4 to 6 minutes or until a tester inserted in the center comes out clean. Transfer cake pops to a wire rack to cool. Repeat with the remaining batter.

4. If desired, attach sticks to cake pops (see page 27).

See the step-by-step photographs on photo page D. ▶

Tip

Do you want the sprinkles arranged in a pattern? After coating the cake pop, let it dry. Use melted candy melts to pipe your design onto the cake pop, then immediately sprinkle that design with sprinkles. Or use a small paintbrush dipped in water to paint a design, then immediately sprinkle the moist spots with sprinkles.

Decorating with Sprinkles

1. Select a color or type of sprinkle that complements the color of the candy melt you used for the coating. Pour the sprinkles into a small bowl.

2. Right after coating the cake pop and before the coating has a chance to dry, hold the cake pop over the center of the bowl of sprinkles.

3. Dip the cake pop into the sprinkles.

4. Roll the cake pop in the sprinkles to coat it completely.

5. Gently shake off any excess sprinkles.

6. Set the cake pop in a cake pop stand to dry.

Everyday Yellow Cake Pops

Makes 21 to 22 cake pops

These yellow morsels are simple, yes, but so good you will want to make them every day. And they're so versatile, you can decorate them for any season or occasion.

Tip

Store baked cake pops in an airtight container in the freezer for up to 1 month. Dip them at a moment's notice anytime you want a treat or to give a gift.

1 cup	yellow cake mix	250 mL
1	large egg, at room temperature	1
¼ cup	milk	60 mL
2 tbsp	unsalted butter, melted	30 mL
½ tsp	vanilla extract	5 mL
	Nonstick baking spray	

1. In a medium bowl, using an electric mixer on low speed, beat cake mix, egg, milk, butter and vanilla for 30 seconds or until moistened. Beat on medium speed for 2 minutes.

2. Spray cake pop wells with nonstick baking spray. Fill each well with about 1 tbsp (15 mL) batter (see page 25). Bake for 4 to 6 minutes or until a tester inserted in the center comes out clean. Transfer cake pops to a wire rack to cool. Repeat with the remaining batter.

3. If desired, attach sticks to cake pops (see page 27).

See the step-by-step photographs on photo page E. ▶

Tips

If you want the contrasting color to be more marbleized or less pronounced, pipe the swirls onto a freshly dipped cake pop.

For sparkly swirls, use candy melts in the same color as the coating. Immediately after piping the swirls, sprinkle them with sparkling sanding sugar or edible glitter.

Adding Decorative Swirls

1. After the coating has dried, place 1 cup (250 mL) of candy melts in a contrasting or complementary color in a 2-cup (500 mL) glass measuring cup or small microwave-safe glass bowl. Microwave on High in 30-second intervals, stirring after each, until melted and smooth.

2. Fit a pastry bag or squeeze bottle with a fine writing tip.

3. Fill the pastry bag with melted candy melts.

4. Pipe a swirl in a decorative fashion over the cake pop.

5. Continue to pipe swirls until the cake pop is decorated as you like. You can pipe them in a tight design or a loose design. Set the cake pop in a cake pop stand to dry.

White Velvet Cake Pops

These moist, flavorful cake pops are made with a cake mix, which leaves you with more time to spend with family and friends.

Tips

It's fun to color these cake pops according to your decorating plans. Add a few drops of food coloring to the batter and bake as directed.

Different brands of cake mix have slightly different formulas, so flavors and textures vary. Experiment a bit to find the brand of cake mix you prefer.

1 cup	white cake mix	250 mL
¼ cup	all-purpose flour	60 mL
¼ cup	granulated sugar	60 mL
Pinch	salt	Pinch
1	large egg white, at room temperature	1
⅓ cup	water	75 mL
¼ cup	sour cream	60 mL
¼ tsp	almond extract	1 mL
¼ tsp	vanilla extract	1 mL
	Nonstick baking spray	

1. In a medium bowl, using an electric mixer on low speed, beat cake mix, flour, sugar, salt, egg white, water, sour cream, almond extract and vanilla for 30 seconds or until moistened. Beat on medium speed for 2 minutes.

2. Spray cake pop wells with nonstick baking spray. Fill each well with about 1 tbsp (15 mL) batter (see page 25). Bake for 4 to 6 minutes or until a tester inserted in the center comes out clean. Transfer cake pops to a wire rack to cool. Repeat with the remaining batter.

3. If desired, attach sticks to cake pops (see page 27).

See the step-by-step photographs on photo page F. ▶

Tip

Cake and candy decorating shops and craft stores stock a wide array of sprinkles in various colors, shapes and sizes. Use your creativity and select sprinkles that will help convey the theme. For example, a dusting of iridescent or pearlized edible glitter will be elegant, while multicolored sprinkles in fun seasonal or holiday shapes would be more whimsical.

Adding a Sparkly Spiral

1. Select sparkling sanding sugar or edible glitter in a color that complements the color of the candy melt you used for the coating.

2. After the coating has dried, place 1 cup (250 mL) of candy melts in the same color as the coating (or in a complementary color) in a 2-cup (500 mL) glass measuring cup or small microwave-safe glass bowl. Microwave on High in 30-second intervals, stirring after each, until melted and smooth.

3. Fit a pastry bag or squeeze bottle with a fine writing tip.

4. Fill the pastry bag with melted candy melts.

5. Starting at the top center of the cake pop, pipe a spiral around the cake pop.

6. Immediately sprinkle the spiral with the sanding sugar or glitter. Set the cake pop in a cake pop stand to dry.

Easy Red Velvet Cake Pops

Makes 24 to 26 cake pops

The mild chocolate flavor and intense red color make these cake pops an all-time favorite.

Tips

Non-dairy whipped topping mix comes in boxes containing two or four envelopes. Use 2 tbsp (30 mL) — about half of one envelope — for this recipe and store the remaining mix in a sealable bag at room temperature for up to 6 months.

No buttermilk on hand? Stir ¾ tsp (3 mL) lemon juice or white vinegar into ¼ cup (60 mL) milk. Let stand for 5 to 10 minutes or until thickened. Proceed with the recipe.

1 cup	German or Swiss chocolate cake mix	250 mL
2 tbsp	powdered non-dairy whipped topping mix (see tip, at left)	30 mL
1	large egg, at room temperature	1
¼ cup	buttermilk	60 mL
2 tsp	red food coloring	10 mL
½ tsp	vanilla extract	2 mL
	Nonstick baking spray	

1. In a medium bowl, using an electric mixer on low speed, beat cake mix, whipped topping mix, egg, buttermilk, food coloring and vanilla for 30 seconds or until moistened. Beat on medium speed for 2 minutes.

2. Spray cake pop wells with nonstick baking spray. Fill each well with about 1 tbsp (15 mL) batter (see page 25). Bake for 4 to 6 minutes or until a tester inserted in the center comes out clean. Transfer cake pops to a wire rack to cool. Repeat with the remaining batter.

3. If desired, attach sticks to cake pops (see page 27).

See the step-by-step photographs on photo page G. ▶

Tips

Make sure to let each color dry completely before adding the next.

Using a straight-up-and-down motion to dip will ensure that the edges are straight.

Triple-Dipping

1. Select three colors of candy melts. They can be different shades of the same color or three complementary colors. One of them should be the same color you used to attach the stick.

2. Following the instructions on page 29, coat the cake pop in the color you used to attach the stick. Set the cake pop in a cake pop stand to dry.

3. For the second dip, place 1 cup (250 mL) of the next color of candy melts in another 2-cup (500 mL) glass measuring cup or small microwave-safe glass bowl. Microwave in 30-second intervals, stirring after each, until melted and smooth.

4. Gently dip the coated cake pop straight down into the second color until about two-thirds of the cake pop is covered. Lifting the cake pop straight up, gently tap the stick so excess coating drips off. Set the cake pop in a cake pop stand to dry.

5. For the third dip, place 1 cup (250 mL) of the final color of candy melts in another glass measuring cup or bowl. Microwave in 30-second intervals, stirring after each, until melted and smooth.

6. Gently dip the cake pop straight down into the third color until about one-third of the cake pop is covered. Lifting the cake pop straight up, gently tap the stick so excess coating drips off. Set the cake pop in a cake pop stand to dry.

Classic Red Velvet Cake Pops

Makes 42 to 44 cake pops

Red velvet is one of the most popular cake flavors, and the striking red color is perfect for cake pops. Coat them in white candy melts or White Chocolate Glaze (page 79) for a beautiful contrast in color.

Tips

No buttermilk on hand? Stir 1½ tsp (7 mL) lemon juice or white vinegar into ½ cup (125 mL) milk. Let stand for 5 to 10 minutes or until thickened. Proceed with the recipe.

Cake pops are perfect decorations for cakes or cupcakes. It's a win-win: the cake pops make for a pretty accent for the cake, and the cake serves as a stand for the cake pops.

1¼ cups	all-purpose flour	300 mL
4 tsp	unsweetened cocoa powder	20 mL
½ tsp	baking powder	2 mL
¼ tsp	salt	1 mL
1 cup	granulated sugar	250 mL
½ cup	unsalted butter, softened	125 mL
1	large egg, at room temperature	1
1	large egg yolk, at room temperature	1
1 tbsp	red food coloring	15 mL
½ cup	buttermilk	125 mL
1½ tsp	white vinegar	7 mL
½ tsp	baking soda	2 mL
	Nonstick baking spray	

1. In a small bowl, whisk together flour, cocoa, baking powder and salt. Set aside.

2. In a medium bowl, using an electric mixer on medium-high speed, beat sugar and butter for 1 to 2 minutes or until fluffy. Add egg, then egg yolk, beating well after each addition. Beat in food coloring. Add flour mixture alternately with buttermilk, making three additions of flour and two of buttermilk and beating on low speed until smooth.

3. In another small bowl, combine vinegar and baking soda, stirring until baking soda is dissolved. Beat vinegar mixture into batter.

4. Spray cake pop wells with nonstick baking spray. Fill each well with about 1 tbsp (15 mL) batter (see page 25). Bake for 4 to 6 minutes or until a tester inserted in the center comes out clean. Transfer cake pops to a wire rack to cool. Repeat with the remaining batter.

5. If desired, attach sticks to cake pops (see page 27).

See the step-by-step photographs on photo page H. ▶

Tip
Swirl the two colors together just lightly. Do not overmix or blend the colors completely, or you will lose the marbleized look.

Marbleizing

1. Select two colors of candy melts. Those with a striking contrast are especially attractive. One of the colors should be the same color you used to attach the stick. Place 1 cup (250 mL) of one color in a 2-cup (500 mL) glass measuring cup or small microwave-safe glass bowl. Place ½ cup (125 mL) of the second color in another measuring cup or bowl. Microwave the colors, one at a time, on High in 30-second intervals, stirring after each, until each color is melted and smooth.

2. Spoon about 1 tbsp (15 mL) of the second color into the first color.

3. Stir the mixture with a toothpick, gently and briefly, just enough to swirl the two colors, creating a marbleized effect. Do not blend the colors completely.

4. Dip the cake pop straight down into the swirled colors.

5. Rotate the cake pop in the candy melts.

6. Lifting the cake pop straight up, gently tap the stick so excess coating drips off. Set the cake pop in a cake pop stand to dry.

Lemon Cake Pops

The fresh taste of lemon makes these dainty cake pops an instant classic. They are perfect to serve at a shower, send as a gift or include in a cake pop centerpiece.

Tips

It's easiest to zest the lemon before you juice it. One lemon will yield about 3 tbsp (45 mL) juice and 2 to 3 tsp (10 to 15 mL) zest. Zest only the colored portion of the peel, avoiding the bitter white pith underneath. If you have leftover lemon juice, cover and refrigerate it for up to 5 days, or freeze it for up to 6 months.

Do you have a Babycakes Rotating Cake Pop Maker? If so, see page 8 for information on using it.

½ cup	unsalted butter	125 mL
¾ cup	all-purpose flour	175 mL
½ tsp	baking powder	2 mL
¼ tsp	salt	1 mL
⅔ cup	granulated sugar	150 mL
2	large eggs, at room temperature	2
	Grated zest of 1 lemon	
2 tsp	freshly squeezed lemon juice	10 mL
½ tsp	vanilla extract	2 mL
½ tsp	lemon extract	2 mL
	Nonstick baking spray	

1. In a small microwave-safe glass bowl, microwave butter on High for 40 seconds or until melted. Set aside to cool for 3 minutes.

2. In a small bowl, whisk together flour, baking powder and salt. Set aside.

3. In a medium bowl, using an electric mixer on medium-high speed, beat sugar, eggs, lemon zest and lemon juice for 1 minute. Add melted butter and beat for 2 minutes. Beat in vanilla and lemon extract. Add flour mixture and beat on low speed just until blended.

4. Spray cake pop wells with nonstick baking spray. Fill each well with about 1 tbsp (15 mL) batter (see page 25). Bake for 4 to 6 minutes or until a tester inserted in the center comes out clean. Transfer cake pops to a wire rack to cool. Repeat with the remaining batter.

5. If desired, attach sticks to cake pops (see page 27).

Decorating Tip

- These cake pops are extra delicious when coated with Lemon Glaze (page 80) or Easy Frosting Coating (page 77). Remember, if you plan to glaze your cake pops, leave them off the sticks.

See the step-by-step photographs on photo page I. ▶

Tips

Use tweezers to pick up small decorations and press them onto the cake pop.

If you decide to add decorations after the coating has dried, melt some more candy melts to use as glue. Use a toothpick to place a drop of candy melts on the cake pop, then press the decoration onto the wet drop. Continue until the cake pop is decorated as desired.

Adding Decorations

1. Select your decorations. You might use tiny candies, baking chips, edible eyes, small fondant cutouts or premade royal icing decorations, for example.

2. Following the instructions on page 29, coat the cake pop in melted candy melts, but do not let it dry.

3. Arrange the decorations on the wet coating.

4. Continue until the cake pop is decorated as desired. You might fully cover the cake pop with decorations, or you might choose to make a design or pattern with the decorations. Set the cake pop in a cake pop stand to dry.

Strawberry Cake Pops

∙ ∙

**Makes 20
to 22 cake pops**

These bright pink cake pops will make any birthday or occasion special. For added fun, glaze with Strawberry Glaze (page 79).

Tip

Non-dairy whipped topping mix comes in boxes containing two or four envelopes. Use 2 tbsp (30 mL) — about half of one envelope — for this recipe and store the remaining mix in a sealable bag at room temperature for up to 6 months.

Variation

Cherry Chocolate Cake Pops: Substitute cherry-flavored gelatin and cherry extract for the strawberry. Dip the cake pops in melted chocolate candy melts.

1 cup	white cake mix	250 mL
2 tbsp	powdered non-dairy whipped topping mix (see tip, at left)	30 mL
1 tbsp	strawberry-flavored gelatin powder	15 mL
1	large egg, at room temperature	1
2 tbsp	vegetable oil	30 mL
2 tbsp	water	30 mL
1 tsp	strawberry extract	5 mL
	Nonstick baking spray	

1. In a medium bowl, using an electric mixer on low speed, beat cake mix, whipped topping mix, gelatin, egg, oil, water and strawberry extract for 30 seconds or until moistened. Beat on medium speed for 2 minutes.

2. Spray cake pop wells with nonstick baking spray. Fill each well with about 1 tbsp (15 mL) batter (see page 25). Bake for 4 to 6 minutes or until a tester inserted in the center comes out clean. Transfer cake pops to a wire rack to cool. Repeat with the remaining batter.

3. If desired, attach sticks to cake pops (see page 27).

See the step-by-step photographs on photo page J. ▶

Tip

When selecting candy melts, choose colors typical of roses, such as red, pink, yellow or white.

Creating Rose Buds

1. After the coating has dried, place 1 cup (250 mL) of candy melts in the same color as the coating in a 2-cup (500 mL) glass measuring cup or small microwave-safe glass bowl. Microwave on High in 30-second intervals, stirring after each, until melted and smooth.

2. Fit a pastry bag or squeeze bottle with a fine writing tip.

3. Fill the pastry bag with melted candy melts.

4. Pipe a swirl in a tight circle on top of the cake pop to resemble a rose bud.

5. Tie a green ribbon onto the cake pop stick to create the leaves. Set the cake pop in a cake pop stand to dry.

6. Tie several rose buds into a bouquet, arrange them in a vase or place one rose bud on each place setting for a dinner party.

Orange Cream Cake Pops

Makes 26 to 28 cake pops

These are a cake-like take on your favorite frozen ice cream treat. Slice each cake pop in half and fill with ice cream for double the pleasure.

Tips

If you prefer a deep orange color, add orange food coloring to the batter.

Non-dairy whipped topping mix comes in boxes containing two or four envelopes. Use 2 tbsp (30 mL) — about half of one envelope — for this recipe and store the remaining mix in a sealable bag at room temperature for up to 6 months.

Use regular mayonnaise in this recipe, as the fat is important for the composition and texture of the cake pops.

1 cup	yellow cake mix	250 mL
2 tbsp	powdered non-dairy whipped topping mix (see tip, at left)	30 mL
3 tbsp	orange juice	45 mL
1 tbsp	milk	15 mL
1 tbsp	mayonnaise	15 mL
1	large egg, at room temperature	1
	Nonstick baking spray	

1. In a medium bowl, using an electric mixer on low speed, beat cake mix, whipped topping mix, orange juice, milk, mayonnaise and egg for 30 seconds or until moistened. Beat on medium speed for 2 minutes.

2. Spray cake pop wells with nonstick baking spray. Fill each well with about 1 tbsp (15 mL) batter (see page 25). Bake for 4 to 6 minutes or until a tester inserted in the center comes out clean. Transfer cake pops to a wire rack to cool. Repeat with the remaining batter.

3. If desired, attach sticks to cake pops (see page 27).

See the step-by-step photographs on photo page K. ▶

Tips

Reheat the candy melts as necessary at each stage.

When you're piping mouths or other fine details, very hot or thin candy melts may have a tendency to run, so let them cool a bit in the pastry bag before piping. Experiment a bit and you will soon find the perfect consistency of candy melts to work with.

Making Simple Faces with Curly Hair

1. To create a mixture the color of a light skin tone, combine equal parts of yellow, pink and white candy melts. For darker skin tones, combine white candy melts with a small amount of milk chocolate candy melts. Place 1 cup (250 mL) of the combined candy melts in a 2-cup (500 mL) glass measuring cup or small microwave-safe glass bowl. Microwave on High in 30-second intervals, stirring after each, until melted and smooth. Adjust the tone as desired by adding a little more of one color or the other and reheating to melt.

2. Following the instructions on page 29, coat the cake pop in the flesh-colored candy melts. Set the cake pop in a cake pop stand to dry.

3. For the hair, melt 1 cup (250 mL) of yellow, black, orange, white or milk chocolate candy melts. Stir in 1 tsp (5 mL) shortening until smooth. Fit a pastry bag or squeeze bottle with a fine writing tip. Fill the pastry bag with the candy melts. Pipe tight swirls and circles on the top of the cake pop to resemble hair. Set the cake pop in the stand to dry.

4. For the eyes, melt 2 tbsp (30 mL) of blue, green or milk chocolate candy melts. Stir in 1/2 tsp (2 mL) shortening until smooth. Using the end of a paintbrush with a fine tip (opposite the bristles), make two dots of candy melts where the eyes should be. Set the cake pop in the stand to dry.

5. For the mouth, melt 2 tbsp (30 mL) of red candy melts. Stir in 1/2 tsp (2 mL) shortening until smooth. Fit another pastry bag or squeeze bottle with a fine writing tip. Fill the pastry bag with the candy melts. Pipe the mouth.

6. If desired, still using the red candy melts, make a hair bow by piping a small figure 8 in the hair, then piping a small dot in the center of the figure 8. Set the cake pop in the stand to dry.

Almond Cream Cake Pops

**Makes 26
to 28 cake pops**

The creamy, almond flavor and the dense texture make these cake pops perfect for decorating for your next theme party.

Tip

Non-dairy whipped topping mix comes in boxes containing two or four envelopes. Use 2 tbsp (30 mL) — about half of one envelope — for this recipe and store the remaining mix in a sealable bag at room temperature for up to 6 months.

Variation

For a rich, buttery flavor, substitute butter flavoring for the almond extract.

1 cup	white cake mix	250 mL
2 tbsp	powdered non-dairy whipped topping mix (see tip, at left)	30 mL
1	large egg, at room temperature	1
1/4 cup	milk	60 mL
1/2 tsp	vanilla extract	2 mL
1/2 tsp	almond extract	2 mL
	Nonstick baking spray	

1. In a medium bowl, using an electric mixer on low speed, beat cake mix, whipped topping mix, egg, milk, vanilla and almond extract for 30 seconds or until moistened. Beat on medium speed for 2 minutes.

2. Spray cake pop wells with nonstick baking spray. Fill each well with about 1 tbsp (15 mL) batter (see page 25). Bake for 4 to 6 minutes or until a tester inserted in the center comes out clean. Transfer cake pops to a wire rack to cool. Repeat with the remaining batter.

3. If desired, attach sticks to cake pops (see page 27).

See the step-by-step photographs on photo page L. ▶

Tips

Be sure to purchase food-safe brushes from a cake decorating shop.

Thinning the candy melts with shortening makes painting fine details much easier.

Making Simple Faces with Straight Hair

1. To create a mixture the color of a light skin tone, combine equal parts of yellow, pink and white candy melts. For darker skin tones, combine white candy melts with a small amount of milk chocolate candy melts. Place 1 cup (250 mL) of the combined candy melts in a 2-cup (500 mL) glass measuring cup or small microwave-safe glass bowl. Microwave on High in 30-second intervals, stirring after each, until melted and smooth. Adjust the tone as desired by adding a little more of one color or the other and reheating to melt.

2. Following the instructions on page 29, coat the cake pop in the flesh-colored candy melts. Set the cake pop in a cake pop stand to dry. Reserve the candy melts.

3. For the hair, melt 1 cup (250 mL) of yellow, black, orange, white or milk chocolate candy melts. Stir in 1 tsp (5 mL) shortening until smooth. Fit a pastry bag or squeeze bottle with a fine writing tip. Fill the pastry bag with the candy melts. Pipe loops on the top of the cake pop to resemble straight hair. Set the cake pop in the stand to dry.

4. For the eyes, melt 2 tbsp (30 mL) of blue, green or milk chocolate candy melts. Stir in 1/2 tsp (2 mL) shortening until smooth. Fit another pastry bag or squeeze bottle with a fine writing tip. Fill the pastry bag with the candy melts. Pipe two dots of candy melts where the eyes should be. Set the cake pop in the stand to dry.

5. For the mouth, melt 2 tbsp (30 mL) of red candy melts. Stir in 1/2 tsp (2 mL) shortening until smooth. Fit another pastry bag or squeeze bottle with a fine writing tip. Fill the pastry bag with the candy melts. Pipe a smile. Set the cake pop in the stand to dry.

6. Tie a small bow on the cake pop stick.

Decorating Tips

- A pastry bag or squeeze bottle fitted with a fine writing tip makes it easy to pipe intricate designs or filigree.

- A great way to add texture when piping designs onto cake pops is to use the same color as the original coating.

- When creating complex designs, always work in stages, letting one color dry before proceeding to the next.

- Fondant is a great way to make decorations or details, and it comes in a variety of colors. Roll it out on a surface lightly covered with cornstarch or confectioners' (icing) sugar until it is about $1/8$ inch (3 mm) thick. Cut the fondant into the desired shape or mold it as you would clay, rolling thin strips or pieces into the desired shape. Attach the fondant using melted candy melts.

- Upside-down cake pops are fun too. Coat the cake pop in candy melts (see page 29), then dip the very top in finely chopped nuts, sprinkles or cookie crumbs. Set the cake pop, stick side up, on a sheet of waxed paper and let it dry.

- Injecting a cake pop with filling, such as chocolate ganache, is easy. Use a squeeze bottle or pastry bag fitted with a fine tip to inject the filling into the center of the cake pop. Do not overfill.

- When coating baked treats in granulated or confectioners' (icing) sugar, do so immediately after baking, while they are still quite hot. Work quickly but very gently. Place the sugar in a small paper sack. Lift the treats out of the cake pop maker and place them in the sack. Toss very gently to coat evenly, then place on a wire rack to cool. Sugar-coated treats are best served the day they are made, as the sugar will generally dissolve if they are stored overnight.

Filling the Wells

(see page 25 for detailed step-by-step instructions)

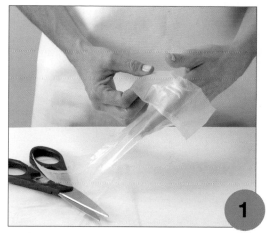

Make a collar on a pastry bag.

Fill the bag with batter.

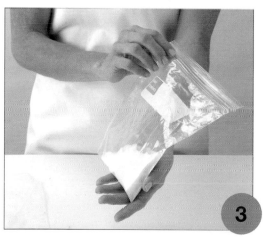

Or use a sealable plastic bag.

Clip the point off the bag.

Fill the wells with batter.

Set the bag upright in a glass between batches.

A.

Attaching the Sticks

(see page 27 for detailed step-by-step instructions)

Lift the cake pops out of the wells.

Transfer cake pops to a wire rack.

Place cake pops in freezer.

Melt candy melts in the microwave.

Dip the stick in the candy melts.

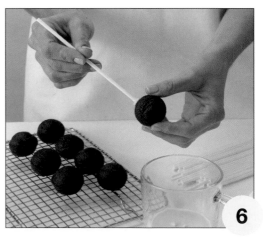

Push the stick into the cake pop.

B.

Coating Cake Pops

(see page 29 for detailed step-by-step instructions)

1

Add more candy melts to the cup.

2

Melt candy melts in the microwave.

3

Dip the cake pop into the coating.

4

Hold the cake pop over the cup.

5

Tap the stick against your fingers.

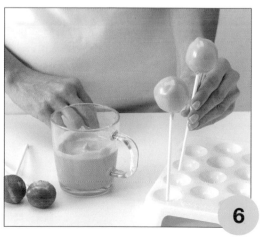

6

Set the cake pop in a cake pop stand.

Decorating with Sprinkles

(see page 31 for detailed step-by-step instructions)

Pour the sprinkles into a small bowl.

Hold the cake pop over the center of the bowl.

Dip the cake pop in the sprinkles.

Roll the cake pop in the sprinkles.

Gently shake off any excess sprinkles.

Set the cake pop in a cake pop stand.

D.

Adding Decorative Swirls

(see page 33 for detailed step-by-step instructions)

Melt candy melts in the microwave.

Fit a pastry bag with a fine writing tip.

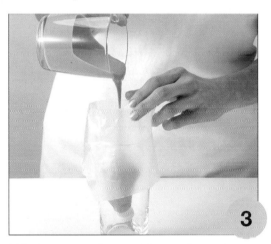

Fill the pastry bag with candy melts.

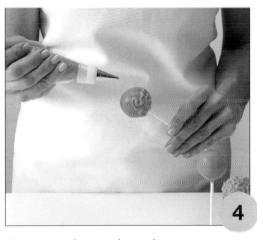

Pipe a swirl over the cake pop.

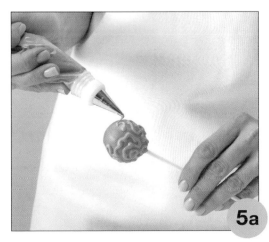

Pipe swirls in a tight design.

Or pipe swirls in a loose design.

E.

Adding a Sparkly Spiral

(see page 35 for detailed step-by-step instructions)

Select your sparkles.

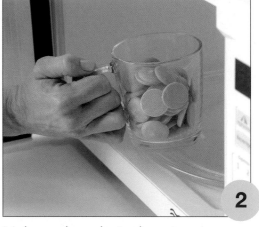

Melt candy melts in the microwave.

Fit a pastry bag with a fine writing tip.

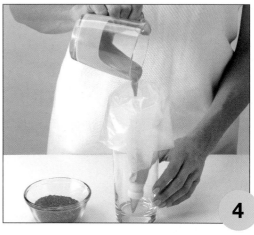

Fill the pastry bag with candy melts.

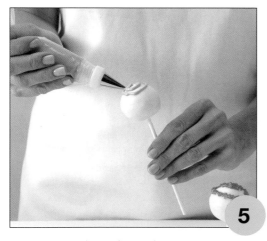

Pipe a spiral on the cake pop.

Sprinkle with sanding sugar or glitter.

F.

Triple-Dipping

(see page 37 for detailed step-by-step instructions)

1

Select three colors of candy melts.

2

Coat the cake pop in the first color. Let dry.

3

Melt the second color in the microwave.

4

Dip the cake pop two-thirds deep in the second color. Let dry.

5

Melt the third color in the microwave.

6

Dip the cake pop one-third deep in the third color. Let dry.

G.

Marbleizing

(see page 39 for detailed step-by-step instructions)

Melt two colors of candy melts.

Spoon about 1 tbsp (15 mL) of the second color into the first.

Swirl the mixture with a toothpick.

Dip the cake pop in the candy melts.

Rotate the cake pop in the candy melts.

Let excess coating drip off, then set in a cake pop stand to dry.

H.

Adding Decorations

(see page 41 for detailed step-by-step instructions)

Select your decorations.

Coat the cake pop in candy melts.

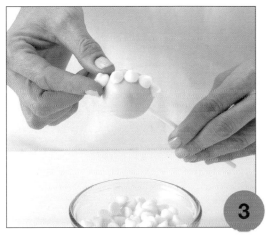

Arrange the decorations on the coating.

Decorate as desired.

Creating Rose Buds

(see page 43 for detailed step-by-step instructions)

Melt candy melts in the microwave.

Fit a pastry bag with a fine writing tip.

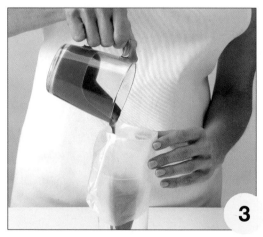

Fill the pastry bag with candy melts.

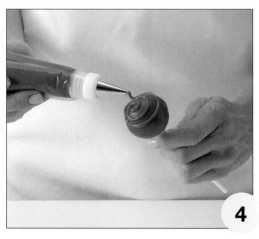

Pipe a swirl on top of the cake pop.

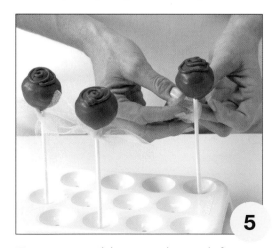

Tie a green ribbon on the stick for leaves.

Tie several rose buds into a bouquet.

J.

Making Simple Faces with Curly Hair

(see page 45 for detailed step-by-step instructions)

Combine candy melts to make a flesh color.

Coat the cake pop in candy melts.

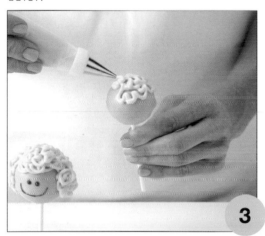

Pipe swirls and circles to resemble hair.

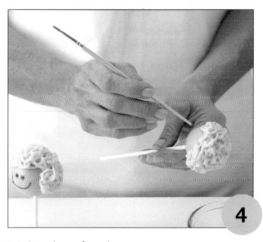

Make dots for the eyes.

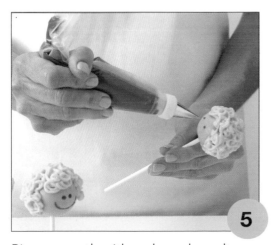

Pipe a mouth with red candy melts.

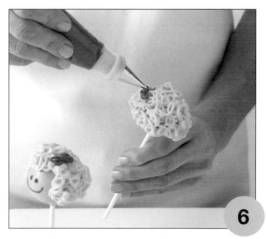

Pipe a hair bow with red candy melts.

K.

Making Simple Faces with Straight Hair

(see page 47 for detailed step-by-step instructions)

Combine candy melts to make a flesh color.

Coat the cake pop in candy melts.

Pipe loops of candy melts to resemble hair.

Make dots for the eyes.

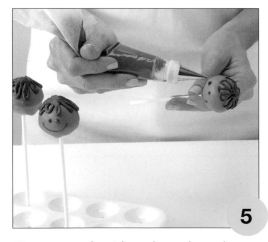

Pipe a mouth with red candy melts.

Tie a small bow on the cake pop stick.

L.

Part 2

Cakes and Sweets

Cake Pop Favorites

White Chocolate Cake Pops. 51

Chocolate Chip Cake Pops. 52

Devil's Food Cake Pops 53

Brownie Cake Pops 54

Root Beer Cake Pops 55

Cola Cake Pops 56

Cherry Cake Pops 57

Banana Cake Pops. 58

Coconut Cake Pops. 59

Peanut Butter Cake Pops 60

Caramel Cake Pops. 61

Spice Cake Pops 62

Gingerbread Cake Pops 63

White Chocolate Cake Pops

**Makes 42
to 44 cake pops**

These elegant white chocolate cake pops taste moist and rich. Kathy's daughter Amanda is a huge fan of white chocolate, so this flavor is a popular request at Kathy's house.

Tip

Be sure to check the baking progress at the minimum time, then continue baking until a tester inserted in the center comes out clean.

3 oz	white chocolate, chopped	90 g
1/4 cup	unsalted butter	60 mL
2 cups	white cake mix	500 mL
2	large eggs, at room temperature	2
1/3 cup	water	75 mL
1 tsp	vanilla extract	5 mL
	Nonstick baking spray	

1. Place white chocolate and butter in a small microwave safe glass bowl. Microwave on High in 30-second intervals, stirring after each, until melted. Set aside to cool for 2 minutes.

2. In a large bowl, using an electric mixer on low speed, beat cake mix, eggs, water, vanilla and melted white chocolate mixture for 30 seconds or until moistened. Beat on medium speed for 2 minutes.

3. Spray cake pop wells with nonstick baking spray. Fill each well with about 1 tbsp (15 mL) batter (see page 25). Bake for 3 to 5 minutes or until a tester inserted in the center comes out clean. Transfer cake pops to a wire rack to cool. Repeat with the remaining batter.

4. If desired, attach sticks to cake pops (see page 27).

Chocolate Chip Cake Pops

1½ cups	all-purpose flour	375 mL
¼ tsp	baking powder	1 mL
¼ tsp	baking soda	1 mL
⅛ tsp	salt	0.5 mL
1 cup	granulated sugar	250 mL
½ cup	unsalted butter, softened	125 mL
2	large eggs, at room temperature	2
1 tsp	vanilla extract	5 mL
⅓ cup	buttermilk	75 mL
½ cup	mini chocolate chips	125 mL
	Nonstick baking spray	

Makes 53 to 55 cake pops

Whether you decide to bake these for after-school snacks or dip them in candy coating for a more intense chocolate treat, these will satisfy that craving for sweets.

Tips

No buttermilk on hand? Stir 1 tsp (5 mL) lemon juice or white vinegar into ⅓ cup (75 mL) milk. Let stand for 5 to 10 minutes or until thickened. Proceed with the recipe.

Did you forget to set out the butter so that it will soften? Cut it into ½-inch (1 cm) slices, place on a microwave-safe glass plate and microwave on Medium-Low (30%) for 10 to 15 seconds or until starting to soften. Let butter stand for about 10 minutes, then proceed with the recipe.

1. In a small bowl, whisk together flour, baking powder, baking soda and salt. Set aside.

2. In a medium bowl, using an electric mixer on medium-high speed, beat sugar and butter for 1 to 2 minutes or until fluffy. Add eggs, one at a time, beating well after each addition. Beat in vanilla. Add flour mixture alternately with buttermilk, making three additions of flour and two of buttermilk and beating on low speed until blended. Gently stir in mini chocolate chips until well blended.

3. Spray cake pop wells with nonstick baking spray. Fill each well with about 1 tbsp (15 mL) batter (see page 25). Bake for 4 to 6 minutes or until a tester inserted in the center comes out clean. Transfer cake pops to a wire rack to cool. Repeat with the remaining batter.

4. If desired, attach sticks to cake pops (see page 27).

Devil's Food Cake Pops

Makes 36 to 38 cake pops

Devil's food cake is a dark, dense and rich chocolate cake that was especially popular during the 19th century.

Tips

No buttermilk on hand? Stir ¾ tsp (3 mL) lemon juice or white vinegar into ¼ cup (60 mL) milk. Let stand for 5 to 10 minutes or until thickened. Proceed with the recipe.

Do you have a Babycakes Rotating Cake Pop Maker? If so, see page 8 for information on using it.

½ cup + 2 tbsp	all-purpose flour	155 mL
¼ cup	unsweetened cocoa powder	60 mL
½ tsp	baking soda	2 mL
¼ tsp	salt	1 mL
⅛ tsp	baking powder	0.5 mL
¼ cup	cold strong brewed coffee or water	60 mL
¼ cup	buttermilk	60 mL
¼ cup	unsalted butter, softened	60 mL
¾ cup	granulated sugar	175 mL
1	large egg, at room temperature	1
½ tsp	vanilla extract	2 mL
	Nonstick baking spray	

1. In a small bowl, whisk together flour, cocoa, baking soda, salt and baking powder. Set aside.

2. In another small bowl, combine coffee and buttermilk. Set aside.

3. In a medium bowl, using an electric mixer on medium speed, beat butter until creamy and light, about 3 minutes. Gradually add sugar and continue beating for 2 minutes. Beat in egg and vanilla. Add flour mixture alternately with coffee mixture, making two additions of flour and one of coffee and beating on low speed until blended.

4. Spray cake pop wells with nonstick baking spray. Fill each well with about 1 tbsp (15 mL) batter (see page 25). Bake for 4 to 6 minutes or until a tester inserted in the center comes out clean. Transfer cake pops to a wire rack to cool. Repeat with the remaining batter.

5. If desired, attach sticks to cake pops (see page 27).

Brownie Cake Pops

Makes 38 to 40 cake pops

Roxanne's husband's family, the Batemans, pride themselves on their family brownie recipe, which has been passed down from generation to generation. Although this recipe is not exactly the same, these cake pops will surely become a fast hit at the Bateman family reunions.

Variation

For extra chocolate flavor, stir 2 tbsp (30 mL) mini chocolate chips into the batter just before baking.

¾ cup	all-purpose flour	175 mL
¼ tsp	baking soda	1 mL
¼ tsp	salt	1 mL
¾ cup	granulated sugar	175 mL
⅓ cup	unsalted butter, cut into pieces	75 mL
2 tbsp	water	30 mL
1 cup	semisweet chocolate chips	250 mL
1 tsp	vanilla extract	5 mL
2	large eggs, at room temperature	2
	Nonstick baking spray	

1. In a small bowl, whisk together flour, baking soda and salt. Set aside.

2. In a small saucepan, over medium-high heat, combine sugar, butter and water; bring just to a boil. Remove from heat and stir in chocolate chips and vanilla. Continue stirring until chocolate chips are melted. Pour chocolate mixture into a medium bowl and let cool for 10 minutes.

3. Add eggs, one at a time, to chocolate mixture, whisking well after each addition. Stir in flour mixture until combined.

4. Spray cake pop wells with nonstick baking spray. Fill each well with about 1 tbsp (15 mL) batter (see page 25). Bake for 5 to 7 minutes or until a tester inserted in the center comes out clean. Transfer cake pops to a wire rack to cool. Repeat with the remaining batter.

5. If desired, attach sticks to cake pops (see page 27).

Root Beer Cake Pops

Makes 44 to 46 cake pops

If you love the flavor of an ice-cold root beer, this recipe is for you.

Tip

This recipe was tested using regular root beer. While it may be tempting to substitute diet or sugar-free root beer, it is not recommended. The sweeteners in these beverages were not developed for cooking, and the results may be less than satisfactory.

Decorating Tip

- Glaze the cake pops with Root Beer Glaze (page 82). Remember, if you plan to glaze your cake pops, leave them off the sticks.

1 oz	bittersweet chocolate, cut into small pieces	30 g
½ cup	unsweetened cocoa powder	125 mL
¼ cup	unsalted butter, cut into pieces	60 mL
1¼ cups	root beer	300 mL
½ cup	granulated sugar	125 mL
¼ cup	packed brown sugar	60 mL
1¼ cups	all-purpose flour	300 mL
¾ tsp	baking soda	3 mL
½ tsp	salt	2 mL
¼ tsp	ground nutmeg	1 mL
¼ tsp	ground allspice	1 mL
1	large egg, at room temperature	1
1	large egg yolk, at room temperature	1
	Nonstick baking spray	

1. In a medium saucepan, over medium heat, combine chocolate, cocoa powder, butter and root beer; heat, stirring often, until butter is melted. Whisk in granulated sugar and brown sugar until dissolved. Remove from heat and let cool.

2. In a small bowl, whisk together flour, baking soda, salt, nutmeg and allspice; set aside.

3. Whisk the egg and egg yolk into the cooled root beer mixture. Gently stir in flour mixture until blended (batter may be slightly lumpy).

4. Spray cake pop wells with nonstick baking spray. Fill each well with about 1 tbsp (15 mL) batter (see page 25). Bake for 4 to 6 minutes or until a tester inserted in the center comes out clean. Transfer cake pops to a wire rack to cool. Repeat with the remaining batter.

5. If desired, attach sticks to cake pops (see page 27).

Decorating Tip

- Prepare half the Root Beer Glaze recipe (page 82) and, using a pastry bag or squeeze bottle fitted with a fine tip, inject the glaze into the center of the cake pops. Dip the filled cake pops in melted candy melts.

Cola Cake Pops

Makes 22 to 24 cake pops

Reminiscent of the old South, this tangy chocolate cake will remind you of magnolias and family reunions.

Tip

This recipe was tested using regular cola. While it may be tempting to substitute diet or sugar-free cola, it is not recommended. The sweeteners in these beverages were not developed for cooking, and the results may be less than satisfactory.

Glaze isn't strong enough to hold cake pop sticks securely, so leave glazed cake pops off the sticks.

An adult version of this recipe, Rum and Cola Cake Pops, can be found on page 164.

1¼ cups	chocolate fudge cake mix	300 mL
3½ tbsp	chocolate instant pudding mix	52 mL
1	large egg, at room temperature	1
⅓ cup	cola	75 mL
1 tbsp	vegetable oil	15 mL
	Nonstick baking spray	
	Cola Glaze (variation, page 78)	
1 cup	toasted chopped pecans (see tip, page 120)	250 mL

1. In a medium bowl, using an electric mixer on low speed, beat cake mix, pudding, egg, cola and oil for 30 seconds or until moistened. Beat on medium speed for 2 minutes.

2. Spray cake pop wells with nonstick baking spray. Fill each well with about 1 tbsp (15 mL) batter (see page 25). Bake for 4 to 6 minutes or until a tester inserted in the center comes out clean. Transfer cake pops to a wire rack set over a sheet of foil or waxed paper to cool. Repeat with the remaining batter.

3. Using the fork tool, dip each cake pop in Cola Glaze, allowing excess glaze to drip back into the bowl. Coat cake pops with pecans. Return coated cake pops to the wire rack to set.

Cherry Cake Pops

· ·

**Makes 34
to 36 cake pops**

Dip these pretty pink
cake pops, packed
with cherries, in
chocolate and you
will be reminded of
a chocolate-covered
cherry.

· ·

Tips

Have you ever noticed
that many cherry desserts
include just a tiny amount
of almond extract? That's
because almond extract
seems to intensify the
cherry flavor.

Do you have a Babycakes
Rotating Cake Pop Maker?
If so, see page 8 for
information on using it.

1 cup	all-purpose flour	250 mL
1 tsp	baking powder	5 mL
1/4 tsp	salt	1 mL
1/4 cup	milk	60 mL
2 tbsp	maraschino cherry juice	30 mL
2/3 cup	granulated sugar	150 mL
1/3 cup	shortening	75 mL
2	large eggs, at room temperature	2
2 tbsp	finely chopped drained maraschino cherries	30 mL
1/2 tsp	almond extract	2 mL
4 to 6	drops red food coloring	4 to 6
	Nonstick baking spray	

1. In a small bowl, whisk together flour, baking powder and salt. Set aside.

2. In another small bowl, combine milk and cherry juice. Set aside.

3. In a medium bowl, using an electric mixer on medium-high speed, beat sugar and shortening for 1 to 2 minutes or until fluffy. Add eggs, one a time, beating well after each addition. Add flour mixture alternately with milk mixture, making three additions of flour and two of milk and beating on low speed until smooth. Beat in cherries, almond extract and 4 drops of food coloring until combined. Add more food coloring, if desired.

4. Spray cake pop wells with nonstick baking spray. Fill each well with about 1 tbsp (15 mL) batter (see page 25). Bake for 4 to 6 minutes or until a tester inserted in the center comes out clean. Transfer cake pops to a wire rack to cool. Repeat with the remaining batter.

5. If desired, attach sticks to cake pops (see page 27).

Banana Cake Pops

Makes 48 to 50 cake pops

Banana makes cake pops moist and flavorful. Dip them in chocolate for a universally popular flavor combination.

Tips

Bananas sweeten as they ripen, and very ripe bananas add the best taste and texture to baked goods.

If you have a ripe banana but you don't have time to bake that day, put it in the refrigerator for up to 3 days. Although the peel will turn brown, the fruit will remain good for use in cakes and breads. If you have an overripe banana, mash it and stir in 1 tsp (5 mL) lemon juice. Store in an airtight container in the freezer for up to 6 months. When you're ready to bake, thaw the mashed banana overnight in the refrigerator, then use it in your favorite baked goods.

1½ cups	all-purpose flour	375 mL
½ tsp	baking soda	2 mL
½ tsp	ground cinnamon	2 mL
¼ tsp	salt	1 mL
1 cup	granulated sugar	250 mL
⅓ cup	vegetable oil	75 mL
2	large eggs, at room temperature	2
½ tsp	vanilla extract	2 mL
1 cup	mashed very ripe bananas (about 2)	250 mL
	Nonstick baking spray	

1. In a small bowl, whisk together flour, baking soda, cinnamon and salt. Set aside.

2. In a medium bowl, using an electric mixer on medium-high speed, beat sugar and oil for 1 to 2 minutes or until fluffy. Add eggs, one a time, beating well after each addition. Beat in vanilla. Beat in bananas. Add flour mixture and beat on low speed until smooth.

3. Spray cake pop wells with nonstick baking spray. Fill each well with about 1 tbsp (15 mL) batter (see page 25). Bake for 4 to 6 minutes or until a tester inserted in the center comes out clean. Transfer cake pops to a wire rack to cool. Repeat with the remaining batter.

4. If desired, attach sticks to cake pops (see page 27).

Coconut Cake Pops

Makes 24 to 26 cake pops

If you like chocolate-covered coconut candy bars, these cake pops will be a real treat. Just dip them in milk chocolate candy melts and you'll shout for joy!

Tips

Non-dairy whipped topping mix comes in boxes containing two or four envelopes. Use 2 tbsp (30 mL) — about half of one envelope — for this recipe and store the remaining mix in a sealable bag at room temperature for up to 6 months.

No coconut extract? Substitute vanilla extract. While the coconut flavor will be milder, the pops will still taste great.

• Food processor

½ cup	sweetened flaked coconut	125 mL
1 cup	yellow cake mix (preferably butter recipe)	250 mL
2 tbsp	powdered non-dairy whipped topping mix	30 mL
1	large egg, at room temperature	1
¼ cup	milk	60 mL
1 tsp	coconut extract	5 mL
	Nonstick baking spray	

1. In food processor, process coconut until it resembles fine crumbs.

2. In a medium bowl, using an electric mixer on low speed, beat ground coconut, cake mix, whipped topping mix, egg, milk and coconut extract for 30 seconds or until moistened. Beat for 2 minutes on medium speed.

3. Spray cake pop wells with nonstick baking spray. Fill each well with about 1 tbsp (15 mL) batter (see page 25). Bake for 4 to 6 minutes or until a tester inserted in the center comes out clean. Transfer cake pops to a wire rack to cool. Repeat with the remaining batter.

4. If desired, attach sticks to cake pops (see page 27).

Decorating Tip

• Dip the cake pops in melted chocolate candy melts, then, if desired, sprinkle immediately with toasted finely chopped almonds and/or sweetened flaked coconut.

Peanut Butter Cake Pops

Makes 31 to 33 cake pops

Dip these peanut butter cake pops in chocolate for a classic flavor combo. Kathy served these one evening to friends, and everyone was clamoring for more.

Tip

Do you have a Babycakes Rotating Cake Pop Maker? If so, see page 8 for information on using it.

1½ cups	yellow cake mix	375 mL
1	large egg, at room temperature	1
1	large egg yolk, at room temperature	1
⅓ cup	water	75 mL
¼ cup	creamy peanut butter	60 mL
2 tbsp	vegetable oil	30 mL
	Nonstick baking spray	

1. In a large bowl, using an electric mixer on low speed, beat cake mix, egg, egg yolk, water, peanut butter and oil for 30 seconds or until moistened. Beat for 2 minutes on medium speed.

2. Spray cake pop wells with nonstick baking spray. Fill each well with about 1 tbsp (15 mL) batter (see page 25). Bake for 4 to 6 minutes or until a tester inserted in the center comes out clean. Transfer cake pops to a wire rack to cool. Repeat with the remaining batter.

3. If desired, attach sticks to cake pops (see page 27).

Decorating Tip

- Dip the cake pops in melted chocolate candy melts and immediately sprinkle with chopped peanuts.

Caramel Cake Pops

**Makes 38
to 40 cake pops**

Do you remember this old-fashioned cake? Moist, with a slight caramel flavor, this recipe makes perfect cake pops that are delicious plain, dipped or glazed.

Variation

Stir in ¼ cup (60 mL) toffee bits to batter before baking.

1⅓ cups	all-purpose flour	325 mL
1 tsp	baking powder	5 mL
¼ tsp	salt	1 mL
½ cup	sour cream	125 mL
2 tbsp	milk	30 mL
½ cup	unsalted butter, softened	125 mL
1 cup	granulated sugar	250 mL
2	large eggs, at room temperature	2
½ tsp	vanilla extract	2 mL
	Nonstick baking spray	

1. In a small bowl, whisk together flour, baking powder and salt. Set aside.

2. In another small bowl, whisk together sour cream and milk. Set aside.

3. In a medium bowl, using an electric mixer on medium-high speed, beat butter for 1 minute or until creamy. Gradually add sugar and continue beating for 2 minutes. Add eggs, one at a time, beating after each addition. Beat in vanilla. Add flour mixture alternately with sour cream mixture, making three additions of flour and two of sour cream and beating on low speed until smooth.

4. Spray cake pop wells with nonstick baking spray. Fill each well with about 1 tbsp (15 mL) batter (see page 25). Bake for 4 to 6 minutes or until a tester inserted in the center comes out clean. Transfer cake pops to a wire rack to cool. Repeat with the remaining batter.

5. If desired, attach sticks to cake pops (see page 27).

Decorating Tip

- Glaze the cake pops with Caramel Glaze (variation, page 84). Remember, if you plan to glaze your cake pops, leave them off the sticks.

Spice Cake Pops

Makes 46 to 48 cake pops

For some — Kathy included — nothing is more comforting than the smell of spice cake baking in the oven. Make some memories with this old-fashioned spice cake recipe.

Tip

No buttermilk on hand? Stir 1½ tsp (7 mL) lemon juice or white vinegar into ½ cup (125 mL) milk. Let stand for 5 to 10 minutes or until thickened. Proceed with the recipe.

1⅓ cups	all purpose flour	325 mL
½ tsp	baking soda	2 mL
½ tsp	baking powder	2 mL
½ tsp	ground cinnamon	2 mL
½ tsp	ground nutmeg	2 mL
¼ tsp	ground cloves	1 mL
Pinch	salt	Pinch
1 cup	packed brown sugar	250 mL
½ cup	unsalted butter, softened	125 mL
3	large eggs, at room temperature	3
½ cup	buttermilk	125 mL
	Nonstick baking spray	

1. In a small bowl, whisk together flour, baking soda, baking powder, cinnamon, nutmeg, cloves and salt. Set aside.

2. In a large bowl, using an electric mixer on medium-high speed, beat brown sugar and butter for 1 to 2 minutes or until fluffy. Add eggs, one a time, beating well after each addition. Add flour mixture alternately with buttermilk, making three additions of flour and two of buttermilk and beating on low speed until smooth.

3. Spray cake pop wells with nonstick baking spray. Fill each well with about 1 tbsp (15 mL) batter (see page 25). Bake for 4 to 6 minutes or until a tester inserted in the center comes out clean. Transfer cake pops to a wire rack to cool. Repeat with the remaining batter.

4. If desired, attach sticks to cake pops (see page 27).

Decorating Tip

- Dip the cake pops in Tennessee Bourbon Glaze (page 84) or Caramel Glaze (variation, page 84) for a truly wonderful flavor. Remember, if you plan to glaze your cake pops, leave them off the sticks.

Gingerbread Cake Pops

Makes 38 to 40 cake pops

The aroma and flavor of classic baking spices combined with the richness of molasses make cake pops that are ideal for fall, winter and the holidays. They are wonderful dipped in vanilla candy melts, or try them dipped in Lemon Glaze (page 80) for a lighter, delightfully different treat.

Tip

No buttermilk on hand? Stir 1 tsp (5 mL) lemon juice or white vinegar into ⅓ cup (75 mL) milk. Let stand for 5 to 10 minutes or until thickened. Proceed with the recipe.

Molasses comes from boiling the juice that is extracted from processing sugar cane or beets into sugar. Light (fancy) and dark (cooking) molasses can be used interchangeably in this recipe, but dark molasses gives the cake pops a more robust flavor. Unsulfured molasses (no sulfur was used in the processing) is preferred, as the flavor is lighter.

1⅓ cups	all-purpose flour	325 mL
1 tsp	ground ginger	5 mL
1 tsp	ground cinnamon	5 mL
½ tsp	baking powder	2 mL
½ tsp	baking soda	2 mL
¼ tsp	salt	1 mL
¼ tsp	ground cloves	1 mL
½ cup	packed brown sugar	125 mL
⅓ cup	unsalted butter, softened	75 mL
1	large egg, at room temperature	1
1	large egg yolk, at room temperature	1
⅓ cup	unsulfured dark (cooking) molasses	75 mL
⅓ cup	buttermilk	75 mL
	Nonstick baking spray	

1. In a small bowl, whisk together flour, ginger, cinnamon, baking powder, baking soda, salt and cloves. Set aside.

2. In a medium bowl, using an electric mixer on medium-high speed, beat brown sugar and butter for 1 to 2 minutes or until fluffy. Beat in egg and egg yolk. Beat in molasses. Add flour mixture alternately with buttermilk, making three additions of flour and two of buttermilk and beating on low speed until smooth.

3. Spray cake pop wells with nonstick baking spray. Fill each well with about 1 tbsp (15 mL) batter (see page 25). Bake for 4 to 6 minutes or until a tester inserted in the center comes out clean. Transfer cake pops to a wire rack to cool. Repeat with the remaining batter.

4. If desired, attach sticks to cake pops (see page 27).

Sweet Treats and Desserts

Neapolitan Cake Pops 65

Cream-Filled Chocolate Cake Pops. 66

Chocolate Malt Cake Pops 67

Thin Mint Cake Pops 68

Chocolate Cherry Cake Pops 69

Chocolate Truffle Cake Pops 70

Key Lime Cake Pops 71

Cheesecake Surprise Cake Pops 72

Strawberry Shortcakes. 73

Mini Banana Splits 74

Mini Ice Cream Sandwich Sundaes 75

Neapolitan Cake Pops

**Makes
72 to 78
cake pops (24 to
26 cake pops of
each flavor)**

One batter divides to make vanilla, strawberry and chocolate cake pops in this special Neapolitan dessert.

Tip

To melt semisweet chocolate, place chocolate in a small microwave-safe glass bowl and microwave on High in 30-second intervals, stirring after each, until melted. Let cool slightly.

Decorating Tip

- Dip each flavor of cake pop in a different flavor or color of candy melt, complementing the flavor of the cake with the coating — white for the vanilla cake, pink for the strawberry cake and chocolate for the chocolate cake. Or dip them all into melted chocolate candy melts and add decorative swirls in complementary colors and flavors.

2⅔ cups	all-purpose flour	650 mL
1½ tsp	baking powder	7 mL
½ tsp	baking soda	2 mL
¼ tsp	salt	1 mL
1⅔ cups	granulated sugar	400 mL
1 cup	unsalted butter, softened	250 mL
3	large eggs, at room temperature	3
¾ cup	sour cream, at room temperature	175 mL
1 tsp	vanilla extract	5 mL
2 tbsp	milk	30 mL
2 tbsp	strawberry-flavored gelatin powder	30 mL
1 tbsp	water	15 mL
2 oz	semisweet chocolate, melted (see tip, at left)	60 g
	Nonstick baking spray	

1. In a small bowl, whisk together flour, baking powder, baking soda and salt. Set aside.

2. In a large bowl, using an electric mixer on medium-high speed, beat together sugar and butter for 1 to 2 minutes or until fluffy. Add eggs, one a time, beating well after each addition. Beat in sour cream and vanilla. Add flour mixture and beat on low speed just until smooth.

3. Measure out 1⅔ cups (400 mL) batter and place into a small bowl. Using an electric mixer on medium-high speed, beat in milk. Set aside.

4. Measure out another 1⅔ cups (400 mL) batter and place in another small bowl. Using an electric mixer on medium-high speed, beat in gelatin and water. Set aside.

5. Using an electric mixer with clean beaters on medium-high speed, beat melted chocolate into the remaining batter.

6. Spray cake pop wells with nonstick baking spray. Fill each well with about 1 tbsp (15 mL) batter (see page 25), keeping the flavors separate. Bake for 4 to 6 minutes or until a tester inserted in the center comes out clean. Transfer cake pops to a wire rack to cool. Repeat with the remaining batter.

7. If desired, attach sticks to cake pops (see page 27).

Cream-Filled Chocolate Cake Pops

Makes 22 to 24 cake pops

The cream filling makes these morsels a winning recipe.

Tips

Non-dairy whipped topping mix comes in boxes containing two or four envelopes. Use 2 tbsp (30 mL) — about half of one envelope — for this recipe and store the remaining mix in a sealable bag at room temperature for up to 6 months.

Store cream-filled cake pops in an airtight container in the refrigerator for up to 3 days.

1 cup	devil's food cake mix	250 mL
2 tbsp	powdered non-dairy whipped topping mix (see tip, at left)	30 mL
1	large egg, at room temperature	1
¼ cup	water	60 mL
½ tsp	vanilla extract	2 mL
	Nonstick baking spray	
	Marshmallow Cream Filling (page 86)	

1. In a medium bowl, using an electric mixer on low speed, beat cake mix, whipped topping mix, egg, water and vanilla for 30 seconds or until moistened. Beat on medium speed for 2 minutes.

2. Spray cake pop wells with nonstick baking spray. Fill each well with about 1 tbsp (15 mL) batter (see page 25). Bake for 4 to 6 minutes or until a tester inserted in the center comes out clean. Transfer cake pops to a wire rack to cool. Repeat with the remaining batter.

3. Cut each cake pop in half, spread one half with Marshmallow Cream Filling, then stick the halves back together.

Decorating Tip

- For an added treat, freeze the filled cake pops, then use the fork tool to dip them in chocolate or vanilla candy melts. Place the coated cake pops on a wire rack over a sheet of foil or waxed paper to set.

Chocolate Malt Cake Pops

**Makes 26
to 28 cake pops**

If you like chocolate malts and chocolate malt candies, these are the treats for you.

Tip
Do you have a Babycakes Rotating Cake Pop Maker? If so, see page 8 for information on using it.

Decorating Tip

- Dip cake pops in melted chocolate candy melts, then immediately sprinkle with additional finely chopped chocolate malt candies. If you've chosen not to attach sticks, use the fork tool to dip the cake pops, then place them on a wire rack over a sheet of foil or waxed paper to set.

⅔ cup	all-purpose flour	150 mL
¼ cup	chocolate malted milk powder	60 mL
½ tsp	baking powder	2 mL
½ tsp	baking soda	2 mL
Pinch	salt	Pinch
3 oz	semisweet chocolate, chopped	90 g
⅓ cup	unsalted butter	75 mL
¼ cup	packed brown sugar	60 mL
2 tbsp	granulated sugar	30 mL
1	large egg, at room temperature	1
1	large egg yolk, at room temperature	1
1 tsp	vanilla extract	5 mL
2 tbsp	sour cream	30 mL
2 tbsp	milk	30 mL
¼ cup	finely chopped chocolate malt candies	60 mL
	Nonstick baking spray	

1. In a small bowl, whisk together flour, chocolate malted milk powder, baking powder, baking soda and salt. Set aside.

2. Place semisweet chocolate and butter in a large microwave-safe glass bowl. Microwave on High in 30-second intervals, stirring after each, until melted. Set aside to cool for 2 minutes.

3. Using an electric mixer on medium-high speed, beat brown sugar and granulated sugar into melted chocolate mixture. Add egg and beat well. Add egg yolk and beat well. Beat in vanilla. Reduce mixer speed to low and beat in one-third of the flour mixture. Beat in sour cream, then another one-third of the flour mixture, then milk. Beat in the remaining flour mixture. Stir in chopped candies.

4. Spray cake pop wells with nonstick baking spray. Fill each well with about 1 tbsp (15 mL) batter (see page 25). Bake for 4 to 6 minutes or until a tester inserted in the center comes out clean. Transfer cake pops to a wire rack to cool. Repeat with the remaining batter.

5. If desired, attach sticks to cake pops (see page 27).

Thin Mint Cake Pops

**Makes 28
to 30 cake pops**

The combination of chocolate and mint is an all-time favorite.

1 oz	unsweetened chocolate, chopped	30 g
2 tbsp	unsalted butter	30 mL
2/3 cup	all-purpose flour	150 mL
2/3 cup	granulated sugar	150 mL
1/4 cup	unsweetened cocoa powder	60 mL
1/2 tsp	baking soda	2 mL
1/4 tsp	baking powder	1 mL
Pinch	salt	Pinch
1	large egg, at room temperature	1
6 tbsp	sour cream	90 mL
3 tbsp	water	45 mL
1/2 tsp	peppermint extract	2 mL
1/4 cup	chopped chocolate thin mint candies	60 mL
	Nonstick baking spray	

Decorating Tip

- Dip cake pops in melted chocolate candy melts, then immediately sprinkle them with finely crushed hard peppermint candies. Alternatively, flavor the melted chocolate candy melts with peppermint candy flavoring. Peppermint candy flavoring is very concentrated, so add just a drop or two, taste and add additional drops as needed. Be sure to use special candy flavoring, an oil-based product.

1. Place chocolate and butter in a small microwave-safe glass bowl. Microwave on High in 30-second intervals, stirring after each, until melted. Set aside to cool for 2 minutes.

2. In a large bowl, whisk together flour, sugar, cocoa, baking soda, baking powder and salt. Add egg, sour cream, water, peppermint extract and melted chocolate mixture. Using an electric mixer on medium-high speed, beat for 1 minute or until well blended. Stir in chopped candies.

3. Spray cake pop wells with nonstick baking spray. Fill each well with about 1 tbsp (15 mL) batter (see page 25). Bake for 4 to 6 minutes or until a tester inserted in the center comes out clean. Transfer cake pops to a wire rack to cool. Repeat with the remaining batter.

4. If desired, attach sticks to cake pops (see page 27).

Decorating Tip

- Dip cake pops in a gently swirled mixture of melted green candy melts and chocolate candy melts. If you've chosen not to attach sticks, use the fork tool to dip the cake pops, then place them on a wire rack over a sheet of foil or waxed paper to set.

Chocolate Cherry Cake Pops

Makes 31 to 33 cake pops

Do you love chocolate-covered cherries? If so, this sweet treat is for you.

Decorating Tip

- Dip cake pops in melted chocolate candy melts. If you've chosen not to attach sticks, use the fork tool to dip the cake pops, then place them on a wire rack over a sheet of foil or waxed paper to set.

2 tbsp	unsalted butter	30 mL
1 oz	unsweetened chocolate, chopped	30 g
2/3 cup	all-purpose flour	150 mL
2/3 cup	granulated sugar	150 mL
1/4 cup	unsweetened cocoa powder	60 mL
1/2 tsp	baking soda	2 mL
1/4 tsp	baking powder	1 mL
Pinch	salt	Pinch
1	large egg, at room temperature	1
6 tbsp	sour cream	90 mL
2 tbsp	maraschino cherry juice	30 mL
1/2 tsp	almond extract	2 mL
1/4 cup	finely chopped drained maraschino cherries	60 mL
	Nonstick baking spray	

1. Place butter and chocolate in a small microwave-safe glass bowl. Microwave on High in 30-second intervals, stirring after each, until melted. Set aside to cool for 2 minutes.

2. In a large bowl, whisk together flour, sugar, cocoa, baking soda, baking powder and salt. Add egg, sour cream, juice, almond extract and melted chocolate mixture. Using an electric mixer on medium-high speed, beat for 1 minute or until well blended. Stir in maraschino cherries.

3. Spray cake pop wells with nonstick baking spray. Fill each well with about 1 tbsp (15 mL) batter (see page 25). Bake for 4 to 6 minutes or until a tester inserted in the center comes out clean. Transfer cake pops to a wire rack to cool. Repeat with the remaining batter.

4. If desired, attach sticks to cake pops (see page 27).

Decorating Tip

- For more pizzazz, dip cake pops in melted dark chocolate candy melts, then add decorative swirls with melted milk chocolate, pink or red candy melts (see page 33).

Chocolate Truffle Cake Pops

Makes 28 to 30 cake pops

These chocolate cake bites are over the top — filled with chocolate ganache, dipped in chocolate and garnished so that they resemble truffle candies. From all of the cake pops he tasted, Kathy's husband, David, chose this one as his very favorite.

Tips

There's no need to use melted candy melts to attach the sticks in this recipe; the ganache will set firmly and hold the stick in place.

Do you have a Babycakes Rotating Cake Pop Maker? If so, see page 8 for information on using it.

• Pastry bag or squeeze bottle, fitted with a fine tip

1 oz	unsweetened chocolate, chopped	30 g
2 tbsp	unsalted butter	30 mL
2/3 cup	all-purpose flour	150 mL
2/3 cup	granulated sugar	150 mL
1/4 cup	unsweetened cocoa powder	60 mL
1/2 tsp	baking soda	2 mL
1/4 tsp	baking powder	1 mL
Pinch	salt	Pinch
1	large egg, at room temperature	1
6 tbsp	sour cream	90 mL
2 tbsp	hot brewed coffee	30 mL
1/2 tsp	vanilla extract	2 mL
	Nonstick baking spray	
	Warm Chocolate Ganache Filling (page 86)	
	Chocolate candy melts	
	Toasted finely chopped nuts (optional)	
	Ground chocolate or additional unsweetened cocoa powder (optional)	

1. Place unsweetened chocolate and butter in a small microwave-safe glass bowl. Microwave on High in 30-second intervals, stirring after each, until melted. Set aside to cool for 2 minutes.

2. In a large bowl, whisk together flour, sugar, cocoa, baking soda, baking powder and salt. Add egg, sour cream, coffee, vanilla and melted chocolate mixture. Using an electric mixer on medium speed, beat for 1 minute or until well blended.

3. Spray cake pop wells with nonstick baking spray. Fill each well with about 1 tbsp (15 mL) batter (see page 25). Bake for 4 to 6 minutes or until a tester inserted in the center comes out clean. Transfer cake pops to a wire rack to cool. Repeat with the remaining batter.

4. Using the pastry bag or squeeze bottle, inject Chocolate Ganache Filling into the center of each cake pop. Insert a cake pop stick into the warm ganache center of each cake pop. Place cake pops on a baking sheet and freeze until firm, about 15 minutes.

5. Melt candy melts (see page 18). Dip cake pops in candy melts, then immediately sprinkle with nuts. Alternatively, let the chocolate coating dry, then sprinkle the cake pops with ground chocolate.

Key Lime Cake Pops

Makes 20 to 22 cake pops

Although most of us can't be in the Florida Keys all the time, it's certainly possible to enjoy the flavors of the islands anytime.

Tip

If you can't find Key limes, it's fine to use regular lime zest and juice. For the zest, use 1 tsp (5 mL).

Variation

Omit the dipping sauce and attach sticks to the cake pops (see page 27). Dip in white or lime green candy melts for a Floridian candy treat.

1¼ cups	white cake mix	300 mL
1	large egg, at room temperature	1
	Grated zest of 1 Key lime	
2 tbsp	freshly squeezed Key lime juice	30 mL
2 tbsp	milk	30 mL
	Nonstick baking spray	
	Key Lime Dipping Sauce (page 85)	

1. In a medium bowl, using an electric mixer on low speed, beat cake mix, egg, lime zest, lime juice and milk for 30 seconds or until moistened. Beat on medium speed for 2 minutes.

2. Spray cake pop wells with nonstick baking spray. Fill each well with about 1 tbsp (15 mL) batter (see page 25). Bake for 4 to 6 minutes or until a tester inserted in the center comes out clean. Transfer cake pops to a wire rack to cool. Repeat with the remaining batter.

3. Serve cake pops with Key Lime Dipping Sauce.

Cheesecake Surprise Cake Pops

These cake pops feature a cheesecake filling hidden inside rich, moist cake topped with a cream cheese glaze. What could be better?

Tips

Store cake pops filled with Cream Cheese Filling in an airtight container in the refrigerator for up to 3 days.

Instead of injecting the filling, you could cut each cake pop in half, spread one half with Cream Cheese Filling, then stick the halves back together.

• Pastry bag or squeeze bottle, fitted with a fine tip

1½ cups	all-purpose flour	375 mL
1¼ tsp	baking powder	6 mL
¼ tsp	salt	1 mL
1 cup	granulated sugar	250 mL
6 tbsp	unsalted butter, softened	90 mL
2	large eggs, at room temperature	2
1 tsp	vanilla extract	5 mL
⅔ cup	milk, at room temperature	150 mL
	Nonstick baking spray	
	Cream Cheese Filling (page 85)	
	Cream Cheese Glaze (page 77)	
	Graham wafer crumbs	

1. In a small bowl, whisk together flour, baking powder and salt. Set aside.

2. In a large bowl, using an electric mixer on medium-high speed, beat sugar and butter for 1 to 2 minutes or until fluffy. Add eggs, one at a time, beating well after each addition. Beat in vanilla. Add flour mixture alternately with milk, making three additions of flour and two of milk and beating on low speed until smooth.

3. Spray cake pop wells with nonstick baking spray. Fill each well with about 1 tbsp (15 mL) batter (see page 25). Bake for 4 to 6 minutes or until a tester inserted in the center comes out clean. Transfer cake pops to a wire rack set over a sheet of foil or waxed paper to cool. Repeat with the remaining batter.

4. Using the pastry bag or squeeze bottle, inject Cream Cheese Filling into the center of each cake pop.

5. Drizzle or pipe Cream Cheese Glaze over filled cake pops and immediately sprinkle with graham wafer crumbs. Return cake pops to the wire rack to set.

Strawberry Shortcakes

Have a ball with the best summertime dessert! The Babycakes cake pop maker is such a fun way to make shortcakes, and they turn out so fresh and crispy.

Tips

To make sweetened whipped cream, pour 1 cup (250 mL) heavy or whipping (35%) cream into a chilled deep bowl. Using an electric mixer on medium-high speed, beat cream until frothy. Gradually beat in 1 tbsp (15 mL) confectioners' (icing) sugar until stiff peaks form.

These wonderful shortcake bites can be paired with other fruits too, such as sweetened sliced peaches or other varieties of fresh berries.

Shortcakes

1 cup	all-purpose flour	250 mL
2 tsp	granulated sugar	10 mL
1½ tsp	baking powder	7 mL
Pinch	salt	Pinch
¼ cup	cold butter	60 mL
½ cup	milk	125 mL
1 tbsp	unsalted butter, melted	15 mL

Sweetened Strawberries

4 cups	sliced strawberries (about 1 to 1¼ lbs/500 to 625 g)	1 L
6 to 8 tbsp	granulated sugar	90 to 120 mL
2 cups	sweetened whipped cream (see tip, at left) or thawed whipped topping	500 mL

1. *Shortcakes:* In a medium bowl, combine flour, sugar, baking powder and salt. Using a pastry cutter or two knives, cut in cold butter until mixture resembles coarse crumbs. Using a fork, stir in milk just until moistened.

2. Drizzle about ⅛ tsp (0.5 mL) melted butter into each cake pop well. Fill each well with a mounded teaspoon (5 mL) of dough. Bake for 3 to 4 minutes or until golden brown. Transfer shortcakes to a wire rack to cool. Repeat with the remaining dough.

3. *Sweetened Strawberries:* Meanwhile, in a large bowl, combine strawberries and sugar, sweetening berries to taste. Using the back of a spoon, press lightly on some of the berries to bruise them slightly and release some juice. Let stand at room temperature for about 30 minutes or until strawberries release their juice.

4. Place 3 or 4 shortcakes in each of six dessert dishes. Ladle berries evenly over each serving and dollop with whipped cream.

Mini Banana Splits

Makes 24 to 25 servings

Capture the flavors of banana, pineapple, strawberry and chocolate in one terrific dessert!

Tip

To add to the fun of this dessert, add a small scoop of ice cream drizzled with chocolate or strawberry sauce. Top it all with a dollop of whipped cream and a cherry.

- 2 pastry bags or squeeze bottles, each fitted with a fine tip

1¼ tsp	granulated sugar	6 mL
1 tsp	cornstarch	5 mL
Pinch	ground ginger	Pinch
⅓ cup	unsweetened pineapple juice	75 mL
48 to 50	Banana Cake Pops (page 58) without sticks, cooled	48 to 50
¼ cup	strawberry sundae syrup	60 mL
	Chocolate candy melts, melted (see page 18)	

1. In a 2-cup (500 mL) microwave-safe glass measuring cup or bowl, combine sugar, cornstarch, ginger and pineapple juice. Microwave on High for 1 minute, stirring halfway through, until thickened and bubbly.

2. Pour the warm pineapple syrup into a pastry bag or squeeze bottle and inject this filling into the center of half of the cake pops.

3. Using another pastry bag or squeeze bottle, inject strawberry syrup into the remaining cake pops.

4. Dip all the cake pops in melted candy melts. Place one of each filling flavor in each dessert dish.

Mini Ice Cream Sandwich Sundaes

Makes 4 servings

These bite-size treats are pure magic! They're fun to eat and fun to serve, and you can vary the flavors to suit any taste.

Tips

To make sweetened whipped cream, pour ½ cup (125 mL) heavy or whipping (35%) cream into a chilled deep bowl. Using an electric mixer on medium-high speed, beat cream until frothy. Gradually beat in 1½ tsp (7 mL) confectioners' (icing) sugar until stiff peaks form.

The firmed sandwiches can be stored in an airtight container in the freezer for up to 7 days.

These are also great as traditional ice cream sandwiches. Omit the syrup, whipped cream and cherry — just serve with napkins! They're perfect for a crowd of children of any age. Make plenty, as they are small and people will want seconds.

16	Old-Fashioned Chocolate Cake Pops (page 26) without sticks, cooled	16
½ cup	vanilla ice cream, slightly softened	125 mL
½ cup	chocolate sundae syrup	125 mL
1 cup	sweetened whipped cream (see tip, at left) or frozen whipped topping, thawed	250 mL
4	maraschino cherries, drained	4

1. Using a sharp knife, slice each cake pop in half. For each cake pop, spoon 1½ tsp (7 mL) ice cream onto the center of one half, mounding slightly, then top with the other half. Place sandwiches on a baking sheet and place in the freezer for 10 to 15 minutes or until ice cream is firm.

2. Arrange 4 sandwiches in each of four parfait glasses or serving bowls. Drizzle with syrup, then garnish with whipped cream and top each with a cherry.

Variation

Mix and match the flavors of cake pops and ice cream. For example, fill Lemon Cake Pops (page 40) with lemon or rainbow sherbet, Princess Cake Pops (page 28) with chocolate ice cream, Spice Cake Pops (page 62) with dulce de leche ice cream, or Classic Red Velvet Cake Pops (page 38) with peppermint ice cream. You can take things one step further by customizing the syrup flavor too: drizzle caramel syrup over Spice Cake Pops with dulce de leche ice cream, or chocolate syrup over Classic Red Velvet Cake Pops with peppermint ice cream. Or simply omit the syrup and garnish the sandwiches with a mint leaf.

Coatings and Fillings

Easy Frosting Coating 77

Cream Cheese Glaze 77

Vanilla Glaze 78

Chocolate Glaze 78

White Chocolate Glaze 79

Strawberry Glaze 79

Lemon Glaze 80

Orange Glaze 80

Maple Glaze 81

French Toast Glaze 81

Cinnamon Candy Glaze 82

Root Beer Glaze 82

Champagne Glaze 83

Limoncello Glaze 83

Rum Glaze 84

Tennessee Bourbon Glaze 84

Key Lime Dipping Sauce 85

Cream Cheese Filling 85

Marshmallow Cream Filling 86

Chocolate Ganache Filling 86

Easy Frosting Coating

Makes about 1⅔ cups (400 mL)

This coating — which is not as firm or sweet as candy melts, yet is not as soft as typical glazes or frostings — dries to a semi-firm glossy surface that many people describe as perfect for cake pops.

Tip

It is important to use store-bought prepared frosting for this recipe.

| 1 | container (16 oz/450 g) creamy chocolate, vanilla or lemon frosting | 1 |
| ½ cup | semisweet chocolate or vanilla baking chips | 125 mL |

1. Place frosting in a small microwave-safe glass bowl. Microwave on High for 1 minute. Stir well. Stir in baking chips and microwave on High for 1 minute. Stir well. Let stand for 2 to 3 minutes, then stir until chips are completely melted. If necessary, microwave on High for an additional 10 to 15 seconds to melt chips, then stir until smooth.

Cream Cheese Glaze

Makes about ¾ cup (175 mL)

This cream cheese glaze is perfect to drizzle over almost any flavor of cake ball, doughnut or muffin.

Tip

Store baked goods drizzled with this glaze in the refrigerator.

3 oz	cream cheese, softened	90 g
3 tbsp	butter, melted	45 mL
½ cup	confectioners' (icing) sugar	125 mL
5 to 6 tsp	milk	25 to 30 mL
½ tsp	vanilla extract	2 mL

1. In a medium bowl, using an electric mixer on medium-high speed, beat cream cheese and butter for 1 minute or until light and creamy. Gradually beat in sugar until blended. Beat in 5 tsp (25 mL) milk and vanilla.

2. If a thinner glaze is desired, beat in an additional 1 tsp (5 mL) milk.

Vanilla Glaze

Dip any flavor of cake ball, doughnut or muffin in this universally popular glaze.

Tip
Dip, coat, drizzle or pipe? Any way you want to do it is fine! Some glazes are thinner and work especially well for dipping, while others are thicker and are easier to drizzle or pipe.

1⅓ cups	confectioners' (icing) sugar, sifted	325 mL
¼ cup	butter, melted	60 mL
2 tbsp	hot water	30 mL
1 tsp	vanilla extract	5 mL

1. In a small bowl, whisk together sugar, butter, hot water and vanilla until smooth.

Variation
Almond Glaze: Replace the vanilla extract with ½ tsp (2 mL) almond extract.

Chocolate Glaze

This versatile glaze tastes great on many different kinds of doughnuts and cake balls.

Tip
The consistency of this glaze works well on doughnuts. If dipping cake pops, thin the glaze to the desired consistency by adding more milk, 1 tbsp (15 mL) at a time.

¼ cup	butter	60 mL
2 tbsp	unsweetened cocoa powder	30 mL
2 cups	confectioners' (icing) sugar	500 mL
1½ tbsp	milk	22 mL

1. In a small saucepan, melt butter over medium heat. Add cocoa and stir until smooth. Remove from heat and whisk in sugar and milk until smooth.

Variations
Cola Glaze: Substitute cola for the milk.

Kahlúa Glaze: Substitute Kahlúa for the milk.

White Chocolate Glaze

Makes about 1 cup (250 mL)

Elegant and rich, this glaze sets to a beautiful semi-firm finish. If you wish, stir in food coloring to tint it to the desired color.

Tip

Dip cake pops, doughnuts or muffins in warm glaze. If necessary, reheat the glaze in the microwave on High for 10 to 15 seconds, as needed, to keep the glaze at a dipping consistency.

6 oz	white chocolate, chopped	175 g
3 tbsp	heavy or whipping (35%) cream	45 mL
3 tbsp	butter, cut into thirds and softened	45 mL
1/2 cup	confectioners' (icing) sugar	125 mL
1/2 tsp	vanilla extract	2 mL

1. Place white chocolate and cream in a small microwave-safe glass bowl. Microwave on High for 1 minute. Stir well. Add butter and microwave on High for 30 seconds. Stir well. If necessary, microwave on High for an additional 10 to 15 seconds to melt white chocolate and butter. Stir in sugar and vanilla until smooth.

Strawberry Glaze

Makes about 1 cup (250 mL)

This easy glaze is the perfect partner for chocolate cake pops or Glazed Strawberry Doughnuts (page 96).

Tip

No strawberry-flavored milk? No problem — just use regular milk and increase the strawberry extract to 1 tsp (5 mL).

2 cups	confectioners' (icing) sugar	500 mL
1/3 cup	strawberry-flavored milk	75 mL
1/2 tsp	strawberry extract	2 mL

1. In a medium bowl, whisk together sugar, milk and strawberry extract until smooth.

Lemon Glaze

Makes about 1 cup (250 mL)

This glaze is perfect for Lemon Poppy Seed Muffins (page 118) and White Velvet Cake Pops (page 34).

2 cups	confectioners' (icing) sugar	500 mL
	Grated zest of 1 lemon	
½ cup	freshly squeezed lemon juice	125 mL
2 tsp	butter	10 mL

1. In a medium microwave-safe glass bowl, whisk together sugar and lemon juice. Add lemon zest and butter. Microwave on High for 30 seconds. Whisk until smooth.

Orange Glaze

Makes about 1 cup (250 mL)

Orange juice gives this light glaze a refreshing taste. It's wonderful on any white or yellow cake pop, or on doughnuts or muffins.

Tip

For a thicker, piping glaze, add more confectioners' (icing) sugar, 2 tbsp (30 mL) at a time, until the desired consistency is reached.

1 tbsp	butter	15 mL
2¼ cups	confectioners' (icing) sugar	550 mL
3 to 4 tbsp	orange juice	45 to 60 mL

1. Place butter in a small microwave-safe glass bowl. Microwave on High for 30 seconds or until melted. Whisk in sugar and 3 tbsp (45 mL) orange juice. Microwave on High for 30 seconds. Stir in the remaining orange juice, 1 tsp (5 mL) at a time, until glaze is the desired consistency.

Variations

Margarita Glaze: Substitute 1 tbsp (15 mL) orange liqueur for 1 tbsp (15 mL) of the orange juice.

Mojito Glaze: Substitute 1 tbsp (15 mL) freshly squeezed lime juice and 2 tbsp (30 mL) rum for the 3 tbsp (45 mL) orange juice. Stir in an additional 1½ tsp (7 mL) lime juice and 1½ tsp (7 mL) rum, as needed, to reach the desired consistency. If desired, add 3 drops green food coloring and stir well.

Piña Colada Glaze: Substitute 2 tbsp (30 mL) pineapple juice and 1 tbsp (15 mL) rum for the 3 tbsp (45 mL) orange juice. Stir in an additional 1 tbsp (15 mL) rum, as needed, to reach the desired consistency.

Maple Glaze

Makes about ½ cup (125 mL)

Remember those maple-glazed doughnuts from your childhood? This glaze will create new memories for your family and friends.

Tip

For intense maple flavor, add ½ tsp (2 mL) maple extract to the glaze.

¾ cup	confectioners' (icing) sugar	175 mL
1 tbsp	pure maple syrup	15 mL
1 tbsp	milk	15 mL

1. In a small bowl, whisk together sugar, maple syrup and milk until smooth.

French Toast Glaze

Makes about ⅔ cup (150 mL)

Pancake syrup adds a hint of maple flavor to this glaze. Use it on French Toast Doughnuts (page 97) or on any of your favorite doughnuts or cakes.

Tip

Substitute pure maple syrup for the pancake syrup, if desired.

1 cup	confectioners' (icing) sugar	250 mL
2 tbsp	butter, melted	30 mL
2 tbsp	milk	30 mL
1 tbsp	maple-flavored pancake syrup	15 mL

1. In a small bowl, whisk together sugar, butter, milk and syrup until smooth.

Cinnamon Candy Glaze

Makes about ½ cup (125 mL)

This glaze will remind you of the coating on candy apples, bringing back childhood memories of carnivals, state fairs and rodeos.

½ cup	small round cinnamon-flavored candies	125 mL
2 tbsp	water	30 mL
1 cup	confectioners' (icing) sugar	250 mL
1 to 2 tbsp	milk	15 to 30 mL

1. In a small saucepan, over medium-high heat, combine candies and water. Bring to a boil, stirring constantly. Reduce heat and simmer, stirring, until candies are dissolved.

2. Remove candy mixture from heat and whisk in sugar. Whisk in 1 tbsp (15 mL) milk until smooth. If necessary for the desired consistency, whisk in the remaining milk.

3. Pour mixture through a fine-mesh sieve to remove any candy bits.

Root Beer Glaze

Makes about 2 cups (500 mL)

This soda-based glaze pairs nicely with Root Beer Cake Pops (page 55).

3 cups	confectioners' (icing) sugar	750 mL
½ cup	butter, melted	125 mL
¼ cup	root beer, at room temperature	60 mL
1 tsp	vanilla extract	5 mL

1. In a medium bowl, whisk together sugar, butter, root beer and vanilla until smooth.

Variation
Substitute cola for the root beer.

Champagne Glaze

**Makes
about ²⁄₃ cup
(150 mL)**

Add pizzazz and
elegance to any
white cake pop or to
Champagne Cake Pops
(page 161) — perfect
for wedding showers!

Tip

Tint with a few drops of red
food coloring to make a
light pink glaze.

1 cup	confectioners' (icing) sugar	250 mL
2 tbsp	Champagne or sparkling wine	30 mL
1 tbsp	milk	15 mL

1. In a medium bowl, whisk together sugar, Champagne
and milk until smooth.

Limoncello Glaze

**Makes
about ¹⁄₂ cup
(125 mL)**

What a treat this glaze
is. Use it on Limoncello
Cake Pops (page 162)
or on any white or
yellow cake pops.

Tip

Limoncello, a lemon liqueur,
is an Italian favorite that can
be used to add a refreshing
lemon flavor to many
dishes and baked goods.
Or try adding a splash to
lemonade — one sip and
you may think you are
strolling the quaint streets
of Rome.

1 cup	confectioners' (icing) sugar	250 mL
3 tbsp	limoncello liqueur	45 mL

1. In a small bowl, whisk together sugar and limoncello
until smooth.

Rum Glaze

**Makes
about 7 tbsp
(105 mL)**

Turn any yellow or chocolate cake pops into a special adult treat by dipping them in this rum-spiked glaze.

| 1 cup | confectioners' (icing) sugar | 250 mL |
| 2 tbsp | dark rum | 30 mL |

1. In a small bowl, whisk together sugar and rum until smooth.

> **Tip**
> This glaze is thick and rich, so dip cake pops only halfway. If you'd rather coat the entire cake ball, make a thinner glaze by adding 1 tbsp (15 mL) more rum.

Tennessee Bourbon Glaze

**Makes
about 1¾ cups
(425 mL)**

This rich brown sugar and butter glaze, with just a hint of bourbon, is perfect for Spice Cake Pops (page 62) or Sour Cream Doughnuts (page 90).

Tip

Be sure to dip the cake pops when this glaze is still hot. If it cools off and begins to thicken, transfer it to a microwave-safe glass bowl and microwave on High for about 30 seconds or until hot. Stir until blended.

1½ cups	packed brown sugar	375 mL
6 tbsp	butter, cut into pieces	90 mL
¼ cup	heavy or whipping (35%) cream	60 mL
½ cup	confectioners' (icing) sugar, sifted	125 mL
2 tbsp	bourbon	30 mL

1. In a small saucepan, over medium heat, combine brown sugar, butter and cream. Bring to a boil, stirring often to dissolve brown sugar. Boil, stirring often, for 3 minutes. Remove from heat and whisk in confectioners' sugar and bourbon until smooth.

> **Variations**
> *Applejack Glaze:* Substitute applejack for the bourbon.
>
> *Caramel Glaze:* Replace the bourbon with 1 tsp (5 mL) vanilla extract. Thin the glaze with an additional 1 to 2 tbsp (15 to 30 mL) cream, if desired.

Key Lime Dipping Sauce

Makes about 6 tbsp (90 mL)

Lime adds a great refreshing flavor to many sweet treats. This dip is wonderful with Key Lime Cake Pops (page 71), White Cake Pops (page 24), Mojito Cake Pops (page 165) or any yellow cake pops. Or, for a delightful change of pace, spread a bit on a batch of Tropical Muffins (page 119).

¼ cup	confectioners' (icing) sugar	60 mL
2 oz	cream cheese, softened	60 g
2 tbsp	freshly squeezed Key lime juice or Persian lime juice	30 mL
1 tbsp	butter, softened	15 mL

1. In a medium bowl, using an electric mixer on low speed, beat sugar, cream cheese, lime juice and butter until smooth.

Cream Cheese Filling

Makes about 6 tbsp (90 mL)

Cream cheese makes the creamiest, richest filling, ideal for any cake pop, doughnut or muffin.

Tip

Be sure to store cake pops or doughnuts filled with Cream Cheese Filling in the refrigerator.

2 oz	cream cheese, softened	60 g
1 tbsp	butter, softened	15 mL
¼ cup	confectioners' (icing) sugar	60 mL
½ tsp	vanilla extract	2 mL

1. In a small bowl, using an electric mixer on medium speed, beat cream cheese and butter for 1 minute or until fluffy. Gradually beat in sugar and vanilla.

Marshmallow Cream Filling

This creamy filling can be used in many different cake pops. Use your imagination!

Tip

Add food coloring to tint this filling, choosing a color that complements your cake pops. For instance, a few drops of red food coloring makes the filling light pink, which is perfect for strawberry-flavored cake pops.

1 tsp	hot water	5 mL
Pinch	salt	Pinch
3 tbsp	confectioners' (icing) sugar	45 mL
1 cup	marshmallow cream	250 mL
¼ cup	shortening	60 mL
½ tsp	vanilla extract	2 mL

1. In a medium bowl, stir hot water and salt until salt is dissolved. Add sugar, marshmallow cream, shortening and vanilla. Using an electric mixer on medium speed, beat for 1 to 2 minutes or until fluffy.

Chocolate Ganache Filling

**Makes
about ⅔ cup
(150 mL)**

Chocolate and cream are the basic ingredients for ganache, and nothing could taste more decadent. What flavor of cake pops do you want to fill first? The possibilities are almost endless.

Tip

To fill cake balls, pour warm ganache into a squeeze bottle with a fine tip.

½ cup	semisweet chocolate chips	125 mL
⅓ cup	heavy or whipping (35%) cream	75 mL
½ tsp	vanilla extract	2 mL

1. Place chocolate chips and cream in a small microwave-safe glass bowl. Microwave on High for 1 minute or until cream is hot and chocolate is melted. Stir well. Stir in vanilla. Let cool for 3 minutes, stirring occasionally.

Part 3

Doughnuts, Ebelskivers and Muffins

Doughnuts

Raised Glazed Doughnuts 89

Sour Cream Doughnuts 90

Old-Fashioned Buttermilk Doughnuts. 91

Chocolate Doughnuts. 92

Apple Pie Doughnuts 93

Blueberry Doughnuts 94

Confetti Doughnuts. 95

Glazed Strawberry Doughnuts 96

French Toast Doughnuts. 97

Maple Nut Doughnuts 98

Beignets 99

Raised Glazed Doughnuts

Makes 46 to 48 doughnuts

This traditional doughnut recipe is reminiscent of treats we enjoyed at old-fashioned doughnut shops — only the size and shape are different.

Tips

One ¼-oz (7 g) package of quick-rise or instant yeast contains 2¼ tsp (11 mL) yeast.

Do you have a Babycakes Rotating Cake Pop Maker? If so, see page 8 for information on using it.

Variation

Substitute Chocolate Glaze (page 78) for the Vanilla Glaze.

2 cups	all-purpose flour	500 mL
¼ cup	granulated sugar	60 mL
½ tsp	salt	2 mL
½ tsp	ground nutmeg	2 mL
1	package (¼ oz/7 g) quick-rising (instant) yeast	1
2	large eggs, at room temperature	2
½ cup	warm water	125 mL
⅓ cup	unsalted butter, softened	75 mL
¼ cup	warm milk	60 mL
	Nonstick baking spray	
	Vanilla Glaze (page 78)	

1. In a large bowl, whisk together flour, sugar, salt, nutmeg and yeast. Add eggs, warm water, butter and milk. Using an electric mixer on medium-high speed, beat for 2 minutes. Cover with a towel and let rise in a warm, draft-free place for 30 minutes.

2. Spray cake pop wells with nonstick baking spray. Add about 1½ tsp (7 mL) batter to each well (see page 25). Wells will be about halfway full; do not overfill. Bake for 4 to 5 minutes or until doughnuts are brown and crisp. Transfer doughnuts to a wire rack set over a sheet of foil or waxed paper to cool. Repeat with the remaining batter.

3. Using the fork tool, dip each doughnut in Vanilla Glaze, allowing excess glaze to drip back into the bowl. Return glazed doughnuts to the rack to set.

Sour Cream Doughnuts

Makes 34 to 36 doughnuts

There's timeless flavor packed into this quick and easy recipe.

Tips

Dip the doughnuts in Vanilla Glaze (page 78) or Chocolate Glaze (page 78).

If you prefer sugar-coated doughnuts, immediately toss the hot doughnuts in granulated sugar, cinnamon sugar or confectioners' (icing) sugar.

1⅓ cups	all-purpose flour	325 mL
½ cup	granulated sugar	125 mL
1 tsp	ground nutmeg	5 mL
½ tsp	baking soda	2 mL
½ tsp	baking powder	2 mL
Pinch	salt	Pinch
1	large egg, at room temperature, lightly beaten	1
½ cup	sour cream, at room temperature	125 mL
¼ cup	milk	60 mL
2 tbsp	unsalted butter, melted	30 mL
	Nonstick baking spray	

1. In a large bowl, whisk together flour, sugar, nutmeg, baking soda, baking powder and salt. Set aside.

2. In a small bowl, whisk together egg, sour cream, milk and butter until blended. Stir into flour mixture just until moistened.

3. Spray cake pop wells with nonstick baking spray. Fill each well with about 1 tbsp (15 mL) batter (see page 25). Bake for 4 to 6 minutes or until a tester inserted in the center comes out clean. Transfer doughnuts to a wire rack to cool. Repeat with the remaining batter.

Old-Fashioned Buttermilk Doughnuts

Makes 19 to 21 doughnuts

Old-fashioned doughnuts tend to have crisper crusts, which makes them perfect for glazing (try Vanilla Glaze, page 78, or Chocolate Glaze, page 78) or dipping in butter and then coating in cinnamon sugar.

Tips

No buttermilk on hand? Stir ¾ tsp (3 mL) lemon juice or white vinegar into ¼ cup (60 mL) milk. Let stand for 5 to 10 minutes or until thickened. Proceed with the recipe.

Sugar-coated doughnuts are best served within a day of baking and coating. If you plan to serve them the next day, store doughnuts in an airtight container to keep them fresh. The sugar mixture will dissolve over time, so generously sprinkle the doughnuts with additional cinnamon sugar just before serving.

Variation

Substitute sour cream for the buttermilk.

Doughnuts

1 cup	all-purpose flour	250 mL
1 tsp	baking soda	5 mL
½ tsp	ground cinnamon	2 mL
¼ tsp	ground nutmeg	1 mL
Pinch	salt	Pinch
⅓ cup	granulated sugar	75 mL
¼ cup	buttermilk	60 mL
1 tbsp	vegetable oil	15 mL
	Nonstick baking spray	

Topping

¼ cup	granulated sugar	60 mL
2 tsp	ground cinnamon	10 mL
⅓ cup	unsalted butter, melted	75 mL

1. *Doughnuts:* In a small bowl, whisk together flour, baking soda, cinnamon, nutmeg and salt. Set aside.

2. In a medium bowl, whisk together sugar, buttermilk and oil. Add the flour mixture in four additions, stirring well after each addition. Cover with plastic wrap and refrigerate for 30 minutes.

3. *Topping:* In a small bowl, combine sugar and cinnamon. Set aside.

4. Spray cake pop wells with nonstick baking spray. Fill each well with about 1 tbsp (15 mL) batter (see page 25). Bake for 4 to 6 minutes or until a tester inserted in the center comes out clean.

5. Immediately dip doughnuts in butter, then roll in cinnamon-sugar mixture. Set on a wire rack to cool.

6. Repeat steps 4 and 5 with the remaining batter.

Chocolate Doughnuts

- -

Makes 29 to 31 doughnuts

While these doughnuts taste oh-so-good even plain, they are especially delicious if coated in confectioners' (icing) sugar.

....

Tip

To coat doughnuts with confectioners' (icing) sugar, place 1 to 1½ cups (250 to 375 mL) confectioners' sugar in a paper bag. As you remove the doughnuts from the cake pop maker, add them to the bag and toss gently to coat. Transfer to a wire rack to cool.

Variation

Mocha Doughnuts: Reduce the cocoa powder to 2 tbsp (30 mL).

1 cup	all-purpose flour	250 mL
¼ cup	unsweetened cocoa powder	60 mL
1 tsp	baking powder	5 mL
¼ tsp	baking soda	1 mL
¼ tsp	salt	1 mL
⅔ cup	granulated sugar	150 mL
2 tbsp	cold unsalted butter, cut into small pieces	30 mL
1	large egg, at room temperature	1
½ cup	sour cream, at room temperature	125 mL
2 tbsp	cold strong brewed coffee	30 mL
	Nonstick baking spray	

1. In a large bowl, whisk together flour, cocoa, baking powder, baking soda and salt. Stir in sugar. Using a pastry blender or two knives, cut in butter until mixture resembles coarse crumbs. Set aside.

2. In a small bowl, whisk together egg, sour cream and coffee. Stir into flour mixture just until moistened.

3. Spray cake pop wells with nonstick baking spray. Fill each well with about 1 tbsp (15 mL) batter (see page 25). Bake for 4 to 6 minutes or until a tester inserted in the center comes out clean. Transfer doughnuts to a wire rack to cool. Repeat with the remaining batter.

Apple Pie Doughnuts

The comforting flavors of that all-time favorite pie are captured in these doughnuts.

Tips

This recipe can also be prepared without a food processor. First, finely chop the apple. In a large bowl, toss apple with flour, granulated sugar, brown sugar, baking powder, cinnamon and salt. Using a pastry blender or two knives, cut in butter until mixture resembles coarse crumbs. Stir in milk and lightly beaten egg. Proceed with step 2.

Sugar-coated doughnuts are best served within a day of baking and coating. If you plan to serve them the next day, store doughnuts in an airtight container to keep them fresh. The sugar mixture will dissolve over time, so generously sprinkle the doughnuts with additional cinnamon sugar just before serving.

- Food processor

Doughnuts

1	crisp cooking apple (such as Fuji or Granny Smith), peeled, cored and quartered	1
1½ cups	all-purpose flour	375 mL
¼ cup	granulated sugar	60 mL
¼ cup	packed brown sugar	60 mL
1½ tsp	baking powder	7 mL
½ tsp	ground cinnamon	2 mL
Pinch	salt	Pinch
⅓ cup	cold unsalted butter, cut into 5 pieces	75 mL
1	large egg, at room temperature	1
6 tbsp	milk	90 mL
	Nonstick baking spray	

Topping

½ cup	granulated sugar	125 mL
2 tsp	ground cinnamon	10 mL
⅓ cup	unsalted butter, melted	60 mL

1. *Doughnuts:* In food processor, pulse apple quarters until finely chopped, scraping the bowl to ensure even chopping. Add flour, granulated sugar, brown sugar, baking powder, cinnamon and salt; pulse to combine. Add butter and pulse until mixture resembles coarse crumbs. Add egg and milk; process just until moistened.

2. *Topping:* In a small bowl, stir together sugar and cinnamon. Set aside.

3. Spray cake pop wells with nonstick baking spray. Fill each well with about 1 tbsp (15 mL) batter (see page 25). Bake for 4 to 6 minutes or until a tester inserted in the center comes out clean.

4. Immediately dip doughnuts in butter, then roll in cinnamon-sugar mixture. Set on a wire rack to cool.

5. Repeat steps 3 and 4 with the remaining batter.

Blueberry Doughnuts

Kathy made these one Sunday morning and took them to church. Everyone loved them!

Tips

If your preserves are chunky, pour the warm preserves through a sieve to remove larger pieces of fruit.

Sugar-coated doughnuts are best served within a day of baking and coating. If you plan to serve them the next day, store doughnuts in an airtight container to keep them fresh. The lemon-sugar mixture will dissolve over time, so generously sprinkle the doughnuts with additional lemon sugar just before serving.

Do you have a Babycakes Rotating Cake Pop Maker? If so, see page 8 for information on using it.

- Food processor
- Pastry bag or squeeze bottle, fitted with a fine tip

Doughnuts

1¼ cups	all-purpose flour	300 mL
1 tsp	baking powder	5 mL
½ tsp	ground nutmeg	2 mL
¼ tsp	salt	1 mL
⅓ cup	blueberries	75 mL
¼ cup	granulated sugar	60 mL
2 tbsp	packed brown sugar	30 mL
¼ cup	unsalted butter, softened	60 mL
1	large egg, at room temperature	1
⅔ cup	milk	150 mL
½ tsp	vanilla extract	2 mL
	Nonstick baking spray	

Topping

½ cup	granulated sugar	125 mL
1 tsp	grated lemon zest	5 mL

Filling

¼ cup	blueberry all-fruit spread or preserves	60 mL

1. *Doughnuts:* In food processor, pulse flour, baking powder, nutmeg and salt to combine. Add blueberries and pulse to coarsely chop. Set aside.

2. In a large bowl, using an electric mixer on medium-high speed, beat granulated sugar, brown sugar and butter for 1 to 2 minutes or until fluffy. Beat in egg, milk and vanilla. Stir in flour mixture just until moistened.

3. *Topping:* In a small bowl, combine sugar and lemon zest. Set aside.

4. Spray cake pop wells with nonstick baking spray. Fill each well with about 1 tbsp (15 mL) batter (see page 25). Bake for 4 to 6 minutes or until a tester inserted in the center comes out clean.

5. Immediately roll each doughnut in lemon-sugar topping. Set on a wire rack to cool.

6. Repeat steps 4 and 5 with the remaining batter.

These doughnuts are so good you can omit the filling, if desired. If filling the doughnuts, it is best to fill them just before serving.

7. *Filling:* Place blueberry spread in a small microwave-safe glass bowl. Microwave on High for 30 seconds or until warm and melted.

8. Pour the warm blueberry spread into the pastry bag or squeeze bottle and inject into the center of each doughnut.

Confetti Doughnuts

Makes 22 to 24 doughnuts

Roxanne's daughter, Grace, always chooses glazed confetti doughnuts with sprinkles. They are her all-time favorite.

Tips

Can't find confetti cake mix (sometimes called Funfetti)? Substitute a white cake mix and stir in 2 tbsp (30 mL) sprinkles.

No buttermilk on hand? Stir 1 tsp (5 mL) lemon juice or white vinegar into 1/3 cup (75 mL) milk. Let stand for 5 to 10 minutes or until thickened. Proceed with the recipe.

1 1/2 cups	confetti cake mix	375 mL
1	large egg, at room temperature	1
1/3 cup	buttermilk	75 mL
1 tbsp	unsalted butter, melted	15 mL
	Nonstick baking spray	
	Vanilla Glaze (page 78)	
	Sprinkles	

1. In a medium bowl, using an electric mixer on low speed, beat cake mix, egg, buttermilk and butter for 30 seconds or until moistened.

2. Spray cake pop wells with nonstick baking spray. Fill each well with about 1 tbsp (15 mL) batter (see page 25). Bake for 4 to 6 minutes or until a tester inserted in the center comes out clean. Transfer doughnuts to a wire rack set over a sheet of foil or waxed paper to cool. Repeat with the remaining batter.

3. Using the fork tool, dip each doughnut in Vanilla Glaze, allowing excess glaze to drip back into the bowl. Use your fingers to sprinkle each doughnut lightly with sprinkles, or hold each doughnut over a bowl of sprinkles and use a spoon to coat the entire doughnut. Return doughnuts to the rack to set.

Glazed Strawberry Doughnuts

● ●

**Makes 30
to 32 doughnuts**

Not everyone enjoys chocolate. Here's an easy recipe for those times when the flavor of fresh fruit is in order for a sweet splurge.

● ●

Tips

For a pinker color, add a few drops of red food coloring to the batter before baking.

A single-serving bottle or carton of strawberry milk, often available at convenience stores, will provide enough milk for both this recipe and the Strawberry Glaze.

No strawberry-flavored milk? No problem — just use regular milk and increase the strawberry extract to 1 tsp (5 mL).

1½ cups	white cake mix	375 mL
1	large egg, at room temperature	1
⅓ cup	strawberry-flavored milk	75 mL
1 tbsp	unsalted butter, melted	15 mL
½ tsp	strawberry extract	2 mL
3 to 4	strawberries	3 to 4
	Nonstick baking spray	
	Strawberry Glaze (page 79)	

1. In a medium bowl, using an electric mixer on low speed, beat cake mix, egg, milk, butter and strawberry extract for 30 seconds or until moistened. Set aside.

2. Rinse strawberries so that they are slightly wet and cut into small pieces. Place in a shallow bowl. Using a fork, mash strawberries. Measure 3 tbsp (45 mL) mashed strawberries and gently fold into batter.

3. Spray cake pop wells with nonstick baking spray. Fill each well with about 1 tbsp (15 mL) batter (see page 25). Bake for 4 to 6 minutes or until a tester inserted in the center comes out clean. Transfer doughnuts to a wire rack set over a sheet of foil or waxed paper to cool. Repeat with the remaining batter.

4. Drizzle doughnuts heavily with Strawberry Glaze.

Clockwise from top: Treats for Dog Lovers, White Dog
(page 222), Maple Nut Doughnuts (page 98), Classic
Red Velvet Cake Pops (page 38), Daisy Days (page 219)
and Old-Fashioned Chocolate Cake Pops (page 26)

White Cake Pops,
decorated (page 24)

Cherry Cake Pops (page 57) and
Orange Cream Cake Pops (page 44)

Thin Mint Cake Pops (page 68) and
Cheesecake Surprise Cake Pops (page 72)

Strawberry Shortcakes (page 73)

Clockwise from top left: Chocolate Doughnuts (page 92), Lemon
Blueberry Ebelskivers (page 106) and Confetti Doughnuts (page 95)

Lemon Poppy Seed Muffins (page 118)
and Mini Scones (page 116)

Bacon Cheddar Biscuit Bites (page 115)
and Pancake Bites (page 123)

French Toast Doughnuts

Makes 26
to 28 doughnuts

This recipe was inspired by traditional French toast. The doughnuts are scrumptious when glazed, but can also be enjoyed plain or served with warm pancake or maple syrup.

Variations

Instead of glazing, sprinkle doughnuts with cinnamon sugar. Combine 2 tbsp (30 mL) granulated sugar with 1/4 tsp (1 mL) ground cinnamon and generously sprinkle over hot doughnuts.

Omit the glaze and arrange 5 or 6 doughnuts in each serving bowl or stemmed glass. Drizzle with warm pancake syrup.

1 cup	all-purpose flour	250 mL
1/2 cup	granulated sugar	125 mL
1 tbsp	baking powder	15 mL
1/2 tsp	salt	2 mL
1/2 tsp	ground cinnamon	2 mL
1	large egg, at room temperature	1
1/2 cup	milk	125 mL
3 tbsp	unsalted butter, melted	45 mL
	Nonstick baking spray	
	French Toast Glaze (page 81)	

1. In a medium bowl, whisk together flour, sugar, baking powder, salt and cinnamon. Set aside.

2. In a small bowl, whisk together egg, milk and melted butter. Stir into flour mixture just until moistened.

3. Spray cake pop wells with nonstick baking spray. Fill each well with about 1 tbsp (15 mL) batter (see page 25). Bake for 4 to 6 minutes or until a tester inserted in the center comes out clean. Transfer doughnuts to a wire rack set over a sheet of foil or waxed paper to cool. Repeat with the remaining batter.

4. Glaze doughnuts with French Toast Glaze.

Maple Nut Doughnuts

Makes 28
to 30 doughnuts

Roxanne's husband, Bob Bateman, used to order maple long johns from the local doughnut shop. This recipe cured that habit. Now the entire family enjoys these doughnuts on Saturday mornings.

Tips

No buttermilk on hand? Stir ¾ tsp (3 mL) lemon juice or white vinegar into ¼ cup (60 mL) milk. Let stand for 5 to 10 minutes or until thickened. Proceed with the recipe.

Toasting walnuts intensifies their flavor. Spread finely chopped walnuts in a single layer on a baking sheet. Bake at 350°F (180°C) for 5 to 7 minutes or until lightly browned.

Do you have a Babycakes Rotating Cake Pop Maker? If so, see page 8 for information on using it.

1 cup	all-purpose flour	250 mL
¼ tsp	baking soda	1 mL
¼ tsp	ground cinnamon	1 mL
⅛ tsp	salt	0.5 mL
¼ cup	granulated sugar	60 mL
¼ cup	packed dark brown sugar	60 mL
3 tbsp	unsalted butter, softened	45 mL
1	large egg, at room temperature	1
1	large egg yolk, at room temperature	1
½ tsp	vanilla extract	2 mL
¼ cup	buttermilk	60 mL
	Nonstick baking spray	
	Maple Glaze (page 81)	
⅓ cup	toasted finely chopped walnuts (see tip, at left)	75 mL

1. In a small bowl, whisk together flour, baking soda, cinnamon and salt. Set aside.

2. In a medium bowl, using an electric mixer on medium-high speed, beat granulated sugar, brown sugar and butter for 1 to 2 minutes or until fluffy. Add egg, then egg yolk, beating well after each addition. Stir in vanilla. Add flour mixture alternately with buttermilk, making two additions of flour and one of buttermilk and beating on low speed until smooth.

3. Spray cake pop wells with nonstick baking spray. Fill each well with about 1 tbsp (15 mL) batter (see page 25). Bake for 4 to 6 minutes or until a tester inserted in the center comes out clean. Transfer doughnuts to a wire rack set over a sheet of foil or waxed paper to cool. Repeat with the remaining batter.

4. Drizzle doughnuts with Maple Glaze. Sprinkle with walnuts.

Beignets

**Makes 46
to 48 beignets**

We have worked the International Home and Housewares Show in Chicago together for many, many years, and we have a tradition of sharing a meal at the Grand Lux Café before the show begins. Without fail we order the beignets, and — since days of hard work are ahead — we feel no guilt as we indulge in these New Orleans favorites.

Tips

No paper bag? Place the sugar in a small bowl and use a spoon to gently coat the beignets.

At the Grand Lux Café, the beignets are served with dipping sauces. Try serving yours with chocolate sauce.

Variation

Cream Puff Bites: Split cooled beignets in half, spread one half with prepared pudding (any flavor you like), then stick the halves back together. Glaze with Vanilla Glaze (page 78).

1 tbsp	granulated sugar	15 mL
¼ tsp	salt	1 mL
1 cup	water	250 mL
6 tbsp	unsalted butter, cut into pieces	90 mL
1 cup	all-purpose flour	250 mL
3	large eggs, at room temperature	3
1 to 1½ cups	confectioners' (icing) sugar	250 to 375 mL

1. In a medium saucepan, over medium-high heat, combine granulated sugar, salt, water and butter; bring to a boil. Reduce heat to medium. Using a wooden spoon, stir in flour and cook, stirring, for 3 minutes.

2. Transfer batter to a medium bowl. Stir for 1 minute to cool the batter. Using an electric mixer on medium-high speed, beat in eggs, one at a time, scraping the sides of the bowl after each addition.

3. Add about 1½ tsp (7 mL) batter to each cake pop well (see page 25). Wells will be about halfway full; do not overfill. Bake for 8 to 10 minutes or until beignets are golden brown.

4. Place confectioners' sugar in a paper bag (see tip, at left). Add hot beignets and gently toss to generously coat with sugar. Transfer beignets to a wire rack to cool slightly. Serve warm.

Ebelskivers

Sour Cream and Buttermilk Ebelskivers 101

Milk and Cinnamon Ebelskivers 102

Cherry Almond Ebelskivers. 103

Apple Ebelskivers 104

Bananas Foster Ebelskivers with Rum Sauce 105

Lemon Blueberry Ebelskivers 106

Pumpkin Ebelskivers 107

Maple Ebelskivers 108

Chocolate Chip Ebelskivers 109

Ricotta Herb Ebelskivers. 110

Sour Cream and Buttermilk Ebelskivers

Makes 28 to 30 ebelskivers

Ebelskivers are Danish pancakes. As with many traditional foods, every family has a different recipe for these light, round treats. This version, one of our favorites, includes sour cream and buttermilk.

Tips

No buttermilk on hand? Stir 1½ tsp (7 mL) lemon juice or white vinegar into ½ cup (125 mL) milk. Let stand for 5 to 10 minutes or until thickened. Proceed with the recipe.

Turning the ebelskivers partway through baking improves the evenness of the browning.

Be sure to toss the ebelskivers in the confectioners' (icing) sugar while they're hot.

No paper bag? Place the sugar in a small bowl and use a spoon to gently coat the ebelskivers.

¾ cup	all-purpose flour	175 mL
½ tsp	baking powder	2 mL
¼ tsp	baking soda	1 mL
Pinch	salt	Pinch
1	large egg, at room temperature	1
½ cup	sour cream, at room temperature	125 mL
½ cup	buttermilk, at room temperature	125 mL
2 tbsp	unsalted butter, melted	30 mL
1 to 1½ cups	confectioners' (icing) sugar	250 to 375 mL

1. In a medium bowl, whisk together flour, baking powder, baking soda and salt. Set aside.

2. In a small bowl, whisk together egg, sour cream and buttermilk. Stir into flour mixture until blended.

3. Generously brush cake pop wells with melted butter. Fill each well with about 1 tbsp (15 mL) batter (see page 25).Bake for 2 to 3 minutes or until softly set and golden brown on the bottom. Carefully place the fork tool between each ebelskiver and the edge of the well and gently turn the ebelskiver over. Bake for 2 minutes or until golden brown on the bottom.

4. Place confectioners' sugar in a paper bag (see tip, at left). Add hot ebelskivers and gently toss to generously coat with sugar. Transfer ebelskivers to a wire rack to cool slightly.

5. Repeat steps 3 and 4 with the remaining batter. Serve warm.

Milk and Cinnamon Ebelskivers

Makes 28 to 30 ebelskivers

These ebelskivers are just as rich and tasty as the Sour Cream and Buttermilk Ebelskivers (page 101). Serve them with your favorite fruit preserves — we especially like them with raspberry preserves.

Tips

It is fun to fill these ebelskivers with a small amount of preserves or syrup. Use a pastry bag or squeeze bottle fitted with a fine tip to inject the filling into the center of each ebelskiver.

Ebelskivers coated in confectioners' (icing) sugar are best served within a day of baking and coating. If you plan to serve them the next day, store ebelskivers in an airtight container to keep them fresh. The sugar coating will dissolve over time, so generously sprinkle the ebelskivers with additional confectioners' sugar just before serving.

1 cup	all-purpose flour	250 mL
2 tbsp	granulated sugar	30 mL
2 tsp	baking powder	10 mL
1/4 tsp	salt	1 mL
1/4 tsp	ground cinnamon	1 mL
1	large egg, at room temperature	1
3/4 cup	milk, at room temperature	175 mL
2 tbsp	unsalted butter, melted	30 mL
1 tsp	vanilla extract	5 mL
	Nonstick baking spray	
1 to 1 1/2 cups	confectioners' (icing) sugar	250 to 375 mL

1. In a medium bowl, whisk together flour, granulated sugar, baking powder, salt and cinnamon. Set aside.

2. In a small bowl, whisk together egg, milk, butter and vanilla. Stir into flour mixture until blended.

3. Spray cake pop wells with nonstick baking spray. Fill each well with about 1 tbsp (15 mL) batter (see page 25). Bake for 3 to 5 minutes or until golden brown and crispy.

4. Place confectioners' sugar in a paper bag (see tip, page 101). Add hot ebelskivers and gently toss to generously coat with sugar. Transfer ebelskivers to a wire rack to cool slightly.

5. Repeat steps 3 and 4 with the remaining batter. Serve warm.

Cherry Almond Ebelskivers

Makes 36 to 38 ebelskivers

Tiny pieces of ruby-colored cherries shine out of these baked pancakes, inviting you to eat "just one more."

Tips

Be sure to have the cherries chopped and ready. Fill each well about three-quarters full of batter so there is room for the cherries. Work quickly to add the cherries, because the batter begins to rise and set as soon as it contacts the hot wells.

You can substitute chopped well-drained canned sweet cherries for the fresh.

Toasting almonds intensifies their flavor. Spread chopped almonds in a single layer on a baking sheet. Bake at 350°F (180°C) for 5 to 7 minutes or until lightly browned.

No buttermilk on hand? Stir 1 tbsp (15 mL) lemon juice or white vinegar into 1 cup (250 mL) milk. Let stand for 5 to 10 minutes or until thickened. Proceed with the recipe.

1 cup	all-purpose flour	250 mL
1½ tsp	granulated sugar	7 mL
1 tsp	baking powder	5 mL
¼ tsp	baking soda	1 mL
Pinch	salt	Pinch
1	large egg, separated, at room temperature	1
1 cup	buttermilk	250 mL
4 tbsp	unsalted butter, melted, divided	60 mL
½ tsp	almond extract	2 mL
⅓ cup	finely chopped pitted sweet cherries	75 mL
1 to 1½ cups	confectioners' (icing) sugar	250 to 375 mL

Cherry preserves
Toasted chopped almonds (see tip, at left)

1. In a medium bowl, whisk together flour, granulated sugar, baking powder, baking soda and salt. Set aside.

2. In a small bowl, whisk together egg yolk, buttermilk, 2 tbsp (30 mL) of the butter and almond extract. Stir into flour mixture until blended.

3. In another small bowl, using an electric mixer on high speed, beat egg white until stiff peaks form. Fold egg white into batter.

4. Generously brush cake pop wells with the remaining butter. Fill each well about three-quarters full, using a scant 1 tbsp (15 mL) batter (see page 25). Quickly sprinkle a few pieces of chopped cherries on top of the batter in each well. Bake for 3 to 5 minutes or until golden brown and crispy.

5. Place confectioners' sugar in a paper bag (see tip, page 101). Add hot ebelskivers and gently toss to generously coat with sugar. Transfer ebelskivers to a wire rack to cool slightly.

6. Repeat steps 4 and 5 with the remaining batter.

7. Serve warm ebelskivers garnished with cherry preserves and sprinkled with almonds.

Apple Ebelskivers

Makes 27
to 29 ebelskivers

Apple is an all-time classic flavor for ebelskivers. In fact, a literal translation of the Dutch word *ebelskiver* is "apple slices." This version includes apple juice in the batter and is partnered with cooked apples.

Tips

No buttermilk on hand? Stir 1 tsp (5 mL) lemon juice or white vinegar into ⅓ cup (75 mL) milk. Let stand for 5 to 10 minutes or until thickened. Proceed with the recipe.

Turning the ebelskivers partway through baking improves the evenness of the browning.

No paper bag? Place the sugar in a small bowl and use a spoon to gently coat the ebelskivers.

Do you have a Babycakes Rotating Cake Pop Maker? If so, see page 8 for information on using it.

Ebelskivers

¾ cup	all-purpose flour	175 mL
½ tsp	ground nutmeg	2 mL
½ tsp	baking soda	2 mL
¼ tsp	salt	1 mL
1	large egg, separated, at room temperature	1
⅓ cup	unsweetened apple juice	75 mL
⅓ cup	buttermilk	75 mL
¼ tsp	cider vinegar	1 mL
2 tbsp	melted butter	30 mL
1 to 1½ cups	confectioners' (icing) sugar	250 to 375 mL

Apples

2 tbsp	unsalted butter	30 mL
2	tart apples (such as Granny Smith), peeled and thinly sliced	2
¼ cup	granulated sugar	60 mL
1 tsp	ground cinnamon	5 mL
¼ cup	unsweetened apple juice	60 mL

1. *Ebelskivers:* In a medium bowl, whisk together flour, nutmeg, baking soda and salt. Set aside.

2. In a small bowl, whisk together egg yolk, apple juice, buttermilk and vinegar. Stir into flour mixture until blended.

3. In another small bowl, using an electric mixer on high speed, beat egg white until stiff peaks form. Fold egg white into batter.

4. Generously brush cake pop wells with melted butter. Fill each well with about 1 tbsp (15 mL) batter (see page 25).Bake for 2 to 3 minutes or until softly set and golden brown on the bottom. Carefully place the fork tool between each ebelskiver and the edge of the well and gently turn the ebelskiver over. Bake for 2 minutes or until golden brown on the bottom.

5. Place confectioners' sugar in a paper bag (see tip, at left). Add hot ebelskivers and gently toss to generously coat with sugar. Transfer ebelskivers to a wire rack to cool slightly.

Tip

Ebelskivers are especially good when served warm. They are puffed and rounded, but very delicate. They are not firm enough to put on cake pop sticks and may actually deflate a bit when cooling. A slightly irregular shape is to be expected.

6. Repeat steps 4 and 5 with the remaining batter.

7. *Apples:* In a small saucepan, melt butter over medium heat. Add apples and cook, stirring often, for 7 minutes or until apples are just tender. Stir in sugar, cinnamon and apple juice. Cook, stirring often, for 3 to 4 minutes or until apples are tender and liquid has thickened.

8. Serve warm ebelskivers with cooked apples ladled over top.

Bananas Foster Ebelskivers with Rum Sauce

Makes 4 to 5 servings

These ebelskivers are inspired by the original bananas Foster, named after Richard Foster, a friend of Owen E. Brennan, whose New Orleans restaurant first served them. Roxanne likes to serve this special treat during her annual Mardi Gras party.

Tip

For a dramatic presentation, when you add the rum to the skillet, use a barbecue lighter to ignite the rum to flambé. Be careful, as a flame will shoot up above the pan. When the flame dies down, serve as above.

1/2 cup	unsalted butter	125 mL
3/4 cup	packed dark brown sugar	175 mL
3	large bananas, sliced crosswise in 1/4-inch (0.5 cm) slices	3
1/4 cup	dark rum	60 mL
	Milk and Cinnamon Ebelskivers (page 102)	

1. In a large skillet (not nonstick), melt butter over medium heat. Stir in brown sugar until blended. Add bananas and cook, stirring gently and frequently, for about 3 minutes or until bananas begin to soften and brown slightly. Add rum and cook, stirring constantly, for 2 minutes.

2. Place 5 or 6 ebelskivers in each of four or five small bowls. Spoon banana mixture evenly over each serving.

Lemon Blueberry Ebelskivers

¾ cup	all-purpose flour	175 mL
½ tsp	baking powder	2 mL
¼ tsp	baking soda	1 mL
Pinch	salt	Pinch
1	large egg, at room temperature	1
½ cup	sour cream, at room temperature	125 mL
⅓ cup	buttermilk, at room temperature	75 mL
2 tbsp	freshly squeezed lemon juice	30 mL
2 tbsp	unsalted butter, melted	30 mL
	Nonstick baking spray	
30 to 32	blueberries	30 to 32
1 to 1½ cups	confectioners' (icing) sugar	250 to 375 mL

Makes 30 to 32 ebelskivers

These pancake bites are sweetened only with blueberries, so don't forget to toss them in confectioners' (icing) sugar.

Tips

You can substitute drained thawed frozen blueberries for the fresh.

No buttermilk on hand? Stir 1 tsp (5 mL) lemon juice or white vinegar into ⅓ cup (75 mL) milk. Let stand for 5 to 10 minutes or until thickened. Proceed with the recipe.

Turning the ebelskivers partway through baking improves the evenness of the browning.

Ebelskivers are especially good when served warm. They are puffed and rounded, but very delicate. They are not firm enough to put on cake pop sticks and may actually deflate a bit when cooling. A slightly irregular shape is to be expected.

1. In a medium bowl, whisk together flour, baking powder, baking soda and salt. Set aside.

2. In a small bowl, whisk together egg, sour cream, buttermilk, lemon juice and butter. Stir into flour mixture until blended.

3. Spray cake pop wells with nonstick baking spray. Fill each well with about 1½ tsp (7 mL) batter (see page 25). Add one blueberry to the center of each well. Spoon an additional 1½ tsp (7 mL) batter into each well, covering blueberries. Bake for 3 to 4 minutes or until softly set and golden brown on the bottom. Carefully place the fork tool between each ebelskiver and the edge of the well and gently turn the ebelskiver over. Bake for 3 to 4 minutes or until golden brown on the bottom.

4. Place confectioners' sugar in a paper bag (see tip, page 104). Add hot ebelskivers and gently toss to generously coat with sugar. Transfer ebelskivers to a wire rack to cool slightly.

5. Repeat steps 3 and 4 with the remaining batter. Serve warm.

Pumpkin Ebelskivers

Makes 28 to 30 ebelskivers

Breakfast on a fall morning couldn't get any better than these ebelskivers flavored with pumpkin and spices. They're moist and rich inside, crisp and golden on the outside!

Tips

Serve these ebelskivers with apple butter or drizzle with pure maple syrup.

Refrigerate any leftover canned pumpkin purée in an airtight container for up to 1 week, or freeze it for up to 3 months. To use from frozen, thaw the pumpkin overnight in the refrigerator, then stir well and use it to bake another batch of ebelskivers.

Do you have a Babycakes Rotating Cake Pop Maker? If so, see page 8 for information on using it.

1 cup	all-purpose flour	250 mL
2 tbsp	granulated sugar	30 mL
2 tsp	baking powder	10 mL
1 tsp	pumpkin pie spice	5 mL
1/4 tsp	salt	1 mL
1	large egg, at room temperature	1
1/2 cup	milk, at room temperature	125 mL
1/3 cup	canned pumpkin purée (not pie filling)	75 mL
2 tbsp	unsalted butter, melted	30 mL
1 tsp	vanilla extract	5 mL
	Nonstick baking spray	
1 to 1 1/2 cups	confectioners' (icing) sugar	250 to 375 mL

1. In a medium bowl, whisk together flour, granulated sugar, baking powder, pumpkin pie spice and salt. Set aside.

2. In a small bowl, whisk together egg, milk, pumpkin, butter and vanilla. Stir into flour mixture until blended.

3. Spray cake pop wells with nonstick baking spray. Fill each well with about 1 tbsp (15 mL) batter (see page 25). Bake for 3 to 5 minutes or until golden brown and crispy.

4. Place confectioners' sugar in a paper bag (see tip, page 104). Add hot ebelskivers and gently toss to generously coat with sugar. Transfer ebelskivers to a wire rack to cool slightly.

5. Repeat steps 3 and 4 with the remaining batter. Serve warm.

Maple Ebelskivers

Makes 30 to 32 ebelskivers

The indigenous people of North America first discovered how to tap the maple tree for sap and boil it down to make syrup. Native peoples called it "sweet water"; we call it maple syrup. The addition of maple syrup to this batter makes these ebelskivers sublime.

Tips

For a fun presentation, place ebelskivers on a plate and lightly dust with additional confectioners' (icing) sugar. Drizzle with warm maple syrup.

Do you have a Babycakes Rotating Cake Pop Maker? If so, see page 8 for information on using it.

Variation

Stir 3 tbsp (45 mL) finely chopped toasted pecans into the batter at the end of step 2.

1 cup	all-purpose flour	250 mL
2 tbsp	granulated sugar	30 mL
2 tsp	baking powder	10 mL
1/4 tsp	salt	1 mL
1/4 tsp	ground cinnamon	1 mL
1	large egg, at room temperature	1
2/3 cup	milk, at room temperature	150 mL
2 tbsp	pure maple syrup	30 mL
1 tsp	vanilla extract	5 mL
	Nonstick baking spray	
1 to 1 1/2 cups	confectioners' (icing) sugar	250 to 375 mL

1. In a medium bowl, whisk together flour, granulated sugar, baking powder, salt and cinnamon. Set aside.

2. In a small bowl, whisk together egg, milk, maple syrup and vanilla. Stir into flour mixture until blended.

3. Spray cake pop wells with nonstick baking spray. Fill each well with about 1 tbsp (15 mL) batter (see page 25). Bake for 3 to 5 minutes or until golden brown and crispy.

4. Place confectioners' sugar in a paper bag (see tip, page 109). Add hot ebelskivers and gently toss to generously coat with sugar. Transfer ebelskivers to a wire rack to cool slightly.

5. Repeat steps 3 and 4 with the remaining batter. Serve warm.

Chocolate Chip Ebelskivers

Makes 28 to 30 ebelskivers

These chocolatey ebelskivers are crispy on the outside, moist and rich on the inside. They're great for breakfast or brunch, but you might also enjoy serving them for dessert.

Tips

No paper bag? Place the sugar in a small bowl and use a spoon to gently coat the ebelskivers.

Fill a small basket with freshly baked ebelskivers and deliver it to a neighbor. Nothing says "Welcome to the neighborhood" or "Have a nice day" quite like something freshly baked.

Ebelskivers are especially good when served warm. They are puffed and rounded, but very delicate. They are not firm enough to put on cake pop sticks and may actually deflate a bit when cooling. A slightly irregular shape is to be expected.

1 cup	all-purpose flour	250 mL
2 tbsp	granulated sugar	30 mL
2 tsp	baking powder	10 mL
½ tsp	baking soda	2 mL
¼ tsp	salt	1 mL
1	large egg, at room temperature	1
½ cup	milk, at room temperature	125 mL
¼ cup	sour cream	60 mL
2 tbsp	unsalted butter, melted	30 mL
1 tsp	vanilla extract	5 mL
¼ cup	mini semisweet chocolate chips	60 mL
	Nonstick baking spray	
1 to 1½ cups	confectioners' (icing) sugar	250 to 375 mL

1. In a medium bowl, whisk together flour, granulated sugar, baking powder, baking soda and salt. Set aside.

2. In a small bowl, whisk together egg, milk, sour cream, butter and vanilla. Stir into flour mixture until blended. Stir in chocolate chips.

3. Spray cake pop wells with nonstick baking spray. Fill each well with about 1 tbsp (15 mL) batter (see page 25). Bake for 3 to 5 minutes or until golden brown and crispy.

4. Place confectioners' sugar in a paper bag (see tip, at left). Add hot ebelskivers and gently toss to generously coat with sugar. Transfer ebelskivers to a wire rack to cool slightly.

5. Repeat steps 3 and 4 with the remaining batter. Serve warm.

Ricotta Herb Ebelskivers

¾ cup	all-purpose flour	175 mL
1 tsp	granulated sugar	5 mL
1 tsp	dried basil	5 mL
½ tsp	baking powder	2 mL
½ tsp	salt	2 mL
2	large eggs, separated, at room temperature	2
⅔ cup	buttermilk, at room temperature	150 mL
½ cup	low-fat ricotta cheese	125 mL
	Nonstick baking spray	

Makes 34 to 36 ebelskivers

Ricotta cheese makes these crispy ebelskivers so moist and creamy on the inside. Serve them warm as an accompaniment to a salad or on their own as an appetizer.

Tip

No buttermilk on hand? Stir 2 tsp (10 mL) lemon juice or white vinegar into ⅔ cup (150 mL) milk. Let stand for 5 to 10 minutes or until thickened. Proceed with the recipe.

Variation

Substitute dried herbes de Provence, thyme or another favorite herb for the basil.

1. In a medium bowl, whisk together flour, sugar, basil, baking powder and salt. Set aside.

2. In a small bowl, whisk together egg yolks, buttermilk and ricotta until blended and smooth. Stir into flour mixture until blended.

3. In another small bowl, using an electric mixer on high speed, beat egg whites until stiff peaks form. Fold egg whites into batter.

4. Spray cake pop wells with nonstick baking spray. Fill each well with about 1 tbsp (15 mL) batter (see page 25). Bake for 4 to 6 minutes or until golden brown and crispy. Transfer ebelskivers to a wire rack to cool slightly. Repeat with the remaining batter. Serve warm.

Biscuits, Muffins and Breakfast Bites

Southern Biscuit Bites 112

Biscuits and Gravy 113

Lemon Thyme Biscuit Bites. 114

Bacon Cheddar Biscuit Bites 115

Mini Scones 116

Savory Peppered Cheese Muffins 117

Lemon Poppy Seed Muffins 118

Tropical Muffins 119

Banana Nut Muffins. 120

Rise and Shine Muffins 121

Filled Breakfast Bites. 122

Pancake Bites. 123

Mini Dutch Babies 124

Southern Biscuit Bites

**Makes 22
to 24 biscuits**

Roxanne adores the southern part of the United States. She would move there in a heartbeat if life would allow. Enjoying Southern food such as these biscuit bites keeps her in Kansas just a bit longer!

Tips

No buttermilk on hand? Stir 2¼ tsp (11 mL) lemon juice or white vinegar into ¾ cup (175 mL) milk. Let stand for 5 to 10 minutes or until thickened. Proceed with the recipe.

Even though this is a thicker dough, it is much easier to use a pastry bag to fill the wells. Use a sharp knife to cut away dough as you fill the wells.

Do you have a Babycakes Rotating Cake Pop Maker? If so, see page 8 for information on using it.

1½ cups	self-rising flour	375 mL
3 tbsp	shortening	45 mL
¾ cup	buttermilk	175 mL

1. Place flour in a medium bowl. Using your fingertips or a pastry blender, blend in shortening until mixture resembles coarse crumbs. Using a fork, stir in buttermilk just until dough comes together.

2. Fill each cake pop well with about 1 tbsp (15 mL) dough (see page 25). Bake for 4 to 6 minutes or until golden brown. Transfer biscuits to a wire rack to cool slightly. Repeat with the remaining dough. Serve warm.

Biscuits and Gravy

Roxanne's family owned a cottage at the Lake of the Ozarks in Missouri for 40 years. Roxanne's mother would lovingly prepare biscuits and gravy every Sunday while at the lake. The cottage has been sold, but the memories of those family weekends will always remain — and are celebrated each time her family enjoys this recipe.

Tip

Roxanne grew up enjoying gravy made with coarsely ground black pepper, but if you prefer, you can substitute white pepper so that the white gravy has no flecks of black.

8 oz	sausage (bulk or casings removed)	250 g
6 tbsp	all-purpose flour	90 mL
½ tsp	salt	2 mL
¼ tsp	coarsely ground black pepper	1 mL
3 cups	whole milk	750 mL
22 to 24	warm Southern Biscuit Bites (page 112)	22 to 24

1. In a medium nonstick skillet, cook sausage over medium-high heat, breaking it up with the back of a spoon, for 6 to 8 minutes or until no longer pink. Do not drain. Reduce heat to medium and stir in flour, salt and pepper. Stir in milk and bring to a simmer. Cook, stirring constantly, for 2 to 3 minutes or until gravy is thick.

2. Divide warm Southern Biscuit Bites among four plates and spoon gravy over biscuits.

Lemon Thyme Biscuit Bites

Makes 22 to 24 biscuits

These biscuit bites capture the finest flavor of summer. The combination of lemon and fresh herbs makes these biscuits a perfect partner to a salad at lunch or dinner.

Tips

If additional browning is desired, carefully place the fork tool between each biscuit and the edge of the well and gently turn the biscuit over. Bake for 1 to 2 minutes or until browned. If the wells are generously filled, the biscuits will puff and will not require turning.

Do you have a Babycakes Rotating Cake Pop Maker? If so, see page 8 for information on using it.

1 cup	all-purpose flour	250 mL
1 tbsp	minced fresh thyme	15 mL
2 tsp	granulated sugar	10 mL
1 tsp	grated lemon zest	5 mL
1 tsp	baking powder	5 mL
1/4 tsp	baking soda	1 mL
1/4 tsp	salt	1 mL
2 tbsp	cold unsalted butter, cut into small pieces	30 mL
2/3 cup	buttermilk	150 mL

1. In a medium bowl, whisk together flour, thyme, sugar, lemon zest, baking powder, baking soda and salt. Using a pastry blender or two knives, cut in butter until mixture resembles coarse crumbs. Using a fork, stir in buttermilk just until dough comes together.

2. Fill each cake pop well with about 1 tbsp (15 mL) dough (see page 25). Bake for 4 to 6 minutes or until golden brown. Transfer biscuits to a wire rack to cool slightly. Repeat with the remaining dough. Serve warm.

Bacon Cheddar Biscuit Bites

These savory morsels make a great accompaniment to any home-style meal. They're also great split and filled with a dab of pepper jelly.

Tip

Even though this is a thicker dough, it is much easier to use a pastry bag to fill the wells. Use a sharp knife to cut away dough as you fill the wells.

Variation

Replace the bacon with 3 tbsp (45 mL) finely chopped drained pickled jalapeño peppers.

1 cup	baking mix, such as Bisquick	250 mL
3 tbsp	shredded Cheddar cheese	45 mL
3 tbsp	crumbled crisply cooked bacon	45 mL
1/3 cup	milk	75 mL

1. In a medium bowl, combine biscuit mix, cheese, bacon and milk, stirring with a fork just until dough comes together.

2. Fill each cake pop well with about 1 tbsp (15 mL) dough (see page 25). Bake for 4 to 6 minutes or until golden brown. Transfer biscuits to a wire rack to cool slightly. Repeat with the remaining dough. Serve warm.

Mini Scones

Makes 17 to 19 scones

Can you imagine how much fun a tea party would be with these darling little drops of goodness? Slice scones in half and serve with clotted cream or strawberry jam.

Tip

For tender, flaky scones, use very cold butter and whipping cream, and do not overwork the dough.

1 cup	all-purpose flour	250 mL
3 tbsp	granulated sugar	45 mL
2 tsp	baking powder	10 mL
¼ tsp	salt	1 mL
3 tbsp	very cold unsalted butter, cut into small pieces	45 mL
1	large egg yolk	1
⅓ cup	very cold heavy or whipping (35%) cream	75 mL

1. In a medium bowl, whisk together flour, sugar, baking powder and salt. Using your fingertips or a pastry blender, cut in butter until mixture resembles coarse crumbs.

2. In a small bowl, whisk together egg yolk and cream. Using a fork, stir egg mixture into flour mixture until just combined.

3. Form dough into 1-inch (2.5 cm) balls. Place one ball in each cake pop well. Bake for 5 to 7 minutes or until golden. Transfer scones to a wire rack to cool slightly. Repeat with the remaining dough. Serve warm.

Savory Peppered Cheese Muffins

**Makes
22 to 24 muffins**

Freshly ground black pepper gives these savory muffins a mild yet distinctive flavor punch. They make ideal accompaniments to hot soup or stew or to cold salad.

Tip

Do you have a Babycakes Rotating Cake Pop Maker? If so, see page 8 for information on using it.

Variation

Substitute shredded Cheddar or Colby-Jack cheese for the Monterey Jack.

1 cup	all-purpose flour	250 mL
2 tsp	granulated sugar	10 mL
1½ tsp	baking powder	7 mL
½ tsp	baking soda	2 mL
½ tsp	freshly ground black pepper	2 mL
¼ tsp	salt	1 mL
1	large egg	1
⅓ cup	milk	75 mL
3 tbsp	sour cream	45 mL
3 tbsp	vegetable oil	45 mL
2 tbsp	canned chopped mild green chiles	30 mL
¼ cup	shredded Monterey Jack cheese	60 mL
	Nonstick baking spray	

1. In a large bowl, whisk together flour, sugar, baking powder, baking soda, pepper and salt. Set aside.

2. In a medium bowl, whisk together egg, milk, sour cream, oil and chiles. Stir into flour mixture until just blended. Stir in cheese.

3. Spray cake pop wells with nonstick baking spray. Fill each well with about 1 tbsp (15 mL) batter (see page 25). Bake for 4 to 6 minutes or until a tester inserted in the center comes out clean. Transfer muffins to a wire rack to cool slightly. Repeat with the remaining batter. Serve warm.

Lemon Poppy Seed Muffins

Makes 26 to 28 muffins

You don't have to visit a famous tearoom to enjoy tearoom treats. This recipe is perfect for brunches, showers or ladies' luncheons.

Tips

For a more intense lemon flavor, add 1 tsp (5 mL) lemon extract with the vanilla.

Cover and refrigerate leftover egg whites for up to 3 days. For longer storage, freeze them for up to 6 months. (Be sure to label and date each container.) When you're ready to use them, let egg whites thaw in the refrigerator and use 2 tbsp (30 mL) for 1 egg white.

¾ cup	all-purpose flour	175 mL
⅓ cup	granulated sugar	75 mL
½ tsp	baking powder	2 mL
Pinch	salt	Pinch
1	large egg	1
1	large egg yolk	1
2 tbsp	milk	30 mL
1 tsp	vanilla extract	5 mL
7 tbsp	unsalted butter, softened	105 mL
1 tbsp	poppy seeds	15 mL
	Grated zest of 1 lemon	
	Nonstick baking spray	
	Lemon Glaze (page 80)	

1. In a medium bowl, whisk together flour, sugar, baking powder and salt. Set aside.

2. In a small bowl, whisk together egg, egg yolk, milk and vanilla.

3. Using an electric mixer on low speed, beat butter and half the egg mixture into the flour mixture until blended. Beat in the remaining egg mixture until well blended. Stir in poppy seeds and lemon zest.

4. Spray cake pop wells with nonstick baking spray. Fill each well with about 1 tbsp (15 mL) batter (see page 25). Bake for 4 to 6 minutes or until a tester inserted in the center comes out clean. Transfer muffins to a wire rack set over a sheet of foil or waxed paper to cool. Repeat with the remaining batter.

5. Using the fork tool, dip each muffin in Lemon Glaze, allowing excess glaze to drip back into the bowl. Return glazed muffins to the rack to set.

Tropical Muffins

**Makes
34 to 36 muffins**

Start your day with a tropical escape. The pineapple makes these muffins moist and packed with flavor.

Tips

After measuring out ¼ cup (60 mL) of the pineapple juice in step 1, you'll likely still have some juice left over. Try drizzling it over fruit salad, adding it to salad dressing or incorporating it into a gelatin salad.

For added tropical flavor, dip muffins in Orange Glaze (page 80) or split them in half, spread one half with orange marmalade, then stick the halves back together.

1	can (8 oz/227 mL) crushed pineapple, with juice	1
1½ cups	all-purpose flour	375 mL
¼ cup	granulated sugar	60 mL
¼ cup	packed brown sugar	60 mL
1½ tsp	baking powder	7 mL
¼ tsp	baking soda	1 mL
Pinch	salt	Pinch
1	large egg	1
½ cup	sour cream	125 mL
¼ cup	vegetable oil	60 mL
½ tsp	almond extract	2 mL
	Nonstick baking spray	

1. Pour pineapple into a fine-mesh sieve set over a glass measuring cup. Press down lightly on fruit with the back of a spoon to drain well. Set fruit aside. Measure out ¼ cup (60 mL) juice and set aside (see tip, at left).

2. In a large bowl, whisk together flour, granulated sugar, brown sugar, baking powder, baking soda and salt. Set aside.

3. In a small bowl, whisk together egg, sour cream, oil, almond extract and pineapple juice. Stir into flour mixture until just blended. Stir in pineapple.

4. Spray cake pop wells with nonstick baking spray. Fill each well with about 1 tbsp (15 mL) batter (see page 25). Bake for 4 to 6 minutes or until a tester inserted in the center comes out clean. Transfer muffins to a wire rack to cool slightly. Repeat with the remaining batter. Serve warm.

Banana Nut Muffins

Makes 48 to 50 muffins		

These warm muffin bites — packed with bananas and pecans — are the ultimate comfort food.

Tip

Toasting pecans intensifies their flavor. Spread chopped pecans in a single layer on a baking sheet. Bake at 350°F (180°C) for 5 to 7 minutes or until lightly browned. Let cool, then measure.

1½ cups	all-purpose flour	375 mL
¾ cup	granulated sugar	175 mL
½ tsp	baking powder	2 mL
½ tsp	baking soda	2 mL
¼ tsp	salt	1 mL
1	large egg	1
2	very ripe bananas, mashed	2
½ cup	milk	125 mL
⅓ cup	unsalted butter, melted	75 mL
¼ cup	finely chopped pecans, toasted (see tip, at left)	60 mL
	Nonstick baking spray	

1. In a large bowl, whisk together flour, sugar, baking powder, baking soda and salt. Set aside.

2. In a medium bowl, whisk together egg, mashed bananas, milk and butter. Stir into flour mixture until just blended. Stir in pecans.

3. Spray cake pop wells with nonstick baking spray. Fill each well with about 1 tbsp (15 mL) batter (see page 25). Bake for 3 to 5 minutes or until a tester inserted in the center comes out clean. Transfer muffins to a wire rack to cool. Repeat with the remaining batter.

Rise and Shine Muffins

These little bites pack a lot of nutrition and are perfect for breakfast. The combination of rolled oats, whole-grain flour, cranberries, nuts and applesauce will remind you of a hearty cereal or granola.

Tips

Store leftover muffins in an airtight container and plan to serve within a day or two. Or store in the freezer for up to 3 months.

Do you have a Babycakes Rotating Cake Pop Maker? If so, see page 8 for information on using it.

• Food processor

½ cup	large-flake (old-fashioned) rolled oats	125 mL
¼ cup	whole wheat flour	60 mL
¼ cup	dried sweetened cranberries or raisins	60 mL
¼ cup	chopped pecans, toasted (see tip, page 120)	60 mL
2 tbsp	all-purpose flour	30 mL
2 tbsp	packed brown sugar	30 mL
1 tsp	baking powder	5 mL
½ tsp	ground nutmeg	2 mL
¼ tsp	baking soda	1 mL
Pinch	salt	Pinch
1	large egg	1
½ cup	sweetened applesauce	125 mL
3 tbsp	milk	45 mL
2 tbsp	unsalted butter, melted	30 mL
½ tsp	vanilla extract	2 mL
	Nonstick baking spray	

1. In food processor, combine oats, whole wheat flour, cranberries, pecans, all-purpose flour, brown sugar, baking powder, nutmeg, baking soda and salt; pulse until well combined and cranberries are chopped. Set aside.

2. In a medium bowl, whisk together egg, applesauce, milk, butter and vanilla.

3. Add oat mixture to egg mixture, stirring just until moistened.

4. Spray cake pop wells with nonstick baking spray. Fill each well with about 1 tbsp (15 mL) batter (see page 25). Bake for 5 to 7 minutes or until a tester inserted in the center comes out clean. Transfer muffins to a wire rack to cool. Repeat with the remaining batter.

Filled Breakfast Bites

Makes 40 biscuits

Bundles of biscuit and jam are fun to eat and easy to make. For an added treat, dip them into melted butter, then roll in cinnamon sugar.

Tips

If you can only find a 16.3-oz (462 g) can with 8 larger biscuits, pat or roll out each biscuit into a $6\frac{1}{2}$- to 7-inch (16 to 17.5 cm) circle, then cut it into 6 pieces. Increase the total amount of jam or jelly to $\frac{1}{3}$ cup (75 mL). Makes 48 biscuits.

Be sure to seal the dough around the jam so it doesn't leak out, and avoid piercing the biscuit with the fork tool when turning it over.

If desired, immediately after baking, dip the biscuits in melted butter, then roll them in cinnamon sugar made from $\frac{1}{2}$ cup (125 mL) granulated sugar and $1\frac{1}{2}$ tbsp (22 mL) ground cinnamon. Or place in a paper bag filled with confectioners' (icing) sugar or granulated sugar and toss to coat.

Dip the biscuits in French Toast Glaze (page 81).

| 1 | can (12 oz/350 g) refrigerated flaky biscuits (10 biscuits) | 1 |
| 3 tbsp | fruit jam or jelly | 45 mL |

1. Separate dough into individual biscuits. Pat or roll out each biscuit into a $4\frac{1}{2}$- to 5-inch (11 to 12.5 cm) circle, then cut into quarters. Spoon about $\frac{1}{4}$ tsp (1 mL) jam or jelly into the center of each quarter.

2. Working with one quarter at a time, gently pull up the edges of the dough, covering the jam completely and shaping it into a rounded dumpling by pinching all edges well to seal. Repeat with the remaining quarters.

3. Place one biscuit in each cake pop well. Bake for 3 minutes. Carefully place the fork tool between each biscuit and the edge of the well and gently turn the biscuit over. Bake for 3 minutes or until golden brown. Transfer biscuits to a wire rack to cool slightly. Repeat with the remaining biscuits. Serve warm.

Pancake Bites

Makes
33 to 35 pancakes

Make breakfast fun! These delightful rounds taste like classic buttermilk pancakes, and your family will be delighted when they discover the surprise syrup filling!

Tips

No buttermilk on hand? Stir 1 tbsp (5 mL) lemon juice or white vinegar into 1 cup (250 mL) milk. Let stand for 5 to 10 minutes or until thickened. Proceed with the recipe.

You can also simply serve the warm pancakes drizzled with syrup, rather than injecting them.

Dip the pancakes in French Toast Glaze (page 81).

Variation

Omit the syrup and fill each pancake with your favorite jam or jelly.

• Squeeze bottle or pastry bag, fitted with a fine tip

1 cup	all-purpose flour	250 mL
1 tbsp	granulated sugar	15 mL
2 tsp	baking powder	10 mL
¼ tsp	baking soda	1 mL
¼ tsp	salt	1 mL
1	large egg, at room temperature	1
1 cup	buttermilk, at room temperature	250 mL
2 tbsp	unsalted butter, melted	30 mL
	Nonstick baking spray	
⅓ cup	pure maple syrup or pancake syrup	75 mL

1. In a large bowl, whisk together flour, sugar, baking powder, baking soda and salt. Set aside.

2. In a small bowl, whisk together egg, buttermilk and butter. Stir into flour mixture until just blended.

3. Spray cake pop wells with nonstick baking spray. Fill each well with about 1 tbsp (15 mL) batter (see page 25). Bake for 4 to 6 minutes or until a tester inserted in the center comes out clean. Transfer pancakes to a wire rack to cool slightly. Repeat with the remaining batter.

4. Using the squeeze bottle or pastry bag, inject maple syrup into the center of each pancake. Serve warm.

Mini Dutch Babies

2	large eggs, at room temperature	2
6 tbsp	milk	90 mL
6 tbsp	all-purpose flour	90 mL
½ tsp	grated lemon zest	2 mL
½ tsp	vanilla extract	2 mL
2 tbsp	unsalted butter, melted	30 mL
	Confectioners' (icing) sugar or granulated sugar	
	Fresh berries or other fruit	

Makes 34 to 36 pastries

Dutch babies, a classic German treat, might be described as part pancake, part popover and part soufflé. Traditional Dutch babies are baked in a skillet; they puff up in the oven, then collapse into a bowl-shaped pastry when they're removed from the oven. These miniature versions will do the same, so don't be surprised!

Tips

Select your favorite fresh berries or use a combination of fruits. We love Dutch babies with blueberries, raspberries, strawberries, peach slices and banana slices, among others. Sweeten the fruit to taste, if desired.

If desired, top the Dutch babies with fruit preserves or jam, or drizzle them with pure maple syrup or pancake syrup.

1. In a medium bowl, using an electric mixer on medium-high speed, beat eggs for 1 minute or until fluffy. Beat in milk. Beat in flour, lemon zest and vanilla. Beat for 1 minute. Pour batter into a large glass measuring cup or a small pitcher. Set aside.

2. Generously brush each cake pop well with melted butter. Pour about 1½ tsp (7 mL) batter into each well, filling it about half full. Bake for 4 to 6 minutes or until puffed and golden brown. Transfer Dutch babies to a plate and immediately sprinkle with confectioners' sugar. Repeat with the remaining batter.

3. Serve warm, with fresh berries on the side.

Part 4

Special Times and Special Flavors

Appetizers and Savory Nibbles

Tortilla Scoopers 127

Dinner Roll Bites 127

Wonton Cups. 128

    Creamy Crab Wonton Cups 128

    Pesto Chicken Wonton Cups 129

Homemade Bread Bites 130

Honey Wheat Mini Rolls 131

Hush Puppies. 132

Garlic Bread Bites 133

Cheese Bites 133

Olive Cheese Bites 134

Pizza Bites. 134

Sausage Bites. 135

Brat Rolls. 135

Crab Cake Bites. 136

BBQ Cocktail Meatballs 137

Mexican Meatballs. 138

Swedish Meatballs. 139

Tortilla Scoopers

The fresh taste of homemade tortilla chips, plus the ease with which these are made, may make this recipe the most popular snack in your home. For an added treat, serve these with Taco Dip (page 146) or Creamy Spinach Artichoke Dip (page 144).

Tip

For the second batch, when the cake pop maker is hot, use the end of a wooden spoon to press the tortilla rounds into the wells.

- 2-inch (5 cm) cookie cutter

| 1 | 10-inch (25 cm) flour tortilla | 1 |

1. Using the cookie cutter, cut rounds from the tortilla. Place 12 of the rounds between paper towels and microwave on High for 10 seconds or until just barely warm and pliable.

2. Working with one tortilla round at a time, gently pleat one edge so that the round forms a cup shape. Place the round in a cake pop well, pressing down lightly so it conforms to the shape of the well.

3. Bake for 3 to 4 minutes or until crisp and golden. Transfer tortilla cups to a wire rack to cool. Repeat with the remaining rounds.

Tips

If desired, spray the tortillas with nonstick baking spray before baking. After baking, immediately sprinkle the hot tortilla scoopers with salt.

These tortillas are best served within a few hours after they are baked.

Dinner Roll Bites

These bread basket treats are so simple to prepare you'll make them over and over again. They are not as heavy as dinner rolls, but they make ideal partners for soup or stew.

| 4 | frozen unbaked dinner rolls, thawed | 4 |
| | Nonstick baking spray | |

1. Cut each roll into thirds. Roll each piece into a ball.

2. Spray cake pop wells with nonstick baking spray. Place a dough ball in each well. Bake for 4 to 5 minutes or until golden brown. Transfer rolls to a wire rack to cool slightly. Serve warm.

Tip

Roll hot baked bread bites in melted butter.

Wonton Cups

**Makes
24 wonton cups**

The filling possibilities
for these crisp treats
are just about endless!

Tips

These wontons are best
served shortly after they are
baked but can be stored in
an airtight container for up
to 1 day.

Do you have a Babycakes
Rotating Cake Pop Maker?
If so, see page 8 for
information on using it.

6	wonton wrappers (about 3½ inches/ 8.5 cm square)	6

1. Cut each wonton wrapper into four squares.

2. Place one square in each well, pressing down lightly so it conforms to the shape of the well. Bake for 4 minutes or until crisp and golden. Transfer wonton cups to a wire rack to cool. Repeat with the remaining squares.

> ## Tips
> For the second batch, when the cake pop maker is hot, use the end of a wooden spoon to press the squares into the wells.
>
> For a neater or round look, use a 2-inch (5 cm) cookie cutter to cut rounds from 24 wonton wrappers. Continue with step 2. Deep-fry or bake the scraps until crisp, and add to soups or salads.

Creamy Crab Wonton Cups

**Makes
24 wonton cups**

These crab-filled wonton
cups tastes as rich and
savory as those served
at the finest Chinese
restaurants, yet they
are so quick and easy
to prepare.

Tip

For the herb garnish, try
parsley, dill or chives.

⅓ cup	cooked backfin (lump) crabmeat, drained and picked over to remove cartilage, or canned white crabmeat, drained	75 mL
2 tsp	finely chopped green onion	10 mL
⅛ tsp	garlic powder	0.5 mL
2 oz	cream cheese, softened	60 g
3 tbsp	sour cream	45 mL
¼ tsp	Worcestershire sauce	1 mL
2 to 3	drops hot pepper sauce	2 to 3
	Salt and freshly ground black pepper	
24	baked Wonton Cups (above)	24
	Small sprigs of fresh herbs, diced red bell pepper and/or additional finely chopped green onion (optional)	

Tip

The filling can be made up to 1 day ahead and stored in an airtight container in the refrigerator. Spoon it into the crisp wonton cups just before serving.

1. In a small bowl, combine crabmeat, green onion, garlic powder, cream cheese, sour cream, Worcestershire sauce and hot pepper sauce to taste. Season to taste with salt and pepper.

2. Spoon about 1 tsp (5 mL) crab filling into each wonton cup. Garnish as desired with herbs, red pepper and/or green onion.

Pesto Chicken Wonton Cups

Makes 24 wonton cups

These elegant yet simple delights are equally at home on silver trays at a black-tie gala and on paper plates while you're gathered around the television, watching the big game. You will never struggle with what appetizer to serve again!

Tips

For the chicken, use about half of a 4½-oz (140 g) can of chicken, drained (store the other half in an airtight container in the refrigerator for up to 2 days, or use leftover grilled or roasted chicken.

The filling can be made up to 1 day ahead and stored in an airtight container in the refrigerator. Spoon it into the crisp wonton cups just before serving.

½ cup	finely chopped cooked chicken (see tip, at left)	125 mL
3 tbsp	finely chopped celery	45 mL
2 tsp	finely chopped green onions	10 mL
2 tbsp	mayonnaise	30 mL
4 tsp	prepared basil pesto	20 mL
24	baked Wonton Cups (opposite)	24
	Minced green onion, minced fresh basil, tiny fresh parsley sprigs, finely chopped red bell pepper and/or toasted sliced almonds	

1. In a small bowl, combine chicken, celery and onions. Stir in mayonnaise and pesto.

2. Spoon about 1 tsp (5 mL) pesto chicken filling into each wonton cup. Garnish as desired with green onion, basil, parsley, red pepper and/or almonds.

Homemade Bread Bites

These mini rolls make the perfect accompaniment to any dinner. Or serve them warm as part of a fondue party, pairing them with Beer, Cheddar and Bacon Fondue (page 147) or Mexican Spinach Cheese Dip (page 145).

Tips

One ¼-oz (7 g) package of quick-rising (instant) yeast contains 2¼ tsp (11 mL) yeast.

Filling the wells half to three-quarters full allows room for the rolls to rise, and brushing the tops of the batter lightly with melted butter improves the browning and adds to the flavor. If the wells are under-filled, the rolls may not rise enough to reach the top of the cake pop maker, and they won't brown. If you're worried that your wells are under-filled, bake for 4 minutes, then check on the progress. If desired, use the fork tool to turn each roll over, then continue baking for 2 minutes or until golden brown.

1¾ cups	all-purpose flour	425 mL
2 tbsp	granulated sugar	30 mL
¾ tsp	salt	3 mL
1	package (¼ oz/7 g) quick-rising (instant) yeast	1
1	large egg, at room temperature	1
¾ cup	warm water	175 mL
3 tbsp	unsalted butter, softened	45 mL
2 tbsp	unsalted butter, melted	30 mL

1. In a large bowl, whisk together flour, sugar, salt and yeast. Add egg, water and softened butter. Using an electric mixer on medium speed, beat for 2 minutes. Cover bowl with a towel and let dough rise in a warm, draft-free place for 30 minutes.

2. Brush cake pop wells with melted butter. Drop about 1½ tsp (7 mL) dough into each well, filling it half to three-quarters full. Quickly and lightly brush the tops of the dough with melted butter. Bake for 5 to 6 minutes or until golden brown and crisp. Transfer rolls to a wire rack to cool slightly. Repeat with the remaining dough. Serve warm.

Variations

Herb Rolls: Add ¼ tsp (1 mL) garlic powder, ¼ tsp (1 mL) dried thyme and ¼ tsp (1 mL) crushed dried rosemary to the flour mixture.

Tex-Mex Rolls: Add ¼ tsp (1 mL) garlic powder, ¼ tsp (1 mL) dried oregano and ¼ tsp (1 mL) chili powder to the flour mixture.

Honey Wheat Mini Rolls

These whole wheat rolls are so easy to prepare that you can serve them daily. Serve them anytime you want hot rolls, or plan a fondue night with these rolls, vegetables and your favorite fondue.

Tips

One ¼-oz (7 g) package of quick-rising (instant) yeast contains 2¼ tsp (11 mL) yeast.

Filling the wells half to three-quarters full allows room for the rolls to rise, and brushing the tops of the batter lightly with melted butter improves the browning and adds to the flavor. If the wells are under-filled, the rolls may not rise enough to reach the top of the cake pop maker, and they won't brown. If you're worried that your wells are under-filled, bake for 4 minutes, then check on the progress. If desired, use the fork tool to turn each roll over, then continue baking for 2 minutes or until golden brown.

1 cup	all-purpose flour	250 mL
½ cup	whole wheat flour	125 mL
¾ tsp	salt	3 mL
1	package (¼ oz/7 g) quick-rising (instant) yeast	1
⅔ cup	warm water	150 mL
2 tbsp	milk, at room temperature	30 mL
1 tbsp	unsalted butter, softened	15 mL
1 tbsp	liquid honey	15 mL
2 tbsp	unsalted butter, melted	30 mL

1. In a large bowl, whisk together all-purpose flour, whole wheat flour, salt and yeast. Stir in water, milk, softened butter and honey. Using an electric mixer on medium speed, beat for 2 minutes. Cover bowl with a towel and let dough rise in a warm, draft-free place for 30 minutes.

2. Brush cake pop wells with melted butter. Drop about 1½ tsp (7 mL) dough into each well, filling it half to three-quarters full. Quickly and lightly brush the tops of the dough with melted butter. Bake for 5 to 6 minutes or until golden brown and crisp. Transfer rolls to a wire rack to cool slightly. Repeat with the remaining dough. Serve warm.

Hush Puppies

Makes 16 to 18 hush puppies

Roxanne's dad and husband both enjoy fishing, and they have many fish stories to tell from the hours spent fishing on the Lake of the Ozarks in Missouri. Roxanne likes to fry fresh fish dredged in cornmeal, and she firmly believes it should always be accompanied by hush puppies.

Tips

No buttermilk on hand? Stir 1½ tsp (7 mL) lemon juice or white vinegar into ½ cup (125 mL) milk. Let stand for 5 to 10 minutes or until thickened. Proceed with the recipe.

Do you have a Babycakes Rotating Cake Pop Maker? If so, see page 8 for information on using it.

Variation

Stir in 2 tbsp (30 mL) finely minced onion after whisking the egg mixture into the flour mixture. Replace the onion salt with salt.

¾ cup	all-purpose flour	175 mL
¼ cup	yellow cornmeal	60 mL
1 tsp	granulated sugar	5 mL
1 tsp	onion salt	5 mL
½ tsp	baking powder	2 mL
1	large egg, at room temperature	1
½ cup	buttermilk	125 mL
	Nonstick baking spray	
¼ cup	unsalted butter, melted	60 mL
½ tsp	salt	2 mL

1. In a medium bowl, whisk together flour, cornmeal, sugar, onion salt and baking powder. Set aside.

2. In a small bowl, whisk together egg and buttermilk. Add to flour mixture and whisk until smooth. Cover with plastic wrap and refrigerate for 30 minutes.

3. Spray cake pop wells with nonstick baking spray. Fill each well with about 1 tbsp (15 mL) batter (see page 25). Bake for 4 to 6 minutes or until a tester inserted in the center comes out clean. Using the fork tool, dip hush puppies quickly in melted butter, then set on a wire rack set over a sheet of foil or waxed paper, sprinkle with salt and let cool. Repeat with the remaining batter.

Garlic Bread Bites

Roxanne's family enjoys these warm buttered garlic bites with spaghetti and meatballs or with Baked Pizza Dip (page 143).

Tip

Freeze leftover baked Garlic Bread Bites in an airtight container for up to 1 month. Place frozen rolls on a microwave-safe plate lined with a paper towel and cover with another paper towel. Microwave on High in 30-second intervals until thawed and hot.

8	frozen unbaked dinner rolls, thawed	8
1/4 cup	unsalted butter	60 mL
1/2 tsp	garlic powder	2 mL

1. Cut each roll into thirds. Roll each piece into a ball.

2. Place butter in microwave-safe glass bowl. Microwave on High for 30 to 40 seconds or until melted. Stir in garlic powder.

3. Roll dough balls in garlic butter.

4. Place a dough ball in each cake pop well. Bake for 4 to 5 minutes or until golden brown. Transfer rolls to a wire rack to cool slightly. Repeat with the remaining dough. Serve warm.

Cheese Bites

**Makes
24 rolls**

Cheese and crackers will become ho-hum after you experience Cheese Bites.

Variation

Replace the Cheddar cheese with your favorite cheese — mozzarella, Munster, Colby-Jack and pepper Jack all work well.

| 8 | frozen unbaked dinner rolls, thawed | 8 |
| 24 | 1/2-inch (1 cm) cubes Cheddar cheese | 24 |

1. Cut each dinner roll into thirds. Using your fingers, form each third into a thin, flat circle. Place one cube of cheese in the center of each circle and wrap dough around cheese, pinching the edges to seal securely.

2. Place one roll in each cake pop well. Bake for 4 to 5 minutes or until golden brown. Transfer rolls to a wire rack to cool slightly. Repeat with the remaining rolls. Serve warm.

Olive Cheese Bites

Some people touch
our lives forever. When
you think of them,
your thoughts turn
to smiles and happy
times. Roxanne's friend
Nancy Ryan is one
such special friend.
This is Nancy's recipe,
passed on to her from
her mother. Thanks for
sharing, Nancy!

Variation

For a spicy version, add
1/4 tsp (1 mL) cayenne
pepper with the flour.

1 cup	shredded sharp (old) Cheddar cheese	250 mL
1/2 cup + 2 tbsp	all-purpose flour	155 mL
1/4 cup	unsalted butter, melted	60 mL
12 to 14	small pimento-stuffed green olives, patted dry	12 to 14

1. In a medium bowl, combine cheese, flour and butter (mixture will appear somewhat dry).

2. Using about 1 1/2 tsp (7 mL) dough, form it into a ball around a olive. (The warmth from your hands will help form the dough into a nice, tight ball. Keep working the dough until it does.) Place on a plate. Repeat with the remaining dough and olives. Refrigerate for 30 to 60 minutes or until well chilled.

3. Place one roll in each cake pop well. Bake for 4 minutes. Carefully place the fork tool between each roll and the edge of the well and gently turn the roll over. Bake for 4 minutes. Transfer to a wire rack to cool slightly. Repeat with the remaining rolls. Serve warm.

Pizza Bites

Roxanne's daughter,
Grace, often requests
these as a lunchtime
treat. Shh! Please don't
let her know how very
simple they are to
prepare.

Variation

Substitute small pieces of
Canadian bacon for the
pepperoni.

4	frozen unbaked dinner rolls, thawed	4
1/4 cup	shredded pizza-blend cheese or 5-cheese Italian blend	60 mL
6	slices pepperoni or turkey pepperoni, cut into quarters	6
2 tbsp	pizza sauce or marinara sauce	30 mL

1. Cut each roll into thirds. Using your fingers, spread dough into a flat round. For each pizza bite, pinch about 1 tsp (5 mL) cheese into a loose ball and place in center of dough. Top with 2 quarters of a pepperoni slice and 1/2 tsp (2 mL) pizza sauce. Wrap edges of dough up around filling to form a small ball. Pinch edges to seal securely. Repeat with the remaining dough.

2. Place one roll in each cake pop well. Bake for 4 to 6 minutes or until golden brown. Transfer to a wire rack to cool slightly. Serve warm.

Sausage Bites

**Makes
24 rolls**

Preparing an appetizer or "just a bite" becomes a breeze with this simple recipe. Serve these with Baked Pizza Dip (page 143).

Tip
This recipe is great with any of your favorite sausage. We especially enjoy it with Italian sausage.

Variation
Add ½ tsp (2 mL) shredded Cheddar or mozzarella cheese to the center of the dough with the cooked sausage.

| 4 oz | sausage (bulk or casings removed) | 125 g |
| 8 | frozen unbaked dinner rolls, thawed | 8 |

1. In a small skillet, cook sausage over medium-high heat, breaking it up with the back of a spoon, for 6 to 8 minutes or until no longer pink. Spoon sausage into a small bowl lined with paper towels and let sausage drain well.

2. Cut each roll into thirds. Using your fingers, spread dough into a flat round. For each sausage bite, place about 1½ tsp (7 mL) sausage in center of dough. Wrap edges of dough up around sausage to form a small ball. Pinch edges to seal securely. Repeat with the remaining dough.

3. Place one roll in each cake pop well. Bake for 4 minutes or until browned. Transfer to a wire rack to cool slightly. Repeat with the remaining rolls. Serve warm.

Brat Rolls

**Makes
24 rolls**

Serve these bundles of moist bratwurst snuggled into bread dough at your next Bavarian Brat Party. Honey Mustard Dipping Sauce (page 141) or spicy mustard make ideal accompaniments.

| 2 | cooked bratwurst links, frankfurters or smoked sausage | 2 |
| 8 | frozen unbaked dinner rolls, thawed | 8 |

1. Cut each link into 12 slices. Cut each dinner roll into thirds. Using your fingers, spread dough into a flat round. For each brat roll, place a bratwurst slice in center of dough. Wrap edges of dough up around bratwurst to form a small ball. Pinch edges to seal securely. Repeat with the remaining dough.

2. Place one roll in each cake pop well. Bake for 4 minutes or until browned. Transfer to a wire rack to cool slightly. Repeat with the remaining rolls. Serve warm.

Crab Cake Bites

These crab cake bites make perfect appetizers. Serve them with your favorite tartar sauce or with Honey Mustard Dipping Sauce (page 141).

Tips

If you don't have buttery crackers on hand, you can substitute ¼ cup (60 mL) more panko bread crumbs, saltine cracker crumbs or dry bread crumbs.

You can use a 6-oz (175 g) can of lump crabmeat, drained, for the crabmeat.

In step 2, use a small scoop (one that holds about 1 tbsp/15 mL) to spoon out just the right amount of the crab mixture, then lightly shape the mixture into a ball with your hands.

6	round buttery crackers (about 2 inches/5 cm in diameter), finely crushed	6
2 tbsp	finely chopped green onion	30 mL
1 tbsp	drained chopped pimento	15 mL
¼ tsp	crab boil or seafood seasoning	1 mL
1	large egg white	1
1 tbsp	mayonnaise	15 mL
1 tsp	Dijon mustard	5 mL
¼ tsp	Worcestershire sauce	1 mL
6 oz	cooked backfin (lump) crabmeat, drained and picked over to remove cartilage	175 g
	Salt and freshly ground black pepper	
½ cup	panko bread crumbs	125 mL
2 tbsp	vegetable oil	30 mL

1. In a large bowl, combine cracker crumbs, green onion, pimento, crab boil seasoning, egg white, mayonnaise, mustard and Worcestershire sauce. Gently stir in crabmeat. Season to taste with salt and pepper.

2. Using wet hands, lightly shape mixture into 1-inch (2.5 cm) balls. Roll each ball in panko.

3. Brush cake pop wells with vegetable oil. Place one crab cake in each well. Bake for 8 minutes. Carefully place the fork tool between each crab cake and the edge of the well and gently turn the crab cake over. Bake for 3 minutes or until golden brown. Transfer to a wire rack to cool slightly. Repeat with the remaining crab mixture. Serve warm.

BBQ Cocktail Meatballs

Kansas City, our hometown, is known for a sweet, tomato-based barbecue sauce, and — of course — that sauce is the inspiration for the quick sauce on these meatballs.

Tips

Always use very lean ground beef, such as ground round or sirloin, to reduce the amount of fat that collects in the wells. For optimum performance and to minimize fat, turn the unit off between batches, let it cool completely, wipe away any collected fat with a paper towel, then bake the next batch.

Meatballs are a great make-ahead appetizer. Let baked meatballs cool, then cover and refrigerate, without sauce, for up to 3 days. When ready to serve, prepare sauce as directed, then stir in the chilled meatballs and heat over low heat, stirring gently, for about 10 minutes or until meatballs are heated through.

Do you have a Babycakes Rotating Cake Pop Maker? If so, see page 8 for information on using it.

Meatballs

1 lb	extra-lean ground beef (see tip, at left)	500 g
½ cup	dry bread crumbs	125 mL
2 tbsp	very finely chopped onion	30 mL
½ tsp	salt	2 mL
¼ tsp	freshly ground black pepper	1 mL
¼ tsp	garlic powder	1 mL
1	large egg	1
2 tbsp	milk	30 mL
1 tsp	Worcestershire sauce	5 mL

Sauce

⅓ cup	packed brown sugar	75 mL
1 cup	ketchup	250 mL
⅓ cup	chili sauce	75 mL
¼ cup	cider vinegar	60 mL
4 tsp	Worcestershire sauce	20 mL
1 tbsp	prepared mustard	15 mL
4 to 5	drops hot pepper sauce	4 to 5

1. *Meatballs:* In a large bowl, combine beef, bread crumbs, onion, salt, pepper, garlic powder, egg, milk and Worcestershire sauce. Form into 1-inch (2.5 cm) meatballs (see tip, page 139).

2. Place one meatball in each cake pop well. Bake for 5 to 7 minutes or until no longer pink inside. Transfer meatballs to a covered dish and keep warm. Repeat with the remaining meatballs.

3. *Sauce:* Meanwhile, in a medium saucepan, over low heat, combine brown sugar, ketchup, chili sauce, vinegar, Worcestershire sauce, mustard and hot pepper sauce to taste. Cook, stirring frequently, for 5 to 10 minutes or until sugar is dissolved and sauce is heated through.

4. Pour sauce over meatballs. Serve warm, on toothpicks.

Mexican Meatballs

Makes about 30 meatballs

Although we generally think of these meatballs as appetizers, they are equally good as a main dish. Simply prepare Mexican rice and serve the meatballs on top.

Tips

Always use very lean ground beef, such as ground round or sirloin, to reduce the amount of fat that collects in the wells. For optimum performance and to minimize fat, turn the unit off between batches, let it cool completely, wipe away any collected fat with a paper towel, then bake the next batch.

Meatballs are a great make-ahead appetizer. Let baked meatballs cool, then cover and refrigerate for up to 3 days. To reheat, spread meatballs in a single layer in a shallow baking pan. Bake in a 375°F (190°C) oven for 10 to 15 minutes or until heated through.

Variation

For a spicier version, add 1½ tbsp (22 mL) finely chopped pickled jalapeño peppers to the meat mixture.

1 lb	extra-lean ground beef (see tip, at left)	500 g
¼ cup	crushed tortilla chips	60 mL
1	package (1¼ oz/35 g) taco seasoning	1
1	large egg	1
3 tbsp	salsa	45 mL

1. In a medium bowl, combine beef, chips, taco seasoning, egg and salsa. Cover with plastic wrap and refrigerate for 30 to 60 minutes or until well chilled. Form into 1-inch (2.5 cm) meatballs (see tip, page 139).

2. Place one meatball in each cake pop well. Bake for 5 to 7 minutes or until no longer pink inside. Transfer meatballs to a covered dish and keep warm. Repeat with the remaining meatballs.

Swedish Meatballs

Makes about 36 meatballs

These meatballs may become one of your family's favorite dishes! Serve them often, either as an appetizer or as a main dish over hot cooked rice, noodles or mashed potatoes.

Tips

Always use very lean ground beef, such as ground round or sirloin, to reduce the amount of fat that collects in the wells. For optimum performance and to minimize fat, turn the unit off between batches, let it cool completely, wipe away any collected fat with a paper towel, then bake the next batch.

When forming meatballs, use a small scoop (one that holds about 1 tbsp/15 mL) to spoon out just the right amount of the beef mixture, then lightly shape the mixture into a ball with your hands.

Do you have a Babycakes Rotating Cake Pop Maker? If so, see page 8 for information on using it.

Meatballs

1 lb	extra-lean ground beef (see tip, at left)	500 g
¼ cup	dry bread crumbs	60 mL
½ tsp	paprika	2 mL
¼ tsp	garlic powder	1 mL
1	large egg	1
1 tbsp	Worcestershire sauce	15 mL
	Salt and freshly ground black pepper	

Sauce

2 tbsp	unsalted butter	30 mL
2 tbsp	all-purpose flour	30 mL
1 cup	reduced-sodium beef broth	250 mL
1 cup	sour cream	250 mL
2 tbsp	minced fresh dill	30 mL
1 tsp	Worcestershire sauce	5 mL
	Salt and freshly ground black pepper	
2 tbsp	minced fresh parsley	30 mL

1. *Meatballs:* In a large bowl, combine beef, bread crumbs, paprika, garlic powder, egg and Worcestershire sauce. Season with salt and pepper. Form into 1-inch (2.5 cm) meatballs (see tip, at left).

2. Place one meatball in each cake pop well. Bake for 5 to 7 minutes or until no longer pink inside. Transfer meatballs to a covered dish and keep warm. Repeat with the remaining meatballs.

3. *Sauce:* Meanwhile, in a small saucepan, melt butter over medium-low heat. Add flour and cook, stirring constantly, for 1 minute. Gradually add broth and cook, stirring constantly, until thickened and bubbly. Gradually add sour cream, stirring until smooth. Stir in dill and Worcestershire sauce. Season to taste with salt and pepper. Reduce heat to low and cook, stirring, for 1 to 2 minutes or until hot and smooth.

4. Pour sauce over meatballs and sprinkle with parsley.

Dips and Fondues

Honey Mustard Dipping Sauce 141

Blue Cheese Dipping Sauce. 141

Wasabi Mayo Sauce 142

Onion Dip. 143

Baked Pizza Dip 143

Creamy Spinach Artichoke Dip 144

Mexican Spinach Cheese Dip. 145

Taco Dip 146

Beer, Cheddar and Bacon Fondue. 147

Honey Mustard Dipping Sauce

Makes about ½ cup (125 mL)

This is one of our favorite dipping sauces. Make plenty to serve on Brat Rolls (page 135) or with Crab Cake Bites (page 136).

Tip
Store this dip in an airtight container in the refrigerator for up to 3 days.

¼ cup	sour cream	60 mL
3 tbsp	Dijon mustard	45 mL
4 tsp	liquid honey	20 mL
3 to 5	drops hot pepper sauce	3 to 5

1. In a small bowl, combine sour cream, mustard, honey and hot pepper sauce to taste.

2. Serve immediately or cover and refrigerate for 1 hour, until well chilled.

Blue Cheese Dipping Sauce

Makes about ¾ cup (175 mL)

This dipping sauce makes a great accompaniment to Spicy Buffalo Meatballs (page 155). It also adds a flavor burst to burgers and sandwiches!

Variation
For extra-spicy sauce, reduce the milk to 1 tbsp (15 mL) and increase the wing sauce to 5 tsp (25 mL).

• Small food processor

½ cup	sour cream	125 mL
½ cup	crumbled blue cheese	125 mL
2 tbsp	milk	30 mL
2 tsp	bottled spicy wing sauce	10 mL
1 tsp	Worcestershire sauce	5 mL

1. In food processor, combine sour cream, blue cheese, milk, wing sauce and Worcestershire sauce; process until smooth.

2. Serve immediately or cover and refrigerate for 1 hour, until well chilled, or overnight.

Wasabi Mayo Sauce

Makes about ⅔ cup (150 mL)

Wasabi, a Japanese horseradish, adds great flavor to this sharp, spicy mayonnaise, which partners perfectly with Thai Crab Bites (page 153).

Tip

You can use wasabi powder instead of prepared wasabi in this recipe. In a small bowl, combine 2 tbsp (30 mL) wasabi powder and 1½ tbsp (22 mL) cold water until well blended. Let stand for 10 minutes or until wasabi powder has dissolved. Proceed with the recipe.

½ cup	mayonnaise	125 mL
2 tbsp	prepared wasabi paste	30 mL
2 tsp	finely minced gingerroot	10 mL
1 tsp	soy sauce	5 mL
	Salt and freshly ground black pepper	

1. In a small bowl, combine mayonnaise, wasabi, ginger and soy sauce. Season to taste with salt and pepper. Serve immediately or cover and refrigerate overnight.

Onion Dip

Makes
about 1½ cups
(375 mL)

After making this homemade onion dip, you will no longer want to purchase the little tubs from the grocery. Roxanne's husband, Bob Bateman, rated this as one of his all-time favorite dip recipes.

Tip

Serve with Garlic Bread Bites (page 133) or Dinner Roll Bites (page 127).

1	onion	1
2 tbsp	olive oil	30 mL
½ tsp	garlic powder	2 mL
¼ tsp	salt	1 mL
1 cup	sour cream	250 mL
½ cup	plain Greek yogurt	125 mL

1. Cut onion in half and thinly slice. Cut slices in half again.

2. In a medium skillet, heat oil over medium heat. Add onion and cook, stirring occasionally, for 20 minutes or until caramelized. Remove from heat and let cool.

3. In a medium bowl, combine caramelized onions, garlic powder, salt, sour cream and yogurt. Serve immediately or cover and refrigerate overnight.

Baked Pizza Dip

Makes
about 2½ cups
(625 mL)

There's no need to travel to your local pizza parlor. Prepare this appetizer at home, or add a salad and call it dinner. Roxanne's teenage daughter, Grace, rates this as her favorite dip for parties. Serve with Sausage Bites (page 135) or Garlic Bread Bites (page 133).

- Preheat oven to 350°F (180°C)
- 9-inch (23 cm) microwave-safe glass pie plate

8 oz	cream cheese	250 g
1	can (15 oz/425 mL) pizza sauce	1
1½ cups	shredded mozzarella cheese	375 mL

1. Place cream cheese in pie plate. Microwave on High for 30 to 45 seconds or until just softened and spreadable. Using a flat knife, spread cream cheese evenly over the bottom of the pie plate.

2. Pour pizza sauce over cream cheese. Sprinkle evenly with mozzarella.

3. Bake in preheated oven for 25 to 30 minutes or until heated through and mozzarella is melted.

Creamy Spinach Artichoke Dip

Makes about 2½ cups (625 mL)

Kathy serves this easy-to-prepare, timeless appetizer often — and her family always asks for it again. Use it to fill Wonton Cups (page 128), or serve with Tortilla Scoopers (page 127).

Tips

This dip can be assembled up to 1 day ahead. Prepare through step 2, cover and refrigerate. When ready to serve, bake as directed.

You can also cook this dip in the microwave. Spoon the spinach mixture into a 4-cup (1 L) microwave-safe glass casserole dish. Cover and microwave on High for 5 to 7 minutes, stirring halfway through, until heated through. Sprinkle with Monterey Jack, cover and microwave on High for 30 to 60 seconds or until cheese is melted.

- Preheat oven to 375°F (190°C)
- 4-cup (1 L) baking dish, sprayed with nonstick baking spray

1 cup	frozen chopped spinach (see tip, page 145)	250 mL
1	clove garlic, minced	1
⅓ cup	freshly grated Parmesan cheese	75 mL
½ tsp	onion salt	2 mL
3 oz	cream cheese, softened	90 g
¼ cup	sour cream	60 mL
¼ cup	mayonnaise	60 mL
1	can (14 oz/398 mL) artichoke hearts, drained, chopped	1
½ cup	shredded Monterey Jack cheese	125 mL

1. Place spinach in a colander and rinse with hot water until thawed. Drain well. Squeeze until dry. Set aside.

2. In a large bowl, combine garlic, Parmesan, onion salt, cream cheese, sour cream and mayonnaise. Stir in spinach and artichoke hearts. Spoon into prepared baking dish.

3. Bake in preheated oven for 20 minutes. Sprinkle with Monterey Jack and bake for 10 minutes or until hot and bubbly.

Gluten-Free Lemon Cake Pops (page 175) and
Vegan Easy Yellow Cake Pops, decorated (page 181)

Thai Crab Bites (page 153)
with Wasabi Mayo Sauce (page 142)

Pesto Chicken Wonton Cups (page 129)
and Olive Cheese Bites (page 134)

Margarita Cake Pops (page 168)
and Piña Colada Cake Pops (page 166)

Winter Carnival (page 188)

Welcome Spring (page 190)

Easter (page 192)

Halloween (page 202)

Romantic Roses (page 204)

Sweet Thanks
(page 221)

Tooth Sweet
(page 216)

Treats for Dog Lovers
(page 222)

Mexican Spinach Cheese Dip

**Makes
about 2 cups
(500 mL)**

This rich, warm dip was inspired by Kathy's daughter Laura, who would order it frequently at a local restaurant. One day, she asked Kathy to make something similar at home. You can serve it with any warm bread rolls, but it is especially good with Tex-Mex Rolls (variation, page 130) and Olive Cheese Bites (page 134).

Tips

Purchase a bag of loose-packed frozen chopped spinach so you can measure out what you need, then seal the bag and return it to the freezer.

For a spicier dip, use the whole jalapeño. Or, since the flavor and spiciness of Mexican cheese blend varies by brand, prepare as directed, then taste. Add 2 to 4 drops of hot pepper sauce, or to taste.

½ cup	frozen chopped spinach (see tip, at left)	125 mL
2 tbsp	unsalted butter	30 mL
¼ cup	chopped red bell pepper	60 mL
½	jalapeño pepper, seeded and chopped	½
1 tbsp	all-purpose flour	15 mL
	Salt and freshly ground black pepper	
⅔ cup	milk	150 mL
2 cups	shredded Mexican cheese blend or Monterey Jack cheese	500 mL
½ cup	heavy or whipping (35%) cream	125 mL

1. Place spinach in a colander and rinse with hot water until thawed. Drain well. Squeeze until dry. Set aside.

2. In a medium saucepan, melt butter over medium heat. Add red pepper and jalapeño; cook, stirring often, for 2 to 3 minutes or until tender. Add spinach and cook, stirring often, for 1 minute. Add flour and cook, stirring constantly, for 1 minute. Season to taste with salt and pepper. Gradually stir in milk and cook, stirring constantly, for about 2 minutes or until bubbly, thickened and smooth. Stir in cheese and cream; cook, stirring constantly, until smooth. Serve warm.

Taco Dip

Makes 8 to 10 servings

Taco dips are eternally popular. They always vanish so quickly from the buffet! Try making a tempting platter of Dinner Roll Bites (page 127) or warm Cheese Bites (page 133) and watch the dip disappear in the blink of an eye at your next party.

Variation

Omit the ground beef and the water. Add ½ package of taco seasoning to the refried beans and stir to blend well. Continue with step 3.

• 9-inch (23 cm) glass pie plate

1 lb	lean ground beef	500 g
1	package (1¼ oz/35 g) taco seasoning	1
½ cup	water	125 mL
1	can (16 oz/454 mL) refried beans	1
½ cup	sour cream	125 mL
1	large avocado	1
2 tbsp	freshly squeezed lime juice	30 mL
¾ cup	shredded sharp (old) Cheddar cheese	175 mL
3	plum (Roma) tomatoes, seeded and diced	3
2	green onions, finely chopped	2

1. In a medium skillet, cook beef over medium-high heat, breaking it up with the back of a spoon, for 6 to 8 minutes or until no longer pink. Drain off fat.

2. Add taco seasoning and water to skillet. Reduce heat and simmer, stirring often, for 5 to 7 minutes or until liquid has evaporated. Remove from heat and let cool slightly.

3. Spread refried beans evenly in bottom of pie plate. Spoon meat mixture evenly over beans. Spread sour cream evenly over meat. Set aside.

4. Peel, pit and dice avocado. Place avocado in a shallow bowl and sprinkle with lime juice. Using a fork, mash avocado. Spread avocado mixture over sour cream. Sprinkle evenly with cheese. Sprinkle tomatoes and green onions over cheese.

Beer, Cheddar and Bacon Fondue

Fondue never seems to go out of style. This rich, savory cheese fondue would be wonderful on a cold winter night with any of our bread rolls (pages 130–134) or with Brat Rolls (page 135).

Tips

Any type of beer will work in this fondue. A lager is a good choice, as it has a light flavor that blends well with cheese. An ale, especially a dark ale, will give a more pronounced flavor.

Pour the warm fondue into a ceramic fondue pot or a small slow cooker to keep it hot while you eat.

2 cups	shredded Cheddar cheese	500 mL
1½ cups	shredded Swiss or Gruyère cheese	375 mL
3½ tsp	all-purpose flour	17 mL
⅛ tsp	cayenne pepper	0.5 mL
1 cup	beer	250 mL
3	slices bacon, cooked crisp and crumbled	3
2 tbsp	spicy brown mustard	30 mL
½ tsp	Worcestershire sauce	2 mL

1. In a sealable plastic bag, combine Cheddar, Swiss cheese, flour and cayenne. Seal and toss to coat cheese evenly with the flour.

2. In a medium saucepan, heat beer over medium heat, until just beginning to bubble. Add cheese mixture, one handful at a time, stirring after each addition until cheese is melted. Stir in bacon, mustard and Worcestershire sauce. Serve warm.

Great Balls of Fire

Southern Cayenne Cheese Bites 149

Firecracker Biscuit Bites 150

Jalapeño Poppers 150

Cajun Cornbread Pops 151

Jalapeño, Corn and Cheese Morsels 152

Thai Crab Bites 153

Buffalo Chicken Dumplings 154

Spicy Buffalo Meatballs 155

Mexican Chocolate Chile Cake Pops 156

Cinnamon Candy Cake Pops 157

Southern Cayenne Cheese Bites

Pat Smith and Donna Richardson are two of Roxanne's "sisters of the skillet." These three pals have worked together throughout the southern states with a traveling cooking school, forging a friendship that has lasted for decades. Whenever they get together, Pat is sure to serve a version of this recipe. Thanks so much for sharing it, Pat, and for all the fond memories!

Tips

This recipe is not for the faint of heart. It is very spicy, but it's the spiciness that makes the cheese bites so addictive. If you prefer, you can reduce the amount of cayenne pepper to $\frac{1}{2}$ tsp (2 mL).

Toasting pecans intensifies their flavor. Spread finely chopped pecans in a single layer on a baking sheet. Bake at 350°F (180°C) for 5 to 7 minutes or until lightly browned.

$\frac{1}{2}$ cup	unsalted butter, softened	125 mL
1 cup	all-purpose flour	250 mL
1 cup	shredded sharp Cheddar cheese	250 mL
$\frac{1}{2}$ cup	toasted finely chopped pecans (see tip, at left)	125 mL
$1\frac{1}{2}$ tsp	cayenne pepper	7 mL
$\frac{1}{4}$ tsp	salt	1 mL
	Nonstick baking spray	

1. In a medium bowl, using an electric mixer on medium-high speed, cream butter for 1 to 2 minutes or until fluffy. On low speed, beat in flour, cheese, pecans, cayenne and salt until well blended. Form dough into 1-inch (2.5 cm) balls.

2. Spray cake pop wells with nonstick baking spray. Place one ball in each well. Bake for 8 to 10 minutes or until golden brown. Carefully transfer cheese bites to a wire rack to cool. Repeat with the remaining dough.

Firecracker Biscuit Bites

**Makes
14 to 16 biscuits**

Your taste buds will explode with delight when you make these spicy bites. They are great served with cold beverages and cheese cubes.

Tip

For tender, flaky biscuits, use very cold butter and sour cream, and do not overwork the dough.

1 cup	baking mix, such as Bisquick	250 mL
3 tbsp	freshly grated Parmesan cheese	45 mL
1/2 tsp	cayenne pepper	2 mL
1/4 cup	very cold unsalted butter, cut into small pieces	60 mL
1/2 cup	very cold sour cream	125 mL

1. In a medium bowl, combine biscuit mix, Parmesan and cayenne. Using your fingertips or a pastry blender, cut in butter until mixture resembles coarse crumbs. Using a fork, stir in sour cream just until dough comes together.

2. Form dough into 1-inch (2.5 cm) balls. Place one ball in each cake pop well. Bake for 4 to 5 minutes or until golden. Repeat with the remaining dough.

Jalapeño Poppers

**Makes 12
poppers**

Keep your deep-fryer packed away and enjoy these spicy poppers made in the Babycakes cake pop maker.

Tips

If the pickled jalapeño slices are large, cut them in half and stack them on top of the cheese so that you can still pinch the dough closed.

These are very hot when first removed from the cake pop maker. Let cool slightly before serving.

4	frozen unbaked dinner rolls, thawed	4
12	3/4- by 1/2-inch (2 by 1 cm) cubes sharp (old) Cheddar cheese	12
12	jarred pickled jalapeño slices, drained and patted dry	12

1. Cut each roll into thirds. Using your fingers, form each third into a thin, flat circle. Place one cube of cheese and one jalapeño slice in the center of each circle and wrap dough around filling, pinching the edges to seal securely.

2. Place one popper in each cake pop well. Bake for 4 to 6 minutes or until golden brown. Transfer poppers to a wire rack to cool slightly. Serve warm.

Cajun Cornbread Pops

These are excellent served with chili or red beans and rice. The flavor will transport you to the Louisiana bayou. Serve warm, smeared with butter.

Tips

No buttermilk on hand? Stir 1½ tsp (7 mL) lemon juice or white vinegar into ½ cup (125 mL) milk. Let stand for 5 to 10 minutes or until thickened. Proceed with the recipe.

Do you have a Babycakes Rotating Cake Pop Maker? If so, see page 8 for information on using it.

Variation

For an even spicier version, add 2 tbsp (30 mL) finely chopped drained pickled jalapeños with the cheese.

½ cup	baking mix, such as Bisquick	125 mL
½ cup	yellow cornmeal	125 mL
2 tsp	granulated sugar	10 mL
¼ tsp	salt	1 mL
½ cup	shredded sharp (old) Cheddar cheese	125 mL
1	large egg, at room temperature	1
½ cup	buttermilk, at room temperature	125 mL
2 tbsp	vegetable oil	30 mL
1 tbsp	hot pepper sauce	15 mL
	Nonstick baking spray	

1. In a medium bowl, whisk together baking mix, cornmeal, sugar and salt. Stir in cheese, egg, buttermilk, oil and hot pepper sauce until blended.

2. Spray cake pop wells with nonstick baking spray. Fill each well with about 1 tbsp (15 mL) batter (see page 25). Bake for 3 to 4 minutes or until lightly browned. Transfer cornbread pops to a wire rack to cool slightly. Repeat with the remaining batter. Serve warm.

Jalapeño, Corn and Cheese Morsels

**Makes
34 to 36 morsels**

These morsels come
alive with the flavors of
jalapeño and Cheddar.
They're the perfect
accompaniment to
a bowl of chili or a
salad — or serve warm
as an appetizer.

Tips

Do you want it just a little
milder? Reduce or omit the
cayenne pepper.

Do you have a Babycakes
Rotating Cake Pop Maker?
If so, see page 8 for
information on using it.

¾ cup	yellow cornmeal	175 mL
½ cup	all-purpose flour	125 mL
1 tbsp	granulated sugar	15 mL
1½ tsp	baking powder	7 mL
¼ tsp	salt	1 mL
⅛ tsp	cayenne pepper	0.5 mL
2	large eggs, at room temperature	2
⅔ cup	milk, at room temperature	150 mL
2 tbsp	vegetable oil	30 mL
¾ cup	shredded sharp Cheddar cheese	175 mL
½ cup	frozen corn kernels, thawed and drained	125 mL
3 tbsp	chopped drained pickled jalapeño peppers	45 mL
	Nonstick baking spray	

1. In a large bowl, whisk together cornmeal, flour, sugar, baking powder, salt and cayenne. Set aside.

2. In a small bowl, whisk together eggs, milk and oil. Stir into cornmeal mixture until just blended. Stir in cheese, corn and jalapeños.

3. Spray cake pop wells with nonstick baking spray. Fill each well with about 1 tbsp (15 mL) batter (see page 25). Bake for 4 to 6 minutes or until a tester inserted in the center comes out clean. Transfer morsels to a wire rack to cool slightly. Repeat with the remaining batter. Serve warm.

Thai Crab Bites

Makes 17 to 19 crab bites

Served with Wasabi Mayo Sauce, these Asian-inspired crab bites make a fantastic appetizer.

Tips

If you don't have buttery crackers on hand, you can substitute 1/4 cup (60 mL) more panko bread crumbs, saltine cracker crumbs or dry bread crumbs.

You can use a 6-oz (175 g) can of lump crabmeat, drained, for the crabmeat.

In step 2, use a small scoop (one that holds about 1 tbsp/15 mL) to spoon out just the right amount of the crab mixture, then lightly shape the mixture into a ball with your hands.

6	round buttery crackers (about 2 inches/ 5 cm in diameter), finely crushed	6
2 tbsp	finely chopped green onion	30 mL
1 tbsp	chopped drained pimento	15 mL
1 tsp	finely minced gingerroot	5 mL
1/4 tsp	garlic powder	1 mL
1/4 tsp	crab boil or seafood seasoning	1 mL
1/8 tsp	cayenne pepper	0.5 mL
1	large egg white	1
1 tbsp	mayonnaise	15 mL
1 tsp	Dijon mustard	5 mL
6 oz	backfin (lump) crabmeat, drained and picked over to remove cartilage	175 g
	Freshly ground black pepper	
1/2 cup	panko bread crumbs	125 mL
2 tbsp	vegetable oil	30 mL
	Wasabi Mayo Sauce (page 142)	

1. In a large bowl, combine cracker crumbs, green onion, pimento, ginger, garlic powder, crab boil seasoning, cayenne, egg white, mayonnaise and mustard. Gently stir in crabmeat. Season to taste with black pepper.

2. Using wet hands, lightly shape mixture into 1-inch (2.5 cm) balls. Roll each ball in panko.

3. Brush cake pop wells with vegetable oil. Place one crab bite in each well. Bake for 8 minutes. Carefully place the fork tool between each crab cake and the edge of the well and gently turn the crab cake over. Bake for 3 minutes or until golden brown. Transfer to a wire rack to cool slightly. Repeat with the remaining crab mixture. Serve warm, with Wasabi Mayo Sauce.

Buffalo Chicken Dumplings

**Makes
24 dumplings**

Wonton wrappers make crispy, golden brown casings for the warm, spicy Buffalo chicken hiding inside.

Tips

Spicy wing sauces vary in heat level, so you might first add about 1 tbsp (15 mL) to the filling, taste, then add additional sauce as desired.

Be sure to seal the edges of the dumplings well so that none of the chicken mixture seeps out. The perfectly rounded, crispy dumplings will be worth every minute you took sealing and shaping them.

If the dumpling is very tightly sealed and you desire more even browning, bake for 7 minutes, then carefully place the fork tool between each dumpling and the edge of the well and gently turn the dumpling over. Bake for 3 to 5 minutes or until golden brown.

Do you have a Babycakes Rotating Cake Pop Maker? If so, see page 8 for information on using it.

1	can (4½ oz/128 g) chicken, drained	1
4 oz	cream cheese, softened	125 g
2 tbsp	ranch dressing	30 mL
2 tbsp	bottled spicy wing sauce (see tip, at left)	30 mL
2 tbsp	crumbled blue cheese	30 mL
24	wonton wrappers, about 3½ inches (8.5 cm) square	24

1. In a small bowl, combine chicken, cream cheese, ranch dressing, wing sauce and blue cheese.

2. Lightly moisten edges of a wonton wrapper. Spoon about 2 tsp (10 mL) chicken mixture into the center of the wrapper. Bring the four corners of the wrapper up to a point and press lightly to seal. Press along the sides to seal well, and very gently squeeze out any air. Gently fold over the top of each filled dumpling so that it is more rounded. Repeat with the remaining wrappers and chicken mixture.

3. Place one dumpling, folded side up, in each cake pop well. Bake for 10 to 12 minutes or until golden brown. Transfer to a wire rack to cool slightly. Repeat with the remaining dumplings. Serve warm.

Spicy Buffalo Meatballs

Makes 30 to 32 meatballs

There's no need to deal with messy chicken wings to enjoy Buffalo-style fare. Serve with Blue Cheese Dipping Sauce (page 141) and celery sticks.

Tips

Always use very lean ground beef, such as ground round or sirloin, to reduce the amount of fat that collects in the wells. For optimum performance and to minimize fat, turn the unit off between batches, let it cool completely, wipe away any collected fat with a paper towel, then bake the next batch.

When forming meatballs, use a small scoop (one that holds about 1 tbsp/15 mL) to spoon out just the right amount of the beef mixture, then lightly shape the mixture into a ball with your hands.

Meatballs are a great make-ahead appetizer. Let baked meatballs cool, then store in an airtight container in the freezer for up to 3 months. Thaw in the refrigerator and reheat in a 350°F (180°C) oven for 10 to 15 minutes or until heated through.

1 lb	extra-lean ground beef (see tip, at left)	500 g
1	stalk celery, finely minced	1
⅔ cup	dry bread crumbs	150 mL
½ tsp	salt	2 mL
1	large egg	1
⅓ cup	bottled spicy wing sauce	75 mL

1. In a large bowl, combine beef, celery, bread crumbs, salt, egg and wing sauce. Form into 1-inch (2.5 cm) meatballs.

2. Place one meatball in each cake pop well. Bake for 5 to 7 minutes or until no longer pink inside. Transfer meatballs to a covered dish and keep warm. Repeat with the remaining meatballs.

Mexican Chocolate Chile Cake Pops

Makes 28 to 30 cake pops

The flavor combination of chiles and chocolate is popular today! We bet you'll love the way ancho chile enlivens these rich chocolate cake pops.

Tip

Ancho chile powder is simply ground ancho chiles (dried poblano peppers), with no other ingredients. You can substitute chipotle chile powder (or any other ground chile powder), but keep in mind that this may affect the spiciness of the cake pops. Regular chili powder is a blend of chiles, salt and spices such as cumin and oregano, and is not recommended for these cake pops.

Variation

For even spicier cake pops, increase the ancho chile powder to 1 tbsp (15 mL).

1 oz	unsweetened chocolate, chopped	30 g
3 tbsp	unsalted butter	45 mL
⅔ cup	all-purpose flour	150 mL
⅔ cup	granulated sugar	150 mL
¼ cup	unsweetened cocoa powder	60 mL
2 tsp	ancho chile powder (see tip, at left)	10 mL
1 tsp	ground cinnamon	5 mL
½ tsp	baking soda	2 mL
¼ tsp	baking powder	1 mL
Pinch	salt	Pinch
1	large egg, at room temperature	1
6 tbsp	sour cream	90 mL
¼ cup	water	60 mL
	Nonstick baking spray	

1. Place chocolate and butter in a small microwave-safe glass bowl. Microwave on High in 30-second intervals, stirring after each, until melted. Set aside to cool for 2 minutes.

2. In a large bowl, whisk together flour, sugar, cocoa, ancho chile powder, cinnamon, baking soda, baking powder and salt. Add egg, sour cream, water and melted chocolate mixture. Using an electric mixer on medium-high speed, beat for 1 minute or until blended and smooth.

3. Spray cake pop wells with nonstick baking spray. Fill each well with about 1 tbsp (15 mL) batter (see page 25). Bake for 4 to 6 minutes or until a tester inserted in the center comes out clean. Transfer cake pops to a wire rack to cool. Repeat with the remaining batter.

4. If desired, attach sticks to cake pops (see page 27).

Cinnamon Candy Cake Pops

Makes 24 to 26 cake pops

These cake pops taste like a cross between candy apples and cinnamon jelly beans. They're not exactly traditional, but they are a sweet indulgence that everyone will enjoy.

Tips

No buttermilk on hand? Stir ¾ tsp (3 mL) lemon juice or white vinegar into ¼ cup (60 mL) milk. Let stand for 5 to 10 minutes or until thickened. Proceed with the recipe.

For pink cake pops, beat a few drops of red food coloring into the batter.

Do you have a Babycakes Rotating Cake Pop Maker? If so, see page 8 for information on using it.

1¼ cups	white cake mix	300 mL
1	large egg, at room temperature	1
¼ cup	buttermilk	60 mL
¼ cup	water	60 mL
1 tbsp	vegetable oil	15 mL
	Nonstick baking spray	
	Cinnamon Candy Glaze (page 82)	

1. In a medium bowl, using an electric mixer on low speed, beat cake mix, egg, buttermilk, water and oil for 30 seconds or until moistened. Beat on medium speed for 2 minutes.

2. Spray cake pop wells with nonstick baking spray. Fill each well with about 1 tbsp (15 mL) batter (see page 25). Bake for 4 to 6 minutes or until a tester inserted in the center comes out clean. Transfer cake pops to a wire rack set over a sheet of foil or waxed paper to cool. Repeat with the remaining batter.

3. Using the fork tool, dip each cake pop in Cinnamon Candy Glaze, allowing excess glaze to drip back into the bowl. Return glazed cake pops to the rack to set.

Booze Pops

Applejack Cake Pops 159

Brewmaster's Chocolate Cake Pops 160

Champagne Cake Pops 161

Limoncello Cake Pops. 162

Rum Cake Pops 163

Rum and Cola Cake Pops 164

Mojito Cake Pops 165

Piña Colada Cake Pops. 166

Margarita Cake Pops. 168

Kahlúa Cake Pops 169

Appl?jack Cake Pops

Applejack is made by distilling hard apple cider and has been enjoyed in North America since the colonial days. For these cake pops, chopped apples and applejack combine to whisk you away to a cool fall day.

Tip

Do you have a Babycakes Rotating Cake Pop Maker? If so, see page 8 for information on using it.

Variations

For a non-alcoholic version, substitute unsweetened apple cider for the applejack.

Stir in ¼ cup (60 mL) finely chopped toasted walnuts or pecans with the apple mixture.

1	tart cooking apple (such as Fuji), peeled and very finely chopped	1
3 tbsp	applejack or apple brandy	45 mL
1⅓ cups	all-purpose flour	325 mL
2 tsp	baking powder	10 mL
1 tsp	baking soda	5 mL
1 tsp	ground cinnamon	5 mL
½ tsp	ground nutmeg	2 mL
¼ tsp	salt	1 mL
⅓ cup	granulated sugar	75 mL
¼ cup	packed brown sugar	60 mL
½ cup	unsalted butter, softened	125 mL
2	large eggs, at room temperature	2
½ cup	sour cream	125 mL
1 tsp	vanilla extract	5 mL
	Nonstick baking spray	
	Applejack Glaze (variation, page 84)	

1. In a small bowl, combine apple and applejack. Set aside and let marinate for 10 minutes.

2. In another small bowl, whisk together flour, baking powder, baking soda, cinnamon, nutmeg and salt. Set aside.

3. In a large bowl, using an electric mixer on medium-high speed, beat granulated sugar, brown sugar and butter for 1 to 2 minutes or until fluffy. Add eggs, one at a time, beating well after each addition. Beat in sour cream. Add flour mixture and beat on low speed until smooth. Stir in apple mixture and vanilla.

4. Spray cake pop wells with nonstick baking spray. Fill each well with about 1 tbsp (15 mL) batter (see page 25). Bake for 4 to 6 minutes or until a tester inserted in the center comes out clean. Transfer cake pops to a wire rack set over a sheet of foil or waxed paper to cool. Repeat with the remaining batter.

5. Using the fork tool, dip each cake pop in Applejack Glaze, allowing excess glaze to drip back into the bowl. Return glazed cake pops to the wire rack to set.

Brewmaster's Chocolate Cake Pops

Makes 38 to 40 cake pops

You don't need to be a brewmaster to love these cake pops. The stout perfectly balances the chocolate, resulting in a cake pop that everyone will enjoy.

Tips

Stout is a strong dark beer and provides an ideal flavor for these cake pops, but you can substitute any type of beer you prefer.

Do you have a Babycakes Rotating Cake Pop Maker? If so, see page 8 for information on using it.

½ cup	unsalted butter, cut into 1-inch (2.5 cm) cubes	125 mL
½ cup	Irish stout	125 mL
6 tbsp	unsweetened cocoa powder	90 mL
1¼ cups	all-purpose flour	300 mL
2 tsp	baking powder	10 mL
¾ tsp	baking soda	3 mL
¼ tsp	salt	1 mL
¾ cup	granulated sugar	175 mL
1	large egg, at room temperature	1
1 tsp	vanilla extract	5 mL
½ cup	sour cream	125 mL
	Nonstick baking spray	

1. In a small saucepan, over medium heat, combine butter and stout. Bring to a boil, stirring often. Remove from heat and whisk in cocoa. Let cool for 5 minutes.

2. In a small bowl, whisk together flour, baking powder, baking soda and salt. Set aside.

3. In a large bowl, using an electric mixer on medium-high speed, beat sugar and egg for 1 to 2 minutes or until fluffy. Beat in stout mixture and vanilla. Beat in sour cream. Add flour mixture and beat on low speed until smooth.

4. Spray cake pop wells with nonstick baking spray. Fill each well with about 1 tbsp (15 mL) batter (see page 25). Bake for 4 to 6 minutes or until a tester inserted in the center comes out clean. Transfer cake pops to a wire rack to cool. Repeat with the remaining batter.

5. If desired, attach sticks to cake pops (see page 27).

Champagne Cake Pops

You don't need to plan a party to celebrate. Champagne cake pops are a great way to celebrate each day.

Tip
Glaze isn't strong enough to hold cake pop sticks securely, so leave glazed cake pops off the sticks.

Variation
Substitute white cake mix for the vanilla cake mix.

1 cup	vanilla cake mix	250 mL
3½ tbsp	vanilla instant pudding mix	52 mL
2	large egg whites, at room temperature	2
⅓ cup	Champagne or sparkling wine, at room temperature	75 mL
1 tbsp	vegetable oil	15 mL
	Red food coloring	
	Nonstick baking spray	
	Champagne Glaze (page 83)	

1. In a medium bowl, using an electric mixer on low speed, beat cake mix, pudding, egg whites, Champagne and oil for 30 seconds or until moistened. Beat in food coloring, 1 to 2 drops at a time, until batter is light pink. Beat on medium speed for 2 minutes.

2. Spray cake pop wells with nonstick baking spray. Fill each well with about 1 tbsp (15 mL) batter (see page 25). Bake for 4 to 6 minutes or until a tester inserted in the center comes out clean. Transfer cake pops to a wire rack set over a sheet of foil or waxed paper to cool. Repeat with the remaining batter.

3. Using the fork tool, dip each cake pop in Champagne Glaze, allowing excess glaze to drip back into the bowl. Return glazed cake pops to the wire rack to set.

Limoncello Cake Pops

Have you ever tasted a recipe made with limoncello that wasn't delicious? These moist, lemon-infused bites will have you craving more.

Tip
Glaze isn't strong enough to hold cake pop sticks securely, so leave glazed cake pops off the sticks.

Variation
Substitute orange liqueur (such as Grand Marnier) for the limoncello, and dip the cake pops in Margarita Glaze (variation, page 80).

¾ cup	all-purpose flour	175 mL
½ tsp	baking powder	2 mL
¼ tsp	salt	1 mL
⅔ cup	granulated sugar	150 mL
2	large eggs, at room temperature	2
	Grated zest of 1 lemon	
1 tbsp	freshly squeezed lemon juice	15 mL
1 tbsp	limoncello liqueur	15 mL
½ cup	unsalted butter, melted and cooled	125 mL
	Nonstick baking spray	
	Limoncello Glaze (page 83)	

1. In a small bowl, whisk together flour, baking powder and salt. Set aside.

2. In a large bowl, using an electric mixer on medium-high speed, beat sugar, eggs, lemon zest, lemon juice and limoncello for 1 minute. Add butter and beat for 2 minutes. Add flour mixture and beat on low speed until just blended.

3. Spray cake pop wells with nonstick baking spray. Fill each well with about 1 tbsp (15 mL) batter (see page 25). Bake for 4 to 6 minutes or until a tester inserted in the center comes out clean. Transfer cake pops to a wire rack set over a sheet of foil or waxed paper to cool. Repeat with the remaining batter.

4. Using the fork tool, dip each cake pop in Limoncello Glaze, allowing excess glaze to drip back into the bowl. Return glazed cake pops to the wire rack to set.

Rum Cake Pops

Makes 22 to 24 cake pops

No need to book a trip to the Bahamas — these cake pops will transport you to paradise.

Tips

If you'd like to coat the entire cake pop in glaze, prepare a thinner glaze by increasing the rum to 3 tbsp (45 mL).

For even more nutty flavor, sprinkle freshly glazed cakes with additional finely chopped toasted pecans.

1 cup	yellow cake mix	250 mL
1	large egg, at room temperature	1
3 tbsp	milk	45 mL
2 tbsp	dark rum	30 mL
2 tbsp	unsalted butter, melted	30 mL
1/4 cup	finely chopped toasted pecans (see tip, page 149)	60 mL
	Nonstick baking spray	
	Rum Glaze (page 84)	

1. In a medium bowl, using an electric mixer on low speed, beat cake mix, egg, milk, rum and butter for 30 seconds or until blended. Beat for 2 minutes on medium speed. Stir in pecans.

2. Spray cake pop wells with nonstick baking spray. Fill each well with about 1 tbsp (15 mL) batter (see page 25). Bake for 4 to 6 minutes or until a tester inserted in the center comes out clean. Transfer cake pops to a wire rack set over a sheet of foil or waxed paper to cool. Repeat with the remaining batter.

3. Using the fork tool, dip half of each cake pop in Rum Glaze, allowing excess glaze to drip back into the bowl. Return glazed cake pops to the wire rack to set.

Rum and Cola Cake Pops

Makes 22 to 24 cake pops

The flavors of the classic alcoholic drink combine in these easy cake pops.

Tips

To easily and neatly inject liquor into cake pops, hold the squeeze bottle upright, pierce the center of the cake pop with the tip, turn it upside down and allow the liquor to seep into the cake. Return the bottle to the upright position before removing the cake pop.

Glaze isn't strong enough to hold cake pop sticks securely, so leave glazed cake pops off the sticks.

• Squeeze bottle, fitted with a fine tip

¼ cup	dark rum	60 mL
22 to 24	Cola Cake Pops (page 56), without glaze or pecans, cooled	22 to 24
	Rum Glaze (page 84), prepared with 3 tbsp (45 mL) dark rum	

1. Using the squeeze bottle, inject about ½ tsp (2 mL) rum into the center of each cake pop (see tip, at left).

2. Using the fork tool, dip each filled cake pop in Rum Glaze, allowing excess glaze to drip back into the bowl. Place glazed cake pops on a wire rack set over a sheet of foil or waxed paper to set.

Mojito Cake Pops

**Makes 22
to 24 cake pops**

The mojito is an adventuresome drink, and its history is woven with stories of swashbuckling pirates, Cuba in the 1800s and Ernest Hemingway. One thing is certain: this drink is refreshing. Now all of the drink's flavors — mint, rum and lime — are captured in these cake pops.

Tip

Glaze isn't strong enough to hold cake pop sticks securely, so leave glazed cake pops off the sticks.

Variation

Filled Mojito Cake Pops: In a small bowl, combine ¼ cup (60 mL) lime curd and 1 tbsp (15 mL) gold or dark rum. Using a squeeze bottle or pastry bag fitted with a fine tip, inject this filling into the center of each cake pop before glazing.

¾ cup	all-purpose flour	175 mL
1¼ tsp	baking powder	6 mL
Pinch	salt	Pinch
6 tbsp	granulated sugar	90 mL
1	large egg, at room temperature	1
3 tbsp	vegetable oil	45 mL
2 tbsp	milk	30 mL
2 tbsp	gold or dark rum	30 mL
	Grated zest of 1 lime	
1 tbsp	freshly squeezed lime juice	15 mL
1 tsp	peppermint extract	5 mL
	Nonstick baking spray	
	Mojito Glaze (variation, page 80)	

1. In a small bowl, whisk together flour, baking powder and salt. Set aside.

2. In a large bowl, using an electric mixer on medium-high speed, beat sugar, egg and oil for 1 to 2 minutes or until fluffy. Reduce mixer speed to low and beat in one-third of the flour mixture. Beat in milk, then another third of the flour mixture, then rum, lime zest, lime juice and peppermint extract. Beat in the remaining flour mixture until smooth.

3. Spray cake pop wells with nonstick baking spray. Fill each well with about 1 tbsp (15 mL) batter (see page 25). Bake for 4 to 6 minutes or until a tester inserted in the center comes out clean. Transfer cake pops to a wire rack set over a sheet of foil or waxed paper to cool. Repeat with the remaining batter.

4. Glaze cake pops with Mojito Glaze.

Piña Colada Cake Pops

Makes 43 to 45 cake pops

If you like piña coladas, this is the cake pop for you. The combination of pineapple juice, cream of coconut and rum will remind you of that famous drink — and you might even catch yourself humming a certain song.

Tips

Cream of coconut is thick and sweet and is commonly used in drinks, so it is found canned in the drinks section of grocery stores or at liquor stores. It should not be confused with coconut milk.

For a milder coconut flavor, substitute vanilla extract for the coconut extract.

- Squeeze bottle or pastry bag, fitted with a fine tip

Cake Pops

1¼ cups	all-purpose flour	300 mL
2 tsp	baking powder	10 mL
½ tsp	baking soda	2 mL
¼ tsp	salt	1 mL
½ cup	cream of coconut (see tip, at left)	125 mL
⅓ cup	unsweetened pineapple juice	75 mL
2 tbsp	gold or dark rum	30 mL
⅔ cup	granulated sugar	150 mL
½ cup	unsalted butter, softened	125 mL
2	large eggs, at room temperature	2
1 tsp	coconut extract	5 mL
	Nonstick baking spray	
	Piña Colada Glaze (variation, page 80)	

Filling

1 tbsp	granulated sugar	15 mL
1 tbsp	cornstarch	15 mL
⅔ cup	unsweetened pineapple juice	150 mL
1 tbsp	gold or dark rum	15 mL

1. *Cake Pops:* In a small bowl, whisk together flour, baking powder, baking soda and salt. Set aside.

2. In another small bowl, whisk together cream of coconut, pineapple juice and rum. Set aside.

3. In a large bowl, using an electric mixer on medium-high speed, beat sugar and butter for 1 to 2 minutes or until fluffy. Add eggs, one at a time, beating well after each addition. Beat in coconut extract. Add flour mixture alternately with cream of coconut mixture, making three additions of flour and two of cream of coconut mixture and beating until smooth.

4. Spray cake pop wells with nonstick baking spray. Fill each well with about 1 tbsp (15 mL) batter (see page 25). Bake for 4 to 6 minutes or until a tester inserted in the center comes out clean. Transfer cake pops to a wire rack set over a sheet of foil or waxed paper to cool. Repeat with the remaining batter.

5. *Filling*: In a small microwave-safe glass bowl, whisk together sugar, cornstarch and pineapple juice. Microwave on High for 2 minutes, stirring every 30 seconds, until thickened and bubbly. Stir in rum. Let cool for 5 minutes.

6. Pour filling into the squeeze bottle or pastry bag and inject into the center of the cake pops.

7. Using the fork tool, dip each filled cake pop in Piña Colada Glaze, allowing excess glaze to drip back into the bowl. Return glazed cake pops to the wire rack to set.

Margarita Cake Pops

Makes 46 to 48 cake pops		

The flavors of a classic margarita — lime, tequila and orange liqueur — are captured in these incredible treats.

Tips

Glaze isn't strong enough to hold cake pop sticks securely, so leave glazed cake pops off the sticks.

Do you have a Babycakes Rotating Cake Pop Maker? If so, see page 8 for information on using it.

• Squeeze bottle or pastry bag, fitted with a fine tip

Cake Pops

1½ cups	all-purpose flour	375 mL
1¼ tsp	baking powder	6 mL
Pinch	salt	Pinch
1 cup	granulated sugar	250 mL
6 tbsp	unsalted butter, softened	90 mL
2	large eggs, at room temperature	2
⅓ cup	milk	75 mL
¼ cup	orange juice	60 mL
2 tbsp	tequila	30 mL
	Nonstick baking spray	
	Margarita Glaze (variation, page 80)	

Filling

½ cup	lime curd	125 mL
1 tsp	tequila	5 mL

1. *Cake Pops:* In a small bowl, whisk together flour, baking powder and salt. Set aside.

2. In a medium bowl, using an electric mixer on medium-high speed, beat sugar and butter for 1 to 2 minutes or until fluffy. Add eggs, one at a time, beating well after each addition. Reduce mixer speed to low and beat in one-third of the flour mixture. Beat in milk, then another third of the flour mixture, then orange juice and tequila. Beat in the remaining flour mixture until smooth.

3. Spray cake pop wells with nonstick baking spray. Fill each well with about 1 tbsp (15 mL) batter (see page 25). Bake for 4 to 6 minutes or until a tester inserted in the center comes out clean. Transfer cake pops to a wire rack set over a sheet of foil or waxed paper to cool. Repeat with the remaining batter.

4. *Filling:* In a small bowl, combine lime curd and tequila. Spoon filling into the squeeze bottle or pastry bag and inject into the center of each cake pop.

5. Using the fork tool, dip each filled cake pop in Margarita Glaze, allowing excess glaze to drip back into the bowl. Return glazed cake pops to the wire rack to set.

Kahlúa Cake Pops

Makes 38 to 40 cake pops

Coffee and chocolate combine to make scrumptious cake pops. We bet you'll love them as much as we do.

Tips

Kahlúa is a wonderful coffee liqueur that has been produced in Mexico since the 1930s. While it is our favorite brand, there are many different coffee liqueurs, and you can pick your favorite.

To easily and neatly inject liquor into cake pops, hold the squeeze bottle upright, pierce the center of the cake pop with the tip, turn it upside down and allow the liquor to seep into the cake. Return the bottle to the upright position before removing the cake pop.

For a rich Kahlúa and cream dessert, arrange three Kahlúa Cake Pops in a dessert dish, top with a small scoop of vanilla ice cream and drizzle with 1 tsp (5 mL) Kahlúa.

- Squeeze bottle, fitted with a fine tip

7 tbsp	Kahlúa or other coffee liqueur	105 mL
38 to 40	Old-Fashioned Chocolate Cake Pops (page 26)	38 to 40
	Kahlúa Glaze (variation, page 78)	

1. Using the squeeze bottle, inject about $1/2$ tsp (2 mL) Kahlúa into the center of each cake pop (see tip, at left).

2. Using the fork tool, dip each filled cake pop in Kahlúa Glaze, allowing excess glaze to drip back into the bowl. Place glazed cake pops on a wire rack set over a sheet of foil or waxed paper to set.

Gluten-Free and Vegan Treats

Gluten-Free

Chocolate Cake Pops 171

Easy Red Velvet Cake Pops. 172

Chocolate Banana Cake Pops 173

Berry Tea Cake Bites 174

Lemon Cake Pops 175

Carrot Coconut Cake Pops. 176

Almond Cake Pops 177

Harvest Treats. 178

Rosemary and Goat Cheese Morsels. 179

Italian Rice Balls 180

Vegan

Easy Yellow Cake Pops 181

Dark Chocolate Brownie Pops 182

Applesauce Spice Cake Pops. 183

Banana Nut Cake Pops. 184

New England Cornbread Bites. 185

Chocolate Cake Pops

Makes 26 to 28 cake pops

GLUTEN-FREE RECIPE

This recipe may be quick and easy, but these gluten-free cake pops are full of flavor — perfect for dipping into melted chocolate or vanilla candy melts and decorating any way you like.

Tips

No buttermilk on hand? Stir ¾ tsp (3 mL) lemon juice or white vinegar into ¼ cup (60 mL) milk. Let stand for 5 to 10 minutes or until thickened. Proceed with the recipe.

Always read labels to be sure all products are gluten-free and were not processed in a plant that also produces products that contain gluten.

1 cup	gluten-free chocolate cake mix	250 mL
2	large eggs, at room temperature	2
¼ cup	buttermilk	60 mL
¼ cup	vegetable oil	60 mL
	Nonstick baking spray	

1. In a medium bowl, using an electric mixer on low speed, beat cake mix, eggs, buttermilk and oil for 30 seconds or until moistened. Beat on medium speed for 2 minutes.

2. Spray cake pop wells with nonstick baking spray. Fill each well with about 1 tbsp (15 mL) batter (see page 25). Bake for 4 to 6 minutes or until a tester inserted in the center comes out clean. Transfer cake pops to a wire rack to cool. Repeat with the remaining batter.

3. If desired, attach sticks to cake pops (see page 27).

Easy Red Velvet Cake Pops

Makes 27 to 29 cake pops

GLUTEN-FREE RECIPE

These fun red cake pops are the perfect treat for any party.

Tips

No buttermilk on hand? Stir 1 tsp (5 mL) lemon juice or white vinegar into ⅓ cup (75 mL) milk. Let stand for 5 to 10 minutes or until thickened. Proceed with the recipe.

Do you have a Babycakes Rotating Cake Pop Maker? If so, see page 8 for information on using it.

1 cup	gluten-free yellow cake mix	250 mL
2 tbsp	unsweetened cocoa powder	30 mL
2	large eggs, at room temperature	2
⅓ cup	buttermilk	75 mL
¼ cup	unsalted butter, softened	60 mL
1 tbsp	red food coloring	15 mL
1 tsp	vanilla extract	5 mL
	Nonstick baking spray	

1. In a medium bowl, using an electric mixer on low speed, beat cake mix, cocoa, eggs, buttermilk, butter, food coloring and vanilla for 30 seconds or until moistened. Beat on medium speed for 2 minutes.

2. Spray cake pop wells with nonstick baking spray. Fill each well with about 1 tbsp (15 mL) batter (see page 25). Bake for 4 to 6 minutes or until a tester inserted in the center comes out clean. Transfer cake pops to a wire rack to cool. Repeat with the remaining batter.

3. If desired, attach sticks to cake pops (see page 27).

Decorating Tip

- Dip the cake pops in melted white candy melts, then decorate as desired.

Chocolate Banana Cake Pops

Makes 30 to 32 cake pops

GLUTEN-FREE RECIPE

The combination of chocolate and banana is a timeless favorite. Dip these cake pops in melted chocolate melts for an over-the-top flavor explosion.

Tips

Bananas sweeten as they ripen, and very ripe bananas add the best taste and texture to baked goods.

If you have a ripe banana but you don't have time to bake that day, put it in the refrigerator for up to 3 days. Although the peel will turn brown, the fruit will remain good for use in cakes and breads. If you have an overripe banana, mash it and stir in 1 tsp (5 mL) lemon juice. Store in an airtight container in the freezer for up to 6 months. When you're ready to bake, thaw the mashed banana overnight in the refrigerator, then use it in your favorite baked goods.

No buttermilk on hand? Stir ¾ tsp (3 mL) lemon juice or white vinegar into ¼ cup (60 mL) milk. Let stand for 5 to 10 minutes or until thickened. Proceed with the recipe.

1 cup	gluten-free chocolate cake mix	250 mL
1	large very ripe banana, mashed (about ½ cup/125 mL)	1
1	large egg, at room temperature	1
1	large egg yolk, at room temperature	1
¼ cup	buttermilk	60 mL
3 tbsp	unsalted butter, softened	45 mL
½ tsp	vanilla extract	2 mL
	Nonstick baking spray	

1. In a large bowl, using an electric mixer on low speed, beat cake mix, banana, egg, egg yolk, buttermilk, butter and vanilla for 30 seconds or until moistened. Beat on medium speed for 2 minutes.

2. Spray cake pop wells with nonstick baking spray. Fill each well with about 1 tbsp (15 mL) batter (see page 25). Bake for 4 to 6 minutes or until a tester inserted in the center comes out clean. Transfer cake pops to a wire rack to cool. Repeat with the remaining batter.

3. If desired, attach sticks to cake pops (see page 27).

Berry Tea Cake Bites

GLUTEN-FREE RECIPE

These warm, freshly baked cake bites are perfect for breakfast or brunch, or bring them to the office to share with colleagues. Alternatively, try dipping them in your favorite glaze and serve them for dessert. They are so rich and flavorful, they'll be a hit anytime you serve them.

Tip

Gluten-free all-purpose baking mix is a blend of several kinds of gluten-free flours and starches. The exact blend used varies from brand to brand, so you might prefer the baking qualities and flavor of one over another. Popular brands include King Arthur and Bob's Red Mill, but stores and websites that specialize in gluten-free baking ingredients offer a large array of brands and package sizes.

Variation

Substitute dried blueberries, sweetened cranberries or cherries for the mixed berries.

• **Small food processor**

1/3 cup	dried mixed berries	75 mL
1/4 cup	boiling water	60 mL
1 cup	gluten-free all-purpose baking mix	250 mL
1/3 cup	granulated sugar	75 mL
1 1/2 tsp	baking powder	7 mL
1/2 tsp	ground cinnamon	2 mL
1/4 tsp	salt	1 mL
2	large egg whites, at room temperature, very lightly beaten	2
1/4 cup	unsalted butter, melted	60 mL
2 tbsp	milk	30 mL
1 tsp	freshly squeezed lemon juice	5 mL
	Nonstick baking spray	

1. Place dried berries in a small, deep bowl and pour boiling water over top. Let stand for 15 minutes to cool and reconstitute.

2. Pour berries and any remaining liquid into food processor. Pulse to chop. Set aside.

3. In a large bowl, whisk together baking mix, sugar, baking powder, cinnamon and salt. Stir in chopped berries, egg whites, butter, milk and lemon juice until blended.

4. Spray cake pop wells with nonstick baking spray. Fill each well with about 1 tbsp (15 mL) batter (see page 25). Bake for 4 to 6 minutes or until a tester inserted in the center comes out clean. Transfer cake bites to a wire rack to cool. Repeat with the remaining batter.

5. If desired, attach sticks to cake pops (see page 27).

Lemon Cake Pops

Makes 22 to 24 cake pops

GLUTEN-FREE RECIPE

Fresh and light, these cake pops are packed with lemon flavor. You'd never guess they are gluten-free.

Tips

For ease, zest the lemon before you juice it. One lemon will yield about 3 tbsp (45 mL) juice and 2 to 3 tsp (10 to 15 mL) zest. Zest only the colored portion of the peel, avoiding the bitter white pith underneath. Store leftover lemon juice in an airtight container in the refrigerator for up to 5 days, or freeze it for up to 6 months.

Do you have a Babycakes Rotating Cake Pop Maker? If so, see page 8 for information on using it.

1 cup	gluten-free yellow cake mix	250 mL
2	large eggs, at room temperature	2
	Grated zest of 1 lemon	
1/3 cup	freshly squeezed lemon juice	75 mL
1/4 cup	unsalted butter, softened	60 mL
1 tsp	vanilla extract	5 mL
1/2 tsp	lemon extract (optional)	2 mL
	Nonstick baking spray	

1. In a medium bowl, using an electric mixer on low speed, beat cake mix, eggs, lemon zest, lemon juice, butter, vanilla and lemon extract (if using) for 30 seconds or until moistened. Beat on medium speed for 2 minutes.

2. Spray cake pop wells with nonstick baking spray. Fill each well with about 1 tbsp (15 mL) batter (see page 25). Bake for 4 to 6 minutes or until a tester inserted in the center comes out clean. Transfer cake pops to a wire rack to cool. Repeat with the remaining batter.

3. If desired, attach sticks to cake pops (see page 27).

Decorating Tip

- Dip the cake pops in Lemon Glaze (page 80). Remember, if you plan to glaze your cake pops, leave them off the sticks.

Carrot Coconut Cake Pops

GLUTEN-FREE RECIPE

Both children and adults will love the combination of carrots, coconut and pecans in these yummy cake pops.

Tips

Toasting pecans intensifies their flavor. Spread pecan halves in a single layer on a baking sheet. Bake at 350°F (180°C) for 5 to 7 minutes or until lightly browned. Transfer to a plate and let cool completely before chopping.

Be sure to process the carrots and coconut until they are very finely chopped.

Gluten-free cakes tend to become firm as they cool. Dip or glaze your cake pops soon after baking to avoid dry cake pops.

- Food processor

2	carrots, cut into 1-inch (2.5 cm) chunks (about 1 cup/250 mL)	2
⅓ cup	sweetened flaked coconut	75 mL
¼ cup	chopped toasted pecans (see tip, at left)	60 mL
1 cup	gluten-free all-purpose baking mix	250 mL
2 tsp	baking powder	10 mL
1 tsp	pumpkin pie spice	5 mL
½ tsp	baking soda	2 mL
¼ tsp	salt	1 mL
½ cup	packed brown sugar	125 mL
¼ cup	unsalted butter, softened	60 mL
2	large eggs, at room temperature	2
3 tbsp	sour cream	45 mL
½ tsp	vanilla extract	2 mL
	Nonstick baking spray	

1. In food processor, pulse carrots until chopped. Add coconut and pulse until carrots and coconut are very finely chopped. Add pecans and pulse to combine. Add baking mix, baking powder, pumpkin pie spice, baking soda and salt; pulse to combine.

2. In a large bowl, using an electric mixer on medium-high speed, beat brown sugar and butter for 1 to 2 minutes or until fluffy. Add eggs, one at a time, beating well after each addition. Beat in sour cream and vanilla. Add carrot mixture and beat on low speed until blended.

3. Spray cake pop wells with nonstick baking spray. Fill each well with about 1 tbsp (15 mL) batter (see page 25). Bake for 4 to 6 minutes or until a tester inserted in the center comes out clean. Transfer cake pops to a wire rack to cool. Repeat with the remaining batter.

4. If desired, attach sticks to cake pops (see page 27).

Almond Cake Pops

Makes 46
to 48 cake pops

GLUTEN-FREE RECIPE

These rich, almond-flavored cake bites will become a favorite whether or not you prefer gluten-free baked goods. For an added treat, inject the baked cake pops with honey almond butter.

Tip

Honey almond butter (or plain almond butter) makes a great filling for these cake pops. Honey almond butter is readily available at local health food and grocery stores. Or make your own by processing roasted almonds in a food processor until fine and almost smooth, then flavor to taste with a little honey. Inject about ½ tsp (2 mL) almond butter into the center of each almond cake pop, then dip as desired.

1 cup	gluten-free all-purpose baking mix	250 mL
¼ cup	almond flour	60 mL
2¼ tsp	baking powder	11 mL
¼ tsp	salt	1 mL
¾ cup	granulated sugar	175 mL
½ cup	unsalted butter, softened	125 mL
3	large eggs, at room temperature	3
1 tsp	vanilla extract	5 mL
1 tsp	almond extract	5 mL
½ cup	unsweetened vanilla-flavored almond milk	125 mL
	Nonstick baking spray	

1. In a small bowl, whisk together baking mix, almond flour, baking powder and salt. Set aside.

2. In a medium bowl, using an electric mixer on medium-high speed, beat sugar and butter for 1 to 2 minutes or until fluffy. Add eggs, one at a time, beating well after each addition. Beat in vanilla and almond extract. Add flour mixture alternately with almond milk, making three additions of flour and two of almond milk and beating on low speed until smooth.

3. Spray cake pop wells with nonstick baking spray. Fill each well with about 1 tbsp (15 mL) batter (see page 25). Bake for 4 to 6 minutes or until a tester inserted in the center comes out clean. Transfer cake pops to a wire rack to cool. Repeat with the remaining batter.

4. If desired, attach sticks to cake pops (see page 27).

Harvest Treats

Makes 46
to 48 cake pops

GLUTEN-FREE RECIPE

Families seem to gather together more frequently during autumn and winter — at least they do at our houses. A basket of these warm cakes is perfect at any gathering. No one will suspect they are gluten-free, and everyone will come back for another.

Tip

Refrigerate leftover canned pumpkin purée in an airtight container for up to 1 week, or freeze it for up to 3 months. Thaw overnight in the refrigerator, then stir well and use it to bake another batch of cake pops.

1½ cups	gluten-free all-purpose baking mix	375 mL
2 tsp	pumpkin pie spice	10 mL
1½ tsp	baking powder	7 mL
½ tsp	baking soda	2 mL
¼ tsp	salt	1 mL
½ cup	packed brown sugar	125 mL
2	large eggs, at room temperature	2
1 cup	canned pumpkin purée (not pie filling)	250 mL
½ cup	vegetable oil	125 mL
¼ cup	pure maple syrup	60 mL
1 tsp	vanilla extract	5 mL
	Nonstick baking spray	

1. In a small bowl, whisk together baking mix, pumpkin pie spice, baking powder, baking soda and salt. Set aside.

2. In a medium bowl, using an electric mixer on medium speed, beat brown sugar, eggs, pumpkin, oil, maple syrup and vanilla for 1 minute. Add flour mixture and beat on low speed just until moistened.

3. Spray cake pop wells with nonstick baking spray. Fill each well with about 1 tbsp (15 mL) batter (see page 25). Bake for 4 to 6 minutes or until a tester inserted in the center comes out clean. Transfer cake pops to a wire rack to cool. Repeat with the remaining batter.

Rosemary and Goat Cheese Morsels

• •

Makes 25 to 27 morsels

GLUTEN-FREE RECIPE

Serve these tasty morsels warm as an appetizer. They are the perfect accompaniment to wine and cheese — and so much better than bread or crackers.

Tips

Goat cheese, also known as chèvre, is creamy and adds a distinct flavor to these treats. Cut off the amount you need from a log of goat cheese and let it come to room temperature. (Wrap and return the rest of the log to the refrigerator after cutting).

Not following a gluten-free diet? Substitute all-purpose flour for the gluten-free all-purpose baking mix.

Variation

Substitute other herbs, such as dried thyme or basil, for the rosemary.

²⁄₃ cup	gluten-free all-purpose baking mix	150 mL
1 tsp	baking powder	5 mL
1 tsp	dried rosemary, crushed	5 mL
¼ tsp	salt	1 mL
2	large eggs, at room temperature	2
1½ oz	soft goat cheese, at room temperature	45 g
¼ cup	unsalted butter, softened	60 mL
¼ cup	sour cream	60 mL
3 tbsp	finely chopped toasted walnuts (see tip, page 98)	45 mL
	Nonstick baking spray	

1. In a small bowl, whisk together baking mix, baking powder, rosemary and salt. Set aside.

2. In a large bowl, using an electric mixer on medium speed, beat eggs, goat cheese, butter and sour cream for 1 minute or until smooth. Add flour mixture and beat on low speed just until moistened. Stir in walnuts.

3. Spray cake pop wells with nonstick baking spray. Fill each well with about 1 tbsp (15 mL) batter (see page 25). Bake for 4 to 6 minutes or until golden and crispy. Transfer morsels to a wire rack to cool slightly. Repeat with the remaining batter. Serve warm.

Italian Rice Balls

Makes 24 to 26 rice balls

GLUTEN-FREE RECIPE

These appetizing rice balls are as versatile as they are flavorful. Serve them warm with a marinara dipping sauce as a scrumptious appetizer or side dish.

Tips

Do you have leftover cooked brown rice? Substitute 2 cups (500 mL) cooked brown rice for the uncooked rice, omit the water and start the recipe from step 2.

In step 3, use a small scoop (one that holds about 1 tbsp/15 mL) to spoon out just the right amount of the rice mixture, then lightly shape the mixture into a ball with your hands.

Do you have a Babycakes Rotating Cake Pop Maker? If so, see page 8 for information on using it.

1⅓ cups	water	325 mL
⅔ cup	long-grain brown rice	150 mL
¾ tsp	salt, divided	3 mL
1	clove garlic, minced	1
½ cup	shredded Italian cheese blend or freshly grated Parmesan cheese	125 mL
½ tsp	dried Italian seasoning	2 mL
¼ tsp	freshly ground black pepper	1 mL
1	large egg, lightly beaten	1
2 tbsp	olive oil	30 mL
	Additional shredded Italian cheese blend or freshly grated Parmesan cheese	
	Minced fresh parsley	

1. In a small saucepan, bring water to a boil over high heat. Add rice and ¼ tsp (1 mL) of the salt. Reduce heat to low, cover and simmer for 45 to 55 minutes or until water is absorbed. Remove from heat and let cool for 30 minutes.

2. Add garlic, cheese, Italian seasoning, the remaining salt, pepper and egg to rice and stir until well blended.

3. Using wet hands, lightly shape rice mixture into 1-inch (2.5 cm) balls.

4. Generously brush cake pop wells with olive oil. Place one rice ball in each well. Bake for 8 minutes or until bottoms are golden brown and crispy. Carefully place the fork tool between each rice ball and the edge of the well and gently turn the rice ball over. Bake for 2 to 3 minutes or until bottoms are lightly browned. Transfer rice balls to a serving plate. Repeat with the remaining rice balls.

5. Garnish rice balls with cheese and parsley. Serve warm.

Easy Yellow Cake Pops

VEGAN RECIPE

Pumpkin purée is a great substitute for the fat and eggs in this vegan cake pop recipe. It's mild in flavor, so no one will even know it's there.

Tips

Refrigerate leftover canned pumpkin purée in an airtight container for up to 1 week, or freeze it for up to 3 months. Thaw overnight in the refrigerator, then stir well and use it to bake another batch of cake pops.

To ensure that the cake pops bake into perfect rounds, always fill the wells completely.

¼ cup	cornstarch	60 mL
⅔ cup	cold water	150 mL
2 cups	vegan yellow cake mix	500 mL
⅓ cup	canned pumpkin purée (not pie filling)	75 mL
	Nonstick baking spray	

1. In a large bowl, whisk together cornstarch and water until cornstarch is dissolved. Add cake mix and pumpkin. Using an electric mixer on low speed, beat for 30 seconds or until moistened. Beat on medium-high speed for 2 minutes.

2. Spray cake pop wells with nonstick baking spray. Fill each well with about 1 tbsp (15 mL) batter (see page 25). Bake for 4 to 6 minutes or until a tester inserted in the center comes out clean. Transfer cake pops to a wire rack to cool. Repeat with the remaining batter.

3. If desired, attach sticks to cake pops (see page 27).

Dark Chocolate Brownie Pops

Makes 32 to 34 cake pops

VEGAN RECIPE

These rich and fudgy vegan brownie bites will be a welcome treat anytime you serve them.

Tips

Substitute unsweetened vanilla-flavored soy milk or other non-dairy milk, as desired.

Hot vegan cake pops are especially fragile because they don't contain egg. Be sure to spray the wells thoroughly with nonstick baking spray so that the cake pops are easy to remove. Use the fork tool to remove them, lifting gently from underneath. Be careful not to scratch the nonstick coating.

1 cup	all-purpose flour	250 mL
¾ cup	granulated sugar	175 mL
6 tbsp	unsweetened cocoa powder	90 mL
1 tsp	instant espresso powder	5 mL
1 tsp	baking powder	5 mL
¼ tsp	salt	1 mL
½ cup	unsweetened vanilla-flavored almond milk	125 mL
½ cup	vegetable oil	125 mL
1 tsp	vanilla extract	5 mL
	Nonstick baking spray	

1. In a large bowl, whisk together flour, sugar, cocoa, espresso powder, baking powder and salt. Stir in almond milk, oil and vanilla until blended.

2. Spray cake pop wells with nonstick baking spray. Fill each well with about 1 tbsp (15 mL) batter (see page 25). Bake for 7 to 9 minutes or until a tester inserted in the center comes out clean. Transfer cake pops to a wire rack to cool. Repeat with the remaining batter.

3. If desired, attach sticks to cake pops (see page 27).

Applesauce Spice Cake Pops

VEGAN RECIPE

Is there anything more comforting than the classic combination of apples and spice?

Tips

For a fancy presentation, arrange warm Applesauce Spice Cake Pops in a dessert dish and spoon hot cooked apple slices and toasted pecans over top.

Molasses comes from boiling the juice that is extracted from processing sugar cane or beets into sugar. Light (fancy) and dark (cooking) molasses can be used interchangeably in this recipe, but dark molasses gives the cake pops a more robust flavor. Unsulfured molasses (no sulfur was used in the processing) is preferred, as the flavor is lighter.

1¼ cups	all-purpose flour	300 mL
¼ cup	packed brown sugar	60 mL
2 tsp	pumpkin pie spice	10 mL
1¼ tsp	baking powder	6 mL
½ tsp	baking soda	2 mL
Pinch	salt	Pinch
⅔ cup	unsweetened applesauce	150 mL
⅓ cup	unsulfured dark (cooking) molasses	75 mL
¼ cup	vegetable oil	60 mL
1 tsp	vanilla extract	5 mL
	Nonstick baking spray	

1. In a large bowl, whisk together flour, brown sugar, pumpkin pie spice, baking powder, baking soda and salt. Stir in applesauce, molasses, oil and vanilla until moistened.

2. Spray cake pop wells with nonstick baking spray. Fill each well with about 1 tbsp (15 mL) batter (see page 25). Bake for 4 to 6 minutes or until a tester inserted in the center comes out clean. Transfer cake pops to a wire rack to cool. Repeat with the remaining batter.

3. If desired, attach sticks to cake pops (see page 27).

Decorating Tips

- Sprinkle the hot cake pops with granulated sugar.

- Glaze the cake pops with a vegan version of Maple Glaze (page 81), substituting almond or soy milk for the dairy milk. Remember, if you plan to glaze your cake pops, leave them off the sticks.

Banana Nut Cake Pops

Makes 28 to 30 cake pops

VEGAN RECIPE

These vegan banana cake pops are moist and wonderful. As an added bonus, you can make this recipe gluten-free, if you wish, by substituting gluten-free all-purpose baking mix for the all-purpose flour.

Tips

Hot vegan cake pops are especially fragile because they don't contain egg. Be sure to spray the wells thoroughly with nonstick baking spray so that the cake pops are easy to remove. Use the fork tool to remove them, lifting gently from underneath. Be careful not to scratch the nonstick coating.

Do you have a Babycakes Rotating Cake Pop Maker? If so, see page 8 for information on using it.

¾ cup	all-purpose flour	175 mL
¾ tsp	baking powder	3 mL
¼ tsp	baking soda	1 mL
¼ tsp	ground cinnamon	1 mL
Pinch	salt	Pinch
⅓ cup	unsweetened vanilla-flavored almond milk	75 mL
½ tsp	white vinegar	2 mL
1	large very ripe banana, mashed (about ½ cup/125 mL)	1
⅓ cup	granulated sugar	75 mL
2 tbsp	packed brown sugar	30 mL
2 tbsp	vegetable oil	30 mL
1 tsp	vanilla extract	5 mL
¼ cup	finely chopped toasted walnuts (see tip, page 98)	60 mL
	Nonstick baking spray	

1. In a small bowl, whisk together flour, baking powder, baking soda, cinnamon and salt. Set aside.

2. In another small bowl, combine almond milk and vinegar. Set aside.

3. In a large bowl, using an electric mixer on medium speed, beat banana, granulated sugar, brown sugar, oil and vanilla for 1 minute. Add flour mixture alternately with almond milk mixture, making three additions of flour and two of milk and beating on low speed until smooth. Stir in walnuts.

4. Spray cake pop wells with nonstick baking spray. Fill each well with about 1 tbsp (15 mL) batter (see page 25). Bake for 5 to 7 minutes or until a tester inserted in the center comes out clean. Transfer cake pops to a wire rack to cool. Repeat with the remaining batter.

5. If desired, attach sticks to cake pops (see page 27).

New England Cornbread Bites

VEGAN RECIPE

These cornbread bites are incredibly delicious and tender, with just a hint of maple sweetness. Your family will be thrilled when you serve a basket of these treats, still warm from the Babycakes cake pop maker.

Variation

Substitute unsweetened almond milk for the soy milk.

⅔ cup	yellow cornmeal	150 mL
⅓ cup	all-purpose flour	75 mL
1 tsp	baking powder	5 mL
½ tsp	baking soda	2 mL
¼ tsp	salt	1 mL
½ cup	unsweetened soy milk	125 mL
½ cup	unsweetened applesauce	125 mL
¼ cup	pure maple syrup	60 mL
2 tbsp	vegetable oil	30 mL
	Nonstick baking spray	

1. In a medium bowl, whisk together cornmeal, flour, baking powder, baking soda and salt. Set aside.

2. In a small bowl, whisk together soy milk, applesauce, maple syrup and oil. Stir into cornmeal mixture just until moistened.

3. Spray cake pop wells with nonstick baking spray. Fill each well with about 1 tbsp (15 mL) batter (see page 25). Bake for 4 to 6 minutes or until a tester inserted in the center comes out clean. Transfer cornbread bites to a wire rack to cool slightly. Repeat with the remaining batter.

Show-Stopping Treats for Parties and Gifts

Valentine's Day 187

Winter Carnival 188

Welcome Spring 190

Easter 192

Christmas 195

Graduation 196

Fourth of July or Canada Day 198

Child's Birthday Party 199

Birthday Party 200

Halloween 202

Romantic Roses 204

Wedding Shower 206

Wedding 208

Baby Shower 210

Congratulations 212

Teacher Gift 214

Tooth Sweet 216

Moving Day 218

Daisy Days 219

Happy Faces 220

Sweet Thanks 221

Treats for Dog Lovers 222

Treats for Dogs 225

Valentine's Day

There is no better way to say "Be my Valentine" than with an elegant bouquet of red rose cake pops.

Tips

The cellophane should extend up out of the top of the vase, so that it partially covers the cake pop sticks. Once all of the cake pops are arranged, fluff the cellophane as needed, then trim off any excess.

You can use any cake pop flavor for any of the arrangements in this chapter, though it is wise to use lighter-colored cakes with white or light pastel candy melts. Bright- or dark-colored candy melts will coat even the darkest cake pops. So have fun — choose your favorite flavor, or mix and match!

Ingredients

	Red candy melts	
12	Red Velvet Cake Pops (page 36 or 38)	12

Materials

12	cake pop sticks	12
1	pastry bag or squeeze bottle, fitted with a fine tip	1
1	straight-sided glass vase (about 3 inches/7.5 cm in diameter and 8 inches/20 cm tall)	1
	Styrofoam block (at least 3 by 3 by 6 inches/7.5 by 7.5 by 15 cm)	
1	24-inch (60 cm) square sheet of green cellophane, plus more as needed for filler	1
4 feet	green tulle (about 6 inches/15 cm wide), cut into 4-inch (10 cm) lengths	120 cm

1. Melt $1/2$ cup (125 mL) candy melts (see page 18) and use to attach sticks to cake pops (see page 27). Freeze cake pops for at least 15 minutes to set. Reserve the remaining candy melts.

2. Add 1 cup (250 mL) candy melts to those left in the cup and melt until smooth. Coat cake pops (see page 29). Set in a cake pop stand to dry.

3. Reheat candy melts, adding more as needed. Use the pastry bag to pipe a swirl in a tight circle on top of each cake pop to resemble a rose bud. Set in the stand to dry.

4. Measure the dimensions of the vase and trim the Styrofoam to fit snugly and be 2 inches (5 cm) shorter than the vase. Center the cellophane over the top of the vase. Place the Styrofoam on the cellophane and gently push it down into the vase so that the Styrofoam rests on the bottom and the top edges of the cellophane fluff out from the top of the vase.

5. Tie a length of tulle in a knot around each cake pop stick. Slide knots up to just below cake pops. Push the cake pop sticks into the Styrofoam, arranging the roses at different heights. Cut additional cellophane into small pieces and press down between the cake pops to fill in as desired.

Winter Carnival

**Makes
1 gift or
centerpiece**

Chase away the winter doldrums with a fun treat. Plan a sledding party and give one of these as a gift to each guest. Or prepare some for yourself and display them as a centerpiece. The little snowman cake pops will make winter your favorite season.

· ·

Tip

Substitute orange sprinkles for the orange-candy-and-chocolate-covered sunflower seeds, or pipe a nose with melted orange candy melts.

Ingredients

	White and dark chocolate candy melts	
3	White Velvet Cake Pops (page 34) or White Chocolate Cake Pops (page 51)	3
3	regular-size chocolate sandwich cookies	3
3	orange-candy-and-chocolate-covered sunflower seeds	3
3	miniature or bite-size chocolate sandwich cookies	3

Materials

3	cake pop sticks	3
1	pastry bag or squeeze bottle, fitted with a fine tip	1
1	decorative coffee mug with a snowman or other winter motif	1
	Styrofoam block (at least 4 by 4 by 5 inches/10 by 10 by 12.5 cm)	
	Red metallic paper shred	
12 inches	red ribbon (about ¼ inch/0.5 cm wide), cut into 4-inch (10 cm) lengths	30 cm

1. Melt ¼ cup (60 mL) white candy melts (see page 18) and use to attach sticks to cake pops (see page 27). Freeze cake pops for at least 15 minutes to set. Reserve the remaining candy melts.

2. Using your fingers, twist regular-size sandwich cookies to separate wafers. Try to keep cream icing intact on one half. Set aside (see tip, at right).

3. Add 1 cup (250 mL) white candy melts to those left in the cup and melt until smooth. Coat cake pops (see page 29), one at a time. Immediately place one cookie wafer, icing side down, on top of each cake pop to make the brim of a hat. Stick a sunflower seed into each cake pop to make a nose. Set in a cake pop stand to dry.

Tip

You'll have 3 chocolate wafers (the halves without icing) left over after you've made the snowmen. You can either eat them (a reward for your hard work!) or crush them for another use.

4. Melt ¼ cup (60 mL) chocolate candy melts. Use the pastry bag to pipe dots for eyes and a curved line of dots for a smiling mouth on each cake pop. Pipe a few dots in the center of each hat brim to secure a miniature sandwich cookie. Set in the stand to dry.

5. Measure the dimensions of the mug and trim the Styrofoam to fit snugly and be about 1 inch (2.5 cm) shorter than the mug. Place Styrofoam in the mug and cover with paper shred.

6. Tie a length of ribbon in a knot around each cake pop stick. Slide knots up to just below cake pops. Push the cake pop sticks into the Styrofoam, arranging the snowmen at different heights.

Welcome Spring

Welcome spring in grand style. Whatever the event — a shower, a garden party, Easter dinner — this centerpiece of cheerful bluebirds will set the scene for spring.

Tip

For yellow birds, substitute yellow candy melts for blue. Use orange-candy-and-chocolate-covered sunflower seeds for the beak and feet.

Ingredients

	Blue, green and dark chocolate candy melts	
3	cake pops (any flavor)	3
6	yellow-candy-and-chocolate-covered sunflower seeds	6
	Paramount Crystals or shortening	
3	white jelly beans	3
	Toasted flaked coconut	

Materials

3	cake pop sticks	3
1	pastry bag or squeeze bottle, fitted with a fine tip	1
1	fine paintbrush	1
1	small decorative flowerpot (about 2 inches/5 cm in diameter)	1
	Styrofoam block (at least 2 inches/ 5 cm cubed)	
	Green paper shred	
12 inches	green tulle (about 6 inches/15 cm wide), cut into 4-inch (10 cm) lengths	30 cm

1. Melt $\frac{1}{4}$ cup (60 mL) blue candy melts (see page 18) and use to attach sticks to 2 cake pops (see page 27). Freeze cake pops for at least 15 minutes to set. Reserve the remaining candy melts. Repeat with 2 tbsp (30 mL) green candy melts, attaching a stick to the remaining cake pop.

2. Add $\frac{1}{2}$ cup (125 mL) blue candy melts to those left in the cup and melt until smooth. Coat one of the cake pops secured with blue candy melts (see page 29). Immediately hold the stick horizontally so that the melted liquid flows down to one spot on the cake pop to create the tail. Stick a sunflower seed on the front of the cake pop to make a beak. Stick two seeds on the bottom to make feet. Set in a cake pop stand to dry. Repeat with second blue cake pop.

Tip

When you're coating cake pops, the candy melts need to be deep enough that you can dip the cake pops straight down into the melts. If you're only dipping a few cake pops, there will be some candy melts left over, but they can be melted again and used another time.

3. Reheat blue candy melts, adding more as needed. Use the pastry bag to pipe wings on the sides of the birds. Set in the stand to dry.

4. Melt 2 tbsp (30 mL) chocolate candy melts, using Paramount Crystals or shortening to thin them (see page 18). Use the paintbrush to paint dots for eyes. Set in the stand to dry.

5. Add $\frac{1}{2}$ cup (125 mL) green candy melts to those left in the cup and melt until smooth. Coat the remaining cake pop. Immediately nestle jelly beans on top for the eggs, then pile coconut around the jelly beans to make a nest. Set in the stand to dry.

6. Measure the dimensions of the flowerpot and trim the Styrofoam to fit snugly and be about 1 inch (2.5 cm) shorter than the pot. Place Styrofoam in the pot and cover with paper shred.

7. Tie a length of tulle in a knot around each cake pop stick. Slide knots up to just below cake pops. Push the cake pop sticks into the Styrofoam, arranging the birds behind and slightly higher than the nest.

Easter

**Makes
1 centerpiece**

The Easter bunny and gorgeous eggs sit side by side in this darling arrangement. Make several centerpieces and give one to each of your friends and neighbors!

Tips

You can use any cake pop flavor for this arrangement, though it is wise to use lighter-colored cakes. Have fun — choose your favorite flavor, or mix and match!

When you're coating cake pops, the candy melts need to be deep enough that you can dip the cake pops straight down into the melts. If you're only dipping a few cake pops, there will be some candy melts left over, but they can be melted again and used another time.

Ingredients

	Lavender, white, yellow, pink, blue, black and milk chocolate candy melts	
6	Princess Cake Pops (page 28) or Carrot Coconut Cake Pops (page 176)	6
	Sprinkles	
2	almond slices	2
	Paramount Crystals or shortening	

Materials

1	rectangular tin or basket (about 8 by 3½ by 3 inches/20 by 8.5 by 7.5 cm)	1
	Styrofoam block (at least 8 by 3½ by 3 inches/20 by 8.5 by 7.5 cm)	
	Green paper shred	
8 to 10	craft or Popsicle sticks	8 to 10
	Glue	
	White spray paint	
6	cake pop sticks	6
1	pastry bag or squeeze bottle, fitted with a fine tip	1
4	fine paintbrushes	4
7 inches	pastel-colored ribbon (about ¼ inch/0.5 cm wide)	17.5 cm
1	sheet thick white printer paper	1
1	small square pastel-colored card stock (about 1½ inches/4 cm square)	1

1. Measure the dimensions of the tin and trim the Styrofoam to fit snugly and be about 1 inch (2.5 cm) shorter than the tin. Place Styrofoam in the tin and cover with paper shred.

2. Place 2 craft sticks parallel to each other on a work surface, about 2 inches (5 cm) apart. Arrange 6 to 8 sticks perpendicular to the 2 sticks to resemble a picket fence, keeping the overall length to slightly less than the length of the tin. Glue sticks together. Spray-paint both sides of the fence white and set aside to dry.

Tips

It's up to you which eggs you add sprinkles to and which ones you pipe decorations on; these instructions are just a starting point. Decorations in a color that contrasts with the color of the egg look best. Be creative and make this centerpiece look at little different each time you make it!

You may wish to use tiny candy eyes, available at some craft and cake decorating stores, instead of painting them on with candy melts.

3. Melt 2 tbsp (30 mL) lavender candy melts (see page 18) and use to attach sticks to 2 cake pops (see page 27). Freeze cake pops for at least 15 minutes to set. Reserve the remaining candy melts. Repeat with white, yellow, pink and blue candy melts, using each color to attach a stick to 1 cake pop.

For the Eggs

4. Add ½ cup (125 mL) each of lavender, white, yellow, pink and blue candy melts to the corresponding color of melted candy melts. Melt until smooth. Matching the color used to secure the sticks, use each color to coat one cake pop (see page 29). Decorate the white and lavender eggs with sprinkles. Set in the stand to dry.

5. Reheat white candy melts, adding more as needed. Use the pastry bag to pipe decorative swirls (see page 33), spirals (see page 35) or dots onto the yellow, pink and blue eggs. Set in the stand to dry.

For the Bunny

6. Add 1 cup (250 mL) lavender candy melts and a few white candy melts to the cup of lavender candy melts and melt until smooth. Coat the remaining cake pop. Immediately stick almond slices on top to resemble bunny ears. Set in a cake pop stand to dry.

7. Reheat lavender candy melts, adding more as needed and using Paramount Crystals or shortening to thin them (see page 18). Use a paintbrush to paint fluffy-looking fur all over the bunny's head and up the backs of its ears. Set in the stand to dry.

8. Reheat white candy melts, adding more as needed and using Paramount Crystals or shortening to thin them. Use another paintbrush to paint the whites of the eyes and two large front teeth on the bunny's face. Set in the stand to dry.

9. Melt 2 tbsp (30 mL) black candy melts, using Paramount Crystals or shortening to thin them. Use another paintbrush to paint pupils in the eyes. Set in the stand to dry.

Continued, next page…

• •

Tip

Black candy melts may only be available seasonally, for Halloween. Stock up in October, or make your own by stirring a small amount of black oil-based candy coloring into melted dark chocolate candy melts.

10. Melt 2 tbsp (30 mL) chocolate candy melts, using Paramount Crystals or shortening to thin them. Use another paintbrush to paint a mouth, a nose and an outline around the teeth. Set in the stand to dry.

11. Tie ribbon in a bow around the bunny cake pop stick. Slide bow up so it is just below the cake pop.

Assembly

12. Push the picket fence into the Styrofoam at the back edge of the tin. It should just pierce the Styrofoam.

13. On printer paper, write or print "Welcome to the Bunny Patch!" and trim to fit onto the square of colored card stock, making a small sign. Glue paper to stock and let dry. Glue sign to fence.

14. Push the cake pop sticks into the Styrofoam, arranging the eggs and the bunny in front of the fence.

Christmas

You will never again struggle with what to get those special people on your list. Cake pops nestled in a festive holiday bowl make a distinctive holiday gift that combines sweet treats with good taste.

Tips

If desired, use ribbon to tie bows around cake pop sticks.

For added pizzazz, insert two or three holiday-themed picks (such as ornaments, holly leaves or evergreen branches) among the cake pops.

Styrofoam blocks can be purchased at craft stores and come in a variety of shapes and sizes. You may wish to purchase larger pieces and cut off the amount you need for each project.

Check the sale rack for inexpensive yet elegant holiday bowls. Stores may feature one-of-a-kind bowls or samples at reduced prices, and sales are common in the off-season and right after the holiday.

Ingredients

	Red, white and green candy melts	
12	Red Velvet Cake Pops (page 36 or 38)	12

Materials

12	cake pop sticks	12
3	pastry bags or squeeze bottles, each fitted with a fine tip	3
1	decorative holiday candy or serving bowl (5 to 6 inches/12.5 to 15 cm in diameter)	1
	Styrofoam block (at least 6 by 6 by 4 inches/15 by 15 by 10 cm)	
	Red or green paper shred	

1. Melt $1/4$ cup (60 mL) red candy melts (see page 18) and use to attach sticks to 4 cake pops (see page 27). Freeze cake pops for at least 15 minutes to set. Reserve the remaining candy melts. Repeat with white and green candy melts, using each color to attach sticks to 4 cake pops.

2. Add 1 cup (250 mL) red candy melts to those left in the cup and melt until smooth. Coat the cake pops secured with red candy melts (see page 29). Set in a cake pop stand to dry. Repeat with white and green candy melts, coating 4 cake pops in each color.

3. Reheat red candy melts, adding more as needed. Use a pastry bag to pipe decorative swirls (see page 33), spirals (see page 35) or dots onto white and/or green cake pops. Set in the stand to dry. Repeat with white and green candy melts, piping designs in contrasting colors onto cake pops.

4. Measure the dimensions of the candy bowl and trim the Styrofoam block to fit snugly and be 1 inch (2.5 cm) shorter than the bowl. Place Styrofoam in the bowl and cover with paper shred. Push the cake pop sticks into the Styrofoam, arranging the cake pops so that the colors alternate.

Graduation

**Makes
50 cake pops**

When Kathy's daughters graduated from high school, lots of family and friends shared in the celebration. An open house was the perfect way to entertain everyone. What can you serve to such a crowd? Cake pops in school colors are always a hit — a show-stopping decoration as well as part of the menu.

....

Tip

For larger parties, you may want to double the recipe so you have enough for all of the guests.

Ingredients

	Candy melts in two school colors (blue and yellow used here)	
50	Everyday Yellow Cake Pops (page 32) or Almond Cream Cake Pops (page 46)	50

Materials

50	cake pop sticks	50
2	pastry bags or squeeze bottles, each fitted with a fine tip	2
1	beverage tub (about 12 inches/30 cm in diameter and 8 inches/20 cm tall)	1
	Styrofoam block (at least 12 by 12 by 8 inches/30 by 30 by 20 cm)	
	Paper shred in a metallic or complementary color	
16⅔ feet	ribbon (about ¼ inch/0.5 cm wide), cut into 4-inch (10 cm) lengths	500 cm

1. Melt ½ cup (125 mL) blue candy melts (see page 18) and use to attach sticks to 25 cake pops (see page 27). Freeze cake pops for at least 15 minutes to set. Reserve the remaining candy melts. Repeat with yellow candy melts, attaching sticks to the remaining cake pops.

2. Add 1 cup (250 mL) blue candy melts to those left in the cup and melt until smooth. Coat the cake pops secured with blue candy melts (see page 29), melting more candy melts as needed. Set in a cake pop stand to dry. Repeat with yellow candy melts and the remaining cake pops.

Tips

It may be difficult to find a Styrofoam block deep enough for this arrangement, but you can always stack two or three sheets together, securing them with toothpicks or glue designed to adhere to Styrofoam (found at craft and hardware stores). The height of the Styrofoam and the height of the cake pops should work together to make an attractive arrangement in the tub.

Four inches (10 cm) of ribbon is enough to tie a knot on each stick. Allow for more ribbon if you plan to tie bows.

Make sure you have enough cake pop stands to hold this large number of cake pops. See page 20 for more information on stands.

3. Reheat blue candy melts, adding more as needed. Use a pastry bag to pipe swirls (see page 33), spirals (see page 35) or dots onto yellow cake pops. Set in the stand to dry. Repeat with yellow candy melts and blue cake pops.

4. Measure the dimensions of the beverage tub and trim the Styrofoam to fit snugly and be 1 to 2 inches (2.5 to 5 cm) shorter than the tub. Place Styrofoam in the tub and cover with paper shred.

5. Tie a length of ribbon in a knot around each cake pop stick. Slide knots up to just below cake pops. Push the cake pop sticks into the Styrofoam, arranging the cake pops so that the colors alternate.

Fourth of July or Canada Day

**Makes
1 centerpiece**

Celebrate with
fireworks and sparkling
cake pops. Make this
fun centerpiece, then
serve the treats to all
of your guests.

Tips

Prepare extra cake pops
so you can replenish the
centerpiece throughout
the day as guests gobble
them up.

Be creative when selecting
your container. A bright
red or blue children's
sand bucket or a summer
flowerpot might be cute
instead of the box. If you
find a container you like,
but it's not the right color,
spray-paint it.

Add metallic or festive
picks to the arrangement,
if desired.

Be sure to keep the
centerpiece in an air-
conditioned room so the
cake pops don't melt.

Ingredients

	Red and white candy melts	
18	Red Velvet Cake Pops (page 36 or 38)	18
	Red, white and/or blue sprinkles	

Materials

18	cake pop sticks	18
2	pastry bags or squeeze bottles, each fitted with a fine tip	2
1	red decorative box or red bowl (about 6 inches/15 cm cubed or in diameter)	1
	Styrofoam block (at least 6 inches/ 15 cm cubed)	
	Silver paper shred	

1. Melt $\frac{1}{2}$ cup (125 mL) red candy melts (see page 18) and use to attach sticks to 9 cake pops (see page 27). Freeze cake pops for at least 15 minutes to set. Reserve the remaining candy melts. Repeat with white candy melts, attaching sticks to the remaining cake pops.

2. Add 1 cup (250 mL) red candy melts to those left in the cup and melt until smooth. Coat the cake pops secured with red candy melts (see page 29), immediately decorating some of them with sprinkles. Set in a cake pop stand to dry. Repeat with white candy melts and the remaining cake pops.

3. Reheat red candy melts, adding more as needed. Use a pastry bag to pipe swirls (see page 33), tiny dots or a star onto white cake pops without sprinkles. Set in the stand to dry. Repeat with white candy melts and red cake pops without sprinkles.

4. Measure the dimensions of the box and trim the Styrofoam to fit snugly and be 1 inch (2.5 cm) shorter than the box. Place Styrofoam in the box and cover with paper shred. Push the cake pop sticks into the Styrofoam, arranging the cake pops decoratively.

Child's Birthday Party

Any party is sweeter with ice cream cones. With this recipe, those ice cream cones are made out of cake pops!

Tips

Choose a color of candy melts that looks like an ice cream flavor — milk chocolate for chocolate, white for vanilla or pink for strawberry.

For a fun display, select a shoebox or similar sturdy box about 4 to 5 inches (10 to 12.5 cm) high. Turn the box upside down and cut 1- to 1¼-inch (2.5 to 3 cm) diameter holes about 2 inches (10 cm) apart in the bottom. Spray-paint the box to match the party colors and let dry. Set an "ice cream cone" cake pop in each hole.

Variations

Substitute chopped toasted nuts or finely chopped candies for the sprinkles.

For a sundae look, leave the sprinkles off the whole cake pops after dipping. Let the coating dry, then use a pastry bag or squeeze bottle fitted with a fine tip to drizzle milk chocolate candy melts over the cake pop to look like chocolate sauce. Decorate the moist drizzles with sprinkles.

| 9 | White Cake Pops (page 24) or Golden Yellow Cake Pops (page 30) White candy melts | 9 |
| 6 | sugar cones (1¾ to 2 inches/4.5 to 5 cm in diameter) Sprinkles | 6 |

1. Cut 3 cake pops in half. Freeze all cake pops for 15 minutes or until chilled.

2. Melt 1 cup (250 mL) candy melts (see page 18). Using the fork tool, spear one of the cake pop halves, dip it in candy melts and place it in a sugar cone, rounded side down. Set the cone upright in a small glass. Repeat with the remaining cake pop halves and cones.

3. Using the fork tool, spear a whole cake pop, dip it in candy melts and place it on top of a halved cake pop. Immediately decorate with sprinkles. Return cone to glass and let dry. Repeat with the remaining whole cake pops.

Birthday Party

Makes 1 gift

This arrangement of cake pops serves as both a present and a decoration! The recipient will be touched by your handmade gift, and the colorful treats revealed when the lid comes off will brighten up any celebration.

Tips

Cater your gift to the recipient by choosing flavors and colors you know he or she loves.

Some craft stores sell decorative clear plastic paint cans. If you can't find one, look for a wide-mouth glass or plastic jar or food storage container. Another option would be a large, clear plastic cube with a lid, found at some craft stores.

Make sure to use only new, clean craft paint cans. Avoid used paint cans, which would pose a safety issue.

Ingredients

	Red, blue, yellow and white candy melts	
12	cake pops (any flavor)	12
	Sprinkles in primary colors	

Materials

12	cake pop sticks	12
1	pastry bag or squeeze bottle, fitted with a fine tip	1
1	clear plastic paint can or gallon (4 L) jar, with lid	1
1	Styrofoam disk (at least 6 inches/ 15 cm in diameter and 1 inch/2.5 cm thick)	1
	Paper shred in primary colors	
	Happy Birthday stickers	
7 feet	ribbon (about ¼ inch/0.5 cm wide), cut into 7-inch (17.5 cm) lengths	210 cm
12 feet	ribbon (1 to 2 inches/2.5 to 5 cm wide)	360 cm

1. Melt ¼ cup (60 mL) red candy melts (see page 18) and use to attach sticks to 4 cake pops (see page 27). Freeze cake pops for at least 15 minutes to set. Reserve the remaining candy melts. Repeat with blue and yellow candy melts, using each color to attach sticks to 4 cake pops.

2. Add 1 cup (250 mL) red candy melts to those left in the cup and melt until smooth. Coat the cake pops secured with red candy melts (see page 29). Set in a cake pop stand to dry. Repeat with blue candy melts. Repeat with yellow candy melts, immediately decorating yellow cake pops with sprinkles.

Tips

Look for Happy Birthday stickers in the scrapbooking section of the craft store.

When you're coating cake pops, the candy melts need to be deep enough that you can dip the cake pops straight down into the melts. If you're only dipping a few cake pops, there will be some candy melts left over, but they can be melted again and used another time.

To be sure the finished cake pops will fit inside the can, check the height of the cake pop sticks before coating and decorating. Trim the sticks as necessary.

3. Melt $\frac{1}{4}$ cup (60 mL) white candy melts. Use the pastry bag to pipe swirls (see page 33), spirals (see page 35) or dots onto the red and blue cake pops. Set in the stand to dry.

4. Measure the dimensions of the paint can and trim Styrofoam to fit snugly in the bottom of the can. Place Styrofoam in the can and cover with paper shred. Decorate the outside of the can with Happy Birthday stickers.

5. Tie a length of thin ribbon in a bow around each cake pop stick. Slide bows up to just below cake pops. Push the cake pop sticks into the Styrofoam, deep enough that the cake pops will not touch the underside of the lid. Put the lid on the can.

6. Slide the middle of the thick ribbon under the can. Wrap the ribbon ends up to the top of the can and tie a large bow.

Halloween

● ●

**Makes
1 centerpiece**

Set the stage for your spooky party with Halloween cake pops for everyone. Jack-o'-lanterns, mummies, ghosts and Cyclops eyes make for fun holiday treats.

● ●

Tips

Make one of these centerpieces for your child's classroom — be sure to include enough cake pops for every child in the class to have at least one.

You can use any cake pop flavor for this arrangement, though it is wise to use lighter-colored cakes with white or light pastel candy melts. Bright- or dark-colored candy melts will coat even the darkest cake pops. So have fun — choose your favorite flavor, or mix and match!

Ingredients

	White, orange, lavender, green and black candy melts	
18	Cola Cake Pops (page 56) or Spice Cake Pops (page 62)	18

Materials

18	cake pop sticks	18
3	pastry bags or squeeze bottles, each fitted with a fine tip	3
1	ceramic pumpkin or Halloween motif bowl (7 to 8 inches/17.5 to 20 cm in diameter)	1
	Styrofoam block (at least 8 by 8 by 6 inches/20 by 20 by 15 cm)	
	Black paper shred	

1. Melt $\frac{1}{4}$ cup (60 mL) white candy melts (see page 18) and use to attach sticks to 6 cake pops (see page 27). Freeze cake pops for at least 15 minutes to set. Reserve the remaining candy melts. Repeat with orange and lavender candy melts, using each color to attach sticks to 6 cake pops.

2. Add 1 cup (250 mL) white candy melts to those left in the cup and melt until smooth. Coat the cake pops secured with white candy melts (see page 29). Set in a cake pop stand to dry. Repeat with orange and lavender candy melts, coating 6 cake pops in each color.

3. Melt $\frac{1}{4}$ cup (60 mL) green candy melts. Use a pastry bag to pipe a pumpkin stem onto each orange cake pop. Set in the stand to dry.

4. Pipe two green eyes onto each of 3 white cake pops. Set in the stand to dry.

Tips

Black candy melts may only be available seasonally, for Halloween. Stock up in October, or make your own by stirring a small amount of black oil-based candy coloring into melted dark chocolate candy melts.

Want to hand out the cake pops as individual take-home favors? Once they are dry and set, cover each cake pop with a 7-inch (17.5 cm) square of clear cellophane and secure it with ribbon.

5. Reheat white candy melts, adding more as needed. Use another pastry bag to pipe tight crisscross lines (mummy wrappings) over the white cake pops with eyes, avoiding the eyes. Set in the stand to dry.

6. To make Cyclops eyeballs, pipe a large white dot near the top of each lavender cake pop. Pipe jagged streaks from the eyeball down toward the cake pop stick to create a bloodshot look. Set in the stand to dry.

7. Melt $\frac{1}{2}$ cup (125 mL) black candy melts. Use another pastry bag to pipe triangle-shaped eyes and a nose onto the pumpkins, then add a fine line for a mouth. Set in the stand to dry.

8. To make ghosts, pipe black eyes and a round mouth onto the remaining 3 white cake pops. Set in the stand to dry.

9. Pipe a black pupil in the center of the white Cyclops eyeballs. Set in the stand to dry.

10. Measure the dimensions of the ceramic pumpkin and trim the Styrofoam to fit snugly and be 1 inch (2.5 cm) shorter than the pumpkin. Place Styrofoam in the pumpkin and cover with paper shred. Push the cake pop sticks into the Styrofoam, arranging the cake pops so that the characters alternate.

Romantic Roses

**Makes
1 centerpiece**

Create this show-stopping tiered arrangement of cake pop roses for a sophisticated garden fête, a tea party for a special grandmother or anytime you want to set the stage for a stylish occasion.

Tips

It looks especially dramatic to place just one cake pop without a stick on one side of the middle layer, positioned beside a bow with especially long tails.

Inexpensive glass candlesticks and individual pieces of china can often be found at thrift stores, flea markets and estate sales. Even mismatched pieces can combine for an attractive look.

Ingredients

	Pink and white candy melts	
20 to 24	Princess Cake Pops (page 28)	20 to 24
	White sugar pearls	

Materials

12	cake pop sticks	12
1	pastry bag or squeeze bottle, fitted with a fine tip	1
	Strong craft glue, suitable for glass	
2	glass candlesticks (about 4 inches/ 10 cm tall)	2
1	china dinner plate	1
1	china soup bowl or salad plate	1
1	china sugar bowl or cup	1
	Light green tulle	
	Styrofoam block (at least 3 inches/ 7.5 cm cubed)	
12 feet	green ribbon (1/8 to 1/4 inch/3 to 5 mm wide)	360 cm
	Pearl strings	

1. Melt 1/4 cup (60 mL) pink candy melts (see page 18) and use to attach sticks to 6 cake pops (see page 27). Freeze cake pops for at least 15 minutes to set. Reserve the remaining candy melts. Repeat with white candy melts, attaching sticks to 6 cake pops (8 to 12 cake pops will not have sticks).

2. Add 1 cup (250 mL) pink candy melts to those left in the cup and melt until smooth. Coat the cake pops secured with pink candy melts (see page 29). Set in a cake pop stand to dry. Using the fork tool, dip half of the cake pops without sticks and place them on a wire rack set over a sheet of foil or waxed paper to dry.

3. Add 1 cup (250 mL) white candy melts to those left in the cup and melt until smooth. Coat the cake pops secured with white candy melts and immediately sprinkle with sugar pearls. Set in the stand to dry. Using the fork took, dip the remaining cake pops without sticks and place them on the rack to dry.

Tips

You can substitute tiered glass cake pedestals in graduated sizes for the china and candlesticks.

To complement this centerpiece, fill matching teacups with additional cake pops on sticks, decorated to match the large arrangement, and set the teacups around the room. Make enough cake pops so that each guest can eat one at the party and take one home as a favor.

Capture the days of wine and roses. For a beautiful evening, begin with a Romantic Roses centerpiece, then serve a bottle of Champagne, Prosecco or your favorite wine in your best wineglasses. Pure romance.

4. Reheat pink candy melts, adding more as needed. Use the pastry bag to pipe a swirl in a tight circle on top of each pink cake pop (with and without sticks) to resemble a rose bud. Set cake pops with sticks in the stand to dry. Set cake pops without sticks on the rack to dry.

5. Use craft glue to glue one candlestick to the bottom of the dinner plate to form a large pedestal. Glue the other candlestick to the bottom of the soup bowl to form a smaller pedestal. Let both dry.

6. Place the small pedestal on top of the large pedestal. Place the sugar bowl on top of the small pedestal. If necessary for stability, glue everything together. Decoratively arrange tulle over the bottom two pedestal layers.

7. Measure the dimensions of the sugar bowl and trim the Styrofoam to fit snugly and be about 1 inch (2.5 cm) shorter than the bowl. Place Styrofoam in the bowl.

8. Cut ribbon into twelve 7-inch (17.5 cm) lengths (there will be ribbon left over). Tie a bow around each cake pop stick. Slide bows up to just below cake pops. Push the cake pop sticks into the Styrofoam, arranging the roses at different heights. Fill in around cake pops with small pieces of tulle, hiding the Styrofoam.

9. Arrange the cake pops without sticks in the tulle on the middle and bottom layers. Cut the remaining ribbon into 8-inch (20 cm) lengths and tie small bows with long tails. Arrange the bows next to the cake pops so that the ribbon flows off the plates. Drape pearl strings around the cake pops on the bottom two layers.

Wedding Shower

**Makes
6 bouquets**

Cake pops decorated
to resemble roses
will make any bridal
shower memorable and
beautiful. Make one
bouquet for each guest.

Tip
You can use any cake pop
flavor for this arrangement,
though it is wise to use
lighter-colored cakes. Have
fun — choose your favorite
flavor, or mix and match!

Ingredients

	White and pink candy melts	
18	White Cake Pops (page 24) or White Velvet Cake Pops (page 34)	18
	White sugar pearls	

Materials

18	cake pop sticks	18
1	pastry bag or squeeze bottle, fitted with a fine tip	1
6	paper doilies (about 6 inches/15 cm in diameter)	6
	Stapler	
6	2-inch (5 cm) cubes of Styrofoam	6
12 feet	green tulle (about 6 inches/15 cm wide), cut into 4-inch (10 cm) lengths	360 cm
6 feet	pink ribbon (about ¼ inch/0.5 cm wide), cut into 12-inch (30 cm) lengths	180 cm
	Glue	

1. Melt ½ cup (125 mL) pink candy melts (see page 18) and use to attach sticks to 12 cake pops (see page 27). Freeze cake pops for at least 15 minutes to set. Reserve the remaining candy melts. Repeat with white candy melts, attaching sticks to the remaining cake pops.

2. Add 1 cup (250 mL) pink candy melts to those left in the cup and melt until smooth. Coat the cake pops secured with pink candy melts (see page 29), melting more candy melts as needed. Set in a cake pop stand to dry. Repeat with white candy melts and the remaining cake pops, immediately sprinkling white cake pops with sugar pearls. Set in the stand to dry.

Tip

Write the name of each guest on a piece of card stock, then punch a hole in the card stock so the ribbon can be threaded through it before you tie the bow. Place each bouquet on the table and let the bouquet double as both a favor and a place card.

3. Reheat pink candy melts, adding more as needed. Use the pastry bag to pipe a swirl in a tight circle on top of each pink cake pop to resemble a rose bud. Set in the stand to dry.

4. Roll each doily into a cone shape and staple the overlap to hold it together. Place a Styrofoam cube in each cone.

5. Tie a length of tulle in a knot around each cake pop stick. Slide knots up to just below cake pops. Arrange one white and two pink cake pops in each doily cone, pushing the cake pop sticks into the Styrofoam. Use a few extra pieces of green tulle to fill in around each cake pop.

6. Tie each length of ribbon into a bow. Glue a bow over the staple in the front of each bouquet.

Wedding

Roxanne's neighbor Barbara Bins saw Roxanne's treats from the cake pop maker and contracted a severe case of cake pop fever. She provided inspiration for many of the ideas in this chapter. Barbara made these centerpieces of cake pops set in flowerpots for her goddaughter's wedding.

Tips

Assemble enough cake pops in the flowerpot to account for each guest at the table. Encourage guests to take one home as a favor.

If desired, sprinkle some of the cake pops with white sugar pearls or edible glitter. Be sure to sprinkle just after coating and before the candy melts dry.

Ingredients

	White candy melts	
6 to 8	White Cake Pops (page 24) or White Velvet Cake Pops (page 34)	6 to 8

Materials

8 to 10	cake pop sticks	8 to 10
1	pastry bag or squeeze bottle, fitted with a fine tip	1
1	flowerpot (4 to 6 inches/10 to 15 cm in diameter)	1
	Styrofoam block (at least 6 inches/ 15 cm cubed)	
1½ to 3 feet	green tulle (about 6 inches/15 cm wide)	45 to 90 cm
	Straight pins	
6 to 8 feet	white iridescent or pearlized ribbon (½ to ¾ inch/1 to 2 cm wide), cut into 12-inch (30 cm) lengths	180 to 240 cm
1	sheet thick white printer paper	1
	Silver and black card stock	
	Glue	

1. Melt ¼ cup (60 mL) candy melts (see page 18) and use to attach sticks to 6 to 8 cake pops (see page 27), leaving 2 sticks left over. Freeze cake pops for at least 15 minutes to set. Reserve the remaining candy melts.

2. Add 1 cup (250 mL) candy melts to those left in the cup and melt until smooth. Coat cake pops (see page 29). Set in a cake pop stand to dry.

3. Reheat candy melts, adding more as needed. Use the pastry bag to pipe a spiral (see page 35), filigree or dots on each cake pop. Set in the stand to dry.

Tip

Twelve inches (30 cm) of ribbon allows for a nice bow on each cake pop. But you may want to adjust the length depending on the width and stiffness of the ribbon you choose. Smaller bows could be tied with as little as 7 inches (17.5 cm). Experiment with one bow to determine the best look, and trim the ribbon as needed.

4. Measure the dimensions of the flowerpot and trim the Styrofoam to fit snugly and be about 1 inch (2.5 cm) shorter than the pot. Place Styrofoam in the pot. Loosely gather the tulle, then, using straight pins, pin the tulle to the Styrofoam. (Keep the tulle loosely gathered so that it looks full and generously covers the Styrofoam.)

5. Tie a length of ribbon in a bow around each cake pop stick. Slide bows up to just below cake pops. Push the cake pop sticks into the Styrofoam, arranging the cake pops decoratively.

6. On printer paper, write or print the names of the couple and the date of the wedding (position these separately on the page). Cut out a 3- by 1½-inch (7.5 by 4 cm) rectangle, centering the couple's names in the rectangle. Repeat with the wedding date. Cut two 3¼- by 1¾-inch (8 by 4.5 cm) rectangles out of silver card stock. Glue a white rectangle to each silver rectangle, leaving a margin all the way around. Cut two 3½- by 2-inch (8.5 by 5 cm) rectangles out of black card stock. Glue a silver rectangle to each black rectangle, leaving a margin all the way around. Glue one card to each of the remaining cake pop sticks and insert the sticks into the flowerpot.

Baby Shower

**Makes
1 centerpiece
and 6 favors**

Roxanne's dear friend Sheri Worrel created, inspired and encouraged us with many of the ideas in this chapter. When her first grandchild was born, she decorated cake pops for her daughter to hand out at the hospital, and she prepared even more for her son-in-law to distribute at work.

....

Tips

Set the favors upright in a basket or vase by the door to welcome your guests. Remind guests to take one as they leave.

Tie a card to the ribbon on each favor and write a guest's name on the card. Place the favor on the table to serve as both gift and place card.

Ingredients

30	Pink (or blue) and white candy melts	
	Princess Cake Pops (page 28)	30
	White sparkling sugar	
	White edible glitter (or a color that complements pink or blue)	

Materials

30	cake pop sticks	30
1	pastry bag or squeeze bottle, fitted with a fine tip	1
1	silver galvanized bucket or glass vase (about 6 inches/15 cm in diameter)	1
	Styrofoam block	
	Pink (or blue) paper shred	
6	12-inch (30 cm) squares of clear cellophane	6
6 feet	pink (or blue) ribbon (about $\frac{1}{2}$-inch/ 1 cm wide), cut into 12-inch (30 cm) lengths	180 cm

1. Melt $\frac{1}{2}$ cup (125 mL) pink candy melts (see page 18) and use to attach sticks to 15 cake pops (see page 27). Freeze cake pops for at least 15 minutes to set. Reserve the remaining candy melts. Repeat with white candy melts, attaching sticks to the remaining cake pops.

2. Add 1 cup (250 mL) pink candy melts to those left in the cup and melt until smooth. Coat the cake pops secured with pink candy melts (see page 29), melting more candy melts as needed. Set in a cake pop stand to dry. Repeat with white candy melts and the remaining cake pops, immediately sprinkling white cake pops with sparkling sugar. Set in the stand to dry.

Tips

Vary the colors of the candy melts and ribbon. For example, if the mother-to-be is using green and yellow in the nursery, substitute green and yellow candy melts for the pink. Alternate the green, yellow and white cake pops in the centerpiece, then assemble one of each color for the favors and use green or yellow ribbon to secure them.

For a different look, sprinkle all of the cake pops with sparkling sugar or glitter and leave off the decorative lines.

To make a more substantial-looking bouquet for each favor, wrap each cake pop individually in a 7-inch (17.5 cm) square of clear cellophane, then arrange 3 cake pops in a sheet of tissue paper and tie together with ribbon.

3. Reheat white candy melts, adding more as needed. Use the pastry bag to pipe decorative lines, crisscrossing or swirling, over the pink cake pops. Immediately sprinkle the piped lines with glitter. Set in the stand to dry.

4. For the centerpiece, measure the dimensions of the bucket and trim the Styrofoam to fit snugly and be about 1 inch (2.5 cm) shorter than the bucket. Place Styrofoam in the bucket and cover with paper shred. Push 12 cake pop sticks into the Styrofoam, arranging the cake pops decoratively.

5. For the favors, arrange 3 cake pops in a bouquet in the center of each piece of cellophane. Wrap the cellophane around the cake pops, pulling it tight around the sticks. Tie a length of ribbon in a bow around the sticks, securing the cellophane.

Congratulations

Celebrate that "can"-do spirit. This unpretentious gift of a decorated soda can mounted by a single cake pop is a fun way to recognize accomplishments.

Tips

Be sure to use a 6-inch (15 cm) cake pop stick. This length is ideal because it holds the cake pop just above the can.

When you're coating cake pops, the candy melts need to be deep enough that you can dip the cake pops straight down into the melts. If you're only dipping a few cake pops, there will be some candy melts left over, but they can be melted again and used another time.

Ingredients

	Blue, white and red candy melts	
1	cake pop (any flavor)	1

Materials

1	6-inch (15 cm) cake pop stick	1
	Red and white card stock	
1	can of soda	1
	Double-sided tape	
	1/8-inch (3 mm) hole punch	
1	sheet thick white printer paper	1
12 inches	red curling ribbon	30 cm
12 inches	blue curling ribbon	30 cm

1. Melt $1/2$ cup (125 mL) blue candy melts (see page 18) and use to attach the stick to the cake pop (see page 27). Freeze cake pop for at least 15 minutes to set. Reserve the remaining candy melts.

2. Reheat blue candy melts, adding more as needed. Coat the cake pop (see page 29). Set in a cake pop stand to dry.

3. Melt $1/2$ cup (125 mL) white candy melts. Gently dip the cake pop straight down into the candy melts until about two-thirds of the cake pop is covered. Set in the stand to dry.

4. Melt $1/4$ cup (60 mL) red candy melts. Gently dip the cake pop straight down into the candy melts until about one-third of the cake pop is covered. Set in the stand to dry.

Tips

Keep a supply of cake pops in the freezer so you can quickly make one of these gifts any time you want to recognize someone's achievement.

As an alternative, use an empty soda can and decorate as directed. Insert several decorated cake pops into the opening of the can.

5. Cut a $9\frac{1}{2}$- by 3-inch (24 by 7.5 cm) rectangle out of red card stock. Wrap it around the can, making a sleeve, and secure it with double-sided tape. To create a holder for the cake pop, cut a 3- by $2\frac{1}{2}$-inch (7.5 by 6 cm) rectangle out of red card stock. Fold back a $\frac{3}{4}$-inch (2 cm) portion of the card stock along the narrow end. Punch two holes, about 1 inch (2.5 cm) apart, in the folded portion. Use double-sided tape to secure the holder to the sleeve, positioning it so that the hole-punched portion extends outward from the can.

6. On printer paper, write or print "Success comes in CANS (not can'ts). Congratulations!" Cut out a 4- by $2\frac{1}{2}$-inch (10 by 6 cm) rectangle, centering the words in the rectangle. Use double-sided tape to stick the rectangle to the paper sleeve, in front of the holder.

7. Tie the red ribbon in a knot around the cake pop stick. Slide the knot up so it is just below the cake pop. Use a scissors blade to curl the ribbon. Repeat with the blue ribbon. Slide the cake pop stick through the holes in the card stock holder.

Teacher Gift

Makes 1 gift

Any teacher of young students will love this creative, colorful gift — scrumptious "kid" cake pops peek-a-booing out of a new box of crayons that the class can use after the treats are gone.

Tips

You can change the ratio of boys to girls; simply adjust the amount of ribbon or scalloped collars as needed. You can also vary the colors used for the hair, eyes, hair bows and other details.

For added fun, decorate one of the cake pops to look like your child.

If you don't have a paper punch, trace circles on the card stock with a 2-inch (5 cm) scalloped circle cookie cutter, then use scissors to cut out the shapes.

Ingredients

	Pink, yellow, white, dark chocolate, milk chocolate and red candy melts	
5	White Cake Pops (page 24) or Orange Cream Cake Pops (page 44)	5
	Paramount Crystals or shortening	

Materials

5	cake pop sticks	5
2	pastry bags or squeeze bottles, each fitted with a fine tip	2
2	fine paintbrushes	2
21 inches	black ribbon (about ¼ inch/0.5 cm wide), cut into 7-inch (17.5 cm) lengths	52.5 cm
	2-inch (5 cm) scalloped circle paper punch (see tip, at left)	
	White card stock	
24 to 30 inches	red tulle (about 6 inches/ 15 cm wide)	60 to 75 cm
1	box of 64 crayons	1

1. Melt ¼ cup (60 mL) pink candy melts (see page 18) and use to attach sticks to cake pops (see page 27). Freeze cake pops for at least 15 minutes to set.

2. To create a mixture the color of a light skin tone, combine equal parts of yellow, pink and white candy melts. For darker skin tones, combine white candy melts with a small amount of milk chocolate candy melts. Melt 1 cup (250 mL) of the combined candy melts. Adjust the tone as desired by adding a little more of one color or another and reheating to melt. Coat cake pops (see page 29). Set in a cake pop stand to dry.

3. Melt 2 to 3 tbsp (30 to 45 mL) dark chocolate candy melts. Use a pastry bag to pipe brown hair (some long, some short) onto 2 or 3 cake pops. Repeat with yellow candy melts, piping yellow hair on the remaining cake pops. Set in the stand to dry.

Tips

To make a balanced arrangement, place the cake pops an equal distance from each other and from the edge of the box.

To create a more elaborate bow, add a few stiffer ribbon pieces, about 3 to 5 inches (7.5 to 12.5 cm) long and in a complementary color, to the knot. If needed, use a drop of glue to hold the bow in place.

4. Reheat dark chocolate candy melts, adding more as needed. Use a paintbrush to paint eyes on the cake pops. Set in the stand to dry.

5. Melt 2 to 3 tbsp (30 to 45 mL) red candy melts, using Paramount Crystals or shortening to thin them (see page 18). Use another paintbrush to paint mouths on the cake pops. Set in the stand to dry.

6. Paint freckles, glasses, rosy cheeks, hair bows or other details as desired, reheating and thinning candy melts as needed. Set in the stand to dry.

7. Tie a length of ribbon in a small bow around the cake pop stick for each of the 3 cake pops that will be "boys." Slide bows up to just below the cake pops, resembling bow ties.

8. Use the paper punch to cut out two scalloped circles from the card stock. Punch a very small hole through the center of each circle. Loosely fold each circle in half, then slide a cake pop stick through the hole in the center until the circle is just below the cake pop, resembling a collar. (These will be the "girls.")

9. Tie the tulle horizontally around the crayon box, finishing with a bow at the front of the box. Open the box and arrange the cake pops inside, sliding the sticks between the crayons.

Tooth Sweet

● ●

Makes 1 gift

After years of visiting the orthodontist, you build a special friendship! Just ask Roxanne. So when the braces come off, thank the doctor with this whimsical gift of two "teeth" in a toothbrush holder. It's also perfect for a child facing braces, someone with an upcoming dental procedure or anyone in need of a giggle.

Tip

Substitute any white- or cream-colored cake pop, such as Almond Cream Cake Pops (page 46), White Chocolate Cake Pops (page 51) or Coconut Cake Pops (page 59).

Ingredients

	White, chocolate and red candy melts	
2	White Cake Pops (page 24) or White Velvet Cake Pops (page 34)	2
4	white jelly beans	4
	Paramount Crystals or shortening	

Materials

2	cake pop sticks	2
2	fine paintbrushes	2
6 feet	silver curling ribbon, cut into 12-inch (30 cm) lengths	180 cm
	Toothbrush	
1	toothbrush holder	1

1. Melt ¼ cup (60 mL) white candy melts (see page 18) and use to attach sticks to cake pops (see page 27). Freeze cake pops for at least 15 minutes to set. Reserve the remaining candy melts.

2. Add 1 cup (250 mL) white candy melts to those left in the cup and melt until smooth. Coat cake pops (see page 29), one at a time. Immediately place two jelly beans near the bottom of the cake pop, on either side of the stick, to form the root of the tooth. (You may need to hold the cake pop upside down for several seconds, holding the jelly beans in place, until the candy melts harden.) Once the jelly beans are firmly secured, set the cake pop in a cake pop stand to dry.

3. Reheat white candy melts, adding more as needed. Coat cake pops again so both the cake pop and the jelly beans are covered. Set in the stand to dry.

Tip

When you're coating cake pops, the candy melts need to be deep enough that you can dip the cake pops straight down into the melts. If you're only dipping a few cake pops, there will be some candy melts left over, but they can be melted again and used another time.

4. Melt 2 tbsp (30 mL) chocolate candy melts, using Paramount Crystals or shortening to thin them (see page 18). Use a paintbrush to paint eyes on each tooth. Set in the stand to dry.

5. Melt 2 tbsp (30 mL) red candy melts, using Paramount Crystals or shortening to thin them. Use another paintbrush to paint a smile on each tooth. Set in the stand to dry.

6. Tie two lengths of ribbon in a knot around the toothbrush and use a scissors blade to curl the ribbon. Tie two lengths of curling ribbon in a knot around each cake pop stick. Slide knots up to just below cake pops. Use a scissors blade to curl the ribbons. Place the toothbrush and the cake pops in the toothbrush holder.

Moving Day

- -

**Makes
1 gift**

Chase away sadness
and make the parting
sweet with this
thoughtful treat of
cake pops packed in
a teensy moving box.

- - - - - - - - - - - - - - - - -

Tips

When you're coating cake
pops, the candy melts
need to be deep enough
that you can dip the cake
pops straight down into
the melts. If you're only
dipping a few cake pops,
there will be some candy
melts left over, but they can
be melted again and used
another time.

If the pieces of paper shred
are long enough, tie a few
in knots around the cake
pop sticks.

Ingredients

	Yellow and chocolate candy melts	
6	Golden Yellow Cake Pops (page 30)	6

Materials

6	cake pop sticks	6
2	pastry bags or squeeze bottles, each fitted with a fine tip	2
1	sheet thick white printer paper	1
	Glue	
1	small brown box (about 4 inches/ 10 cm cubed)	1
	Styrofoam block (at least 4 inches/ 10 cm cubed)	
	Light brown paper shred	

1. Melt $1/4$ cup (60 mL) yellow candy melts (see page 18) and use to attach sticks to 3 cake pops (see page 27). Freeze cake pops for at least 15 minutes to set. Reserve the remaining candy melts. Repeat with chocolate candy melts, attaching sticks to the remaining cake pops.

2. Add $1/2$ cup (125 mL) yellow candy melts to those left in the cup and melt until smooth. Coat the cake pops secured with yellow candy melts (see page 29). Set in a cake pop stand to dry. Repeat with chocolate candy melts and the remaining cake pops.

3. Reheat chocolate candy melts, adding more as needed. Use a pastry bag to pipe crisscross lines, a swirl (see page 33) or dots on each yellow cake pop. Set in the stand to dry. Repeat with yellow candy melts, piping lines, a swirl or dots on each chocolate-coated cake pop.

4. On printer paper, write or print phrases such as "This End Up," "Handle with Care" and/or "Fragile." Cut out rectangles around each phrase and glue to the outside of the box.

5. Measure the dimensions of the box and trim the Styrofoam to fit snugly and be about 1 inch (2.5 cm) shorter than the box. Place Styrofoam in the box and cover with paper shred. Push the cake pop sticks into the Styrofoam, arranging the cake pops decoratively.

Daisy Days

This cheery gift of delicious daisies is suitable for any occasion! And it's easy to make, too.

Tips

A cheese shaker is an inexpensive glass jar with a lid that has holes in it so you can easily shake grated cheese over your meal. Look for them at kitchen shops and discount stores.

You can use any cake pop flavor for any of the arrangements in this chapter, though it is wise to use lighter-colored cakes with white or light pastel candy melts. Bright- or dark-colored candy melts will coat even the darkest cake pops. So have fun — choose your favorite flavor, or mix and match!

Ingredients

6	Lemon Cake Pops (page 40)	6
	Yellow candy melts	
	Vanilla baking chips	
	Lemon drop candies	

Materials

6	cake pop sticks	6
1	glass cheese shaker	1
54 inches	green ribbon (about ¼ inch/ 0.5 cm wide)	135 cm

1. Melt ¼ cup (60 mL) candy melts (see page 18) and use to attach sticks to cake pops (see page 27). Freeze cake pops for at least 15 minutes to set. Reserve the remaining candy melts.

2. Add 1 cup (250 mL) candy melts to those left in the cup and melt until smooth. Coat cake pops (see page 29), one at a time. Immediately arrange baking chips in a ring around the outside of each cake pop to make the petals. Set in a cake pop stand to dry.

3. Fill the cheese shaker with candies and screw the lid back on. Cut a 12-inch (30 cm) length of ribbon and use it to tie a bow around the neck of the shaker.

4. Cut the remaining ribbon into 7-inch (17.5 cm) lengths. Tie a length of ribbon in a bow around each cake pop stick. Slide bows up to just below cake pops. Insert the cake pop sticks through the holes of the shaker, arranging the cake pops decoratively.

Happy Faces

Makes 1 gift		

Smiles are contagious. Bring a smile to someone special with this cute gift that's super-easy to make. Whether it's to say "Have a nice day" or "Thanks a lot," these happy faces are sure to brighten someone's day.

Tips

If the basket is lightweight, top the Styrofoam with polished glass gems or stones (instead of paper shred) for added weight. Or omit the Styrofoam and fill the basket with individually wrapped candies.

Prepare a card with a message such as "Thinking of You," "Get Well," "A Happy Hello" or "Never Underestimate the Power of a Smile." Tie the card to the basket.

Ingredients

	Yellow and dark chocolate candy melts	
6	White Cake Pops (page 24) or Lemon Cake Pops (page 40)	6

Materials

6	cake pop sticks	6
1	pastry bag or squeeze bottle, fitted with a fine tip	1
1	small square basket (about 4 inches/10 cm square)	1
	Styrofoam block (at least 4 inches/10 cm cubed)	
	Yellow paper shred	
42 inches	yellow ribbon (about ¼ inch/0.5 cm wide), cut into 7-inch (17.5 cm) lengths	105 cm

1. Melt ¼ cup (60 mL) yellow candy melts (see page 18) and use to attach sticks to cake pops (see page 27). Freeze cake pops for at least 15 minutes to set. Reserve the remaining candy melts.

2. Add 1 cup (250 mL) yellow candy melts to those left in the cup and melt until smooth. Coat cake pops (see page 29). Set in a cake pop stand to dry.

3. Melt ¼ cup (60 mL) chocolate candy melts. Use the pastry bag to pipe eyes and a smile on each cake pop. Set in the stand to dry.

4. Measure the dimensions of the basket and trim the Styrofoam to fit snugly and be about 1 inch (2.5 cm) shorter than the basket. Place Styrofoam in the basket and cover with paper shred.

5. Tie a length of ribbon in a bow around each cake pop stick. Slide bows up to just below cake pops. Push the cake pop sticks into the Styrofoam, arranging the cake pops decoratively.

Sweet Thanks

●●

**Makes
1 gift**

The words "thank you" are so simple, but they carry such meaning — especially when you add a tasty cake pop treat arranged in a jar full of candy!

●●●●●●●●●●●●●●●●●●●●●●●●

Tips

This gift could also be used to say "Happy Birthday," "Thinking of You" or just "Hello."

When you're coating cake pops, the candy melts need to be deep enough that you can dip the cake pops straight down into the melts. If you're only dipping a few cake pops, there will be some candy melts left over, but they can be melted again and used another time.

Ingredients

	Milk chocolate, red, blue, green, orange, yellow and white candy melts	
6	Brownie Cake Pops (page 54) or Strawberry Cake Pops (page 42)	6

Materials

6	cake pop sticks	6
1	pastry bag or squeeze bottle, fitted with a fine tip	1
1	1-pint (500 mL) canning jar	1
	Candy-coated chocolate candies	
	Red paper raffia ribbon	

1. Melt 2 tbsp (30 mL) chocolate candy melts (see page 18) and use to attach a stick to 1 cake pop (see page 27). Freeze cake pop for at least 15 minutes to set. Reserve the remaining candy melts. Repeat with red, blue, green, orange and yellow candy melts, using each color to attach a stick to 1 cake pop.

2. Add $\frac{1}{2}$ cup (125 mL) chocolate candy melts to those left in the cup and melt until smooth. Coat the cake pop secured with chocolate melts (see page 29). Set in a cake pop stand to dry. Repeat with red, blue, green, orange and yellow candy melts. Set in the stand to dry.

3. Melt $\frac{1}{4}$ cup (60 mL) white candy melts. Use the pastry bag to pipe swirls (see page 33) or filigree on each cake pop. Set in the stand to dry.

4. Fill the canning jar with candies. Arrange cake pops in the jar, using the candies to steady them. Tie the ribbon in a bow around the lip of the jar.

Treats for Dog Lovers

Any dog lover would love to get this treat, featuring three cake pops, each decorated to look like a different dog, popping out from a burlap bag. You can spoil the dog, too, with a batch of Treats for Dogs (page 225).

Tips

Although the instructions for this design look long and complicated, trust us — it's all very easy!

For a simpler design, paint paw prints on coated cake pops, using contrasting colors.

Ingredients

	White, milk chocolate, peanut butter and red candy melts	
3	cake pops (any flavor)	3
3	ring-shaped hard candies (any flavor)	3
4	almond slices	4
	Paramount Crystals or shortening	
2	dark brown candy-coated chocolate candies	2
	Individually wrapped hard candies or caramels	

Materials

	Brown paint	
1	small paintbrush	1
1	small burlap bag (just large enough to hold the jar)	1
3	cake pop sticks	3
3	pastry bags or squeeze bottles, each fitted with a fine tip	3
3	fine paintbrushes	3
1	small jar (such as a 1-pint/500 mL jelly jar)	1
	Styrofoam block (at least 3 by 3 by 5 inches/7.5 by 7.5 by 12.5 cm)	

1. Using brown paint and the small paintbrush, paint two paw prints on one side of the burlap bag. Set bag aside to dry.

2. Melt 2 tbsp (30 mL) white candy melts (see page 18) and use to attach a stick to 1 cake pop (see page 27). Freeze cake pop for at least 15 minutes to set. Reserve the remaining candy melts.

3. Combine 2 tbsp (30 mL) white candy melts and 2 tbsp (30 mL) chocolate candy melts and melt until smooth. Use to attach sticks to the remaining cake pops. Freeze cake pops for at least 15 minutes. Reserve the remaining light brown candy melt mixture.

Tips

You can use any cake pop flavor for this arrangement, though it is wise to use lighter-colored cakes with white or light pastel candy melts. Bright- or dark-colored candy melts will coat even the darkest cake pops. So have fun — choose your favorite flavor, or mix and match!

A fluffy black dog would also be really cute.

When you're coating cake pops, the candy melts need to be deep enough that you can dip the cake pops straight down into the melts. If you're only dipping a few cake pops, there will be some candy melts left over, but they can be melted again and used another time.

For the White Dog

4. Add ½ cup (125 mL) white candy melts to those left in the cup and melt until smooth. Coat the cake pop secured with white candy melts (see page 29). Immediately slide a ring-shaped candy up the stick to the cake pop, making a collar. Stick 2 almond slices on top of the cake pop to make perky ears. Set in a cake pop stand to dry.

5. Reheat white candy melts, adding more as needed. Use a pastry bag to pipe shaggy fur all over the dog's head and up the backs of its ears. Set in the stand to dry.

6. Melt ¼ cup (60 mL) chocolate candy melts, using Paramount Crystals or shortening to thin them (see page 18). Use a fine paintbrush to paint eyes, a nose and a mouth. Set in the stand to dry.

7. Melt ¼ cup (60 mL) red candy melts, using Paramount Crystals or shortening to thin them. Use another fine paintbrush to paint a tongue. Set in the stand to dry.

For the Brown Dog

8. Add ¼ cup (60 mL) white candy melts and ¼ cup (60 mL) chocolate candy melts to the remaining light brown candy melt mixture and melt until smooth. Coat one of the remaining cake pops. Immediately slide a ring-shaped candy up the stick to the cake pop, making a collar. Stick 2 chocolate candies on the dog's face to make jowls. Stick an almond slice on either side of the cake pop to make ears that stand outward. Set in the stand to dry.

9. Reheat chocolate candy melts, adding more to thicken them. Use another pastry bag to pipe fur onto the almonds, creating long, curly ears.

10. Use Paramount Crystals or shortening to thin the chocolate candy melts. Paint eyes and a nose. Set in the stand to dry.

Continued, next page...

Treats for Dog Lovers (continued)

Tips

Experiment with the melted candy melts to achieve the right consistency for piping details or painting features or fur. Candy melts are quite thin when warm and thicken as they cool. If too thin, the liquid will run as you pipe a detail; if too thick, it will be harder to pipe.

Use a contrasting color to pipe a small figure 8 on the top of a dog's ear to resemble a bow. Place a dot in the center of the figure 8.

11. Reheat red candy melts. Paint a tongue. Set in the stand to dry.

12. Reheat white candy melts, using Paramount Crystals or shortening to thin them. Use another fine paintbrush to paint tiny dots on the jowls.

For the Golden Dog

13. Melt $1/2$ cup (125 mL) peanut butter candy melts. Coat the remaining cake pop. Immediately slide a ring-shaped hard candy up the stick to the cake pop, making a collar. Set in the stand to dry.

14. Reheat peanut butter candy melts, adding more as needed. Use another pastry bag to pipe floppy ears, jowls and eyebrows. Set in the stand to dry.

15. Reheat chocolate candy melts. Paint eyes, a nose and tiny dots on the jowls. Set in the stand to dry.

16. Reheat red candy melts. Paint a tongue. Set in the stand to dry.

Assembly

17. Measure the dimensions of the jar and trim the Styrofoam to fit snugly and be about 1 inch (2.5 cm) shorter than the jar. Place Styrofoam in the jar.

18. Place the jar inside the burlap bag. Push a few candies to the bottom of the bag to add stability. Push the cake pop sticks into the Styrofoam, arranging the dogs at different heights. Fill the bag with candies.

Treats for Dogs

Makes 19 to 21 treats

Roxanne's toy Bichon, Daisy, gave these treats the 100% taste test approval rating. The neighborhood dogs — Bella, Brody, Murray, Newton and Lizzy — gave them high marks too! Make these for all your canine friends.

Tips

Stick the end of a rawhide stick into a small amount of peanut butter and push it into the center of each dog treat. Do not use cake pop sticks.

Frost with peanut butter or light cream cheese.

1 cup	all-purpose flour	250 mL
3/4 tsp	baking powder	7 mL
1	large egg, at room temperature	1
1/2	jar (2 1/2 oz/71 mL) beef and gravy or beef and vegetable baby food (2 1/2 tbsp/37 mL)	1/2
1/3 cup	unsalted butter, softened	75 mL
2 tbsp	olive oil	30 mL
	Nonstick baking spray	

1. In a small bowl, whisk together flour and baking powder. Set aside.

2. In a large bowl, using an electric mixer on low speed, beat egg, baby food, butter and oil until well blended. Beat in flour mixture until combined.

3. Spray cake pop wells with nonstick baking spray. Fill each well with about 1 tbsp (15 mL) batter (see page 25).Bake for 4 to 6 minutes or until browned. Transfer treats to a wire rack to cool. Repeat with the remaining batter.

Cake Pops
Problem Solver

WHEN IT comes to baking, everyone occasionally runs into difficulties. Let us help you by sharing some of the wisdom we learned in the test kitchen.

Problem	Cause	Prevention/Solution
The cake pops don't brown evenly.	The bottoms of the cake pops begin baking slightly before the tops.	A little of this is to be expected, since as you fill the wells of the hot cake pop maker the bottoms of the cake pops will begin baking right away. It will be most evident when you're baking white or light-colored cakes and less obvious with chocolate treats. In general, don't worry about this: the coating will conceal the problem.
The cake pops are not round.	The wells were not full enough.	Fill each well until the batter is level with the top edge of the well. This should take about 1 tbsp (15 mL) of batter.
	The cake mix you chose doesn't make firm cake pops.	Some cake mix brands bake into firmer, more rounded cake pops than others. Experiment to see if you prefer the results of another brand.
	You underbaked the cake pops.	Be sure to bake the cake pops until a tester inserted in the center comes out clean.
	You weren't gentle enough when removing the cake pops.	Lift each cake pop out by slipping the fork tool gently between the cake pop and the edge of the well, then lifting gently from underneath. Gently place the cake pop on a wire rack to cool completely.
The cake pops have ridges.	You overfilled the wells or batter dripped around the wells.	Fill each well only until level full. If you use too much batter, it may seep around the edges of the cake pop as it bakes and form a ridge. Once the cake pops are completely cool, you can gently rub off the ridges.

Problem	Cause	Prevention/Solution
The cake pops stick to the cake pop maker.	The appliance was not clean.	After each use, let the appliance cool completely, then thoroughly wipe the plates clean.
	You forgot to use baking spray.	Spray the wells with nonstick baking spray before each batch, or as needed.
The melted candy melts are too thick or stiff.	You overheated the candy melts.	Microwave in 30-second intervals, stirring after each, just until the candy melts are melted.
	The candy melts have cooled.	Candy melts thicken as they cool, so dip quickly. Reheat in 30-second intervals as needed.
	The candy melts need to be thinned.	Add 2 to 3 tsp (10 to 15 mL) of Paramount Crystals and melt as usual. Or stir 1 to 2 tbsp (15 to 30 mL) of shortening into the melted candy melts.
	You've chosen a thicker brand.	Candy melts vary by brand, and each brand melts a little differently. Experiment to see which brand you prefer.
	Your bowl, cup or spoon is wet.	Water causes candy melts to stiffen, or "freeze." Be sure the spoons, cups or bowls you use are dry.
	You added food coloring or flavoring made with water or alcohol.	Food colorings and flavorings that have water or alcohol in them also cause candy melts to stiffen. Use only those specifically designed for candy melts.
The cake pops are not evenly coated.	The candy melts were too thick.	Make sure to reheat the candy melts in 30-second intervals as needed. See above for other solutions for thinner candy melts.
	You did not dip evenly.	Be sure to dip the cake pop straight down into the candy melts and coat it completely. Lift it straight up, hold the coated cake pop over the cup and let the excess drip off, gently tapping the stick against your fingers. Place the coated cake pop in a stand to dry.

Problem	Cause	Prevention/Solution
The cake pops fall off their sticks.	You didn't chill the cake pops.	Always chill cooled cake pops in the freezer for about 15 minutes.
	You didn't secure the sticks with candy melts.	See the step-by-step instructions for attaching the sticks on page 27. Make sure to chill the cake pops in the freezer for about 15 minutes to secure the stick firmly.
	The coating is too thick.	Dip cake pops in freshly melted candy melts, and dip just once, coating thoroughly. A thick coating may cause the cake pops to break apart.
	You inserted the sticks into a soft filling.	Filled cake pops are fun and flavorful, but some fillings are too soft to hold the sticks securely. Try serving filled cake pops without sticks.
The cake shows through the coating.	You used a glaze to coat the cake pops.	Glazes are generally thinner than candy melts, so the cake may well show through. This is to be expected, especially with thinner glazes.
	The candy melt color is lighter than the cake color.	Make sure the candy melts you choose are a darker color than your baked cake pops.

Resources

The Electrified Cooks, LLC: www.electrifiedcooks.com

Kathy and Roxanne's blog, filled with recipes, tips, classes and more: www.pluggedintocooking.com

Select Brands: www.selectbrands.com

Babycakes: www.thebabycakesshop.com

Cake Decorating Supplies

Beryl's: www.beryls.com

Fancy Flours: www.fancyflours.com

N.Y. Cake: www.nycake.com

Sweet! Baking & Candy Making Supply: www.sweetbakingsupply.com

Wilton: www.wilton.com

Golda's Kitchen (Canada): www.goldaskitchen.com

McCall's: www.mccalls.ca

Kitchen Utensils, Kitchen Equipment, Spices, Serving Platters and Packaging

Bridge Kitchenware: www.bridgekitchenware.com

Crate & Barrel: www.crateandbarrel.com

Sur la Table: www.surlatable.com

Williams-Sonoma: www.williamssonoma.com

Flours, Sugars, Spices, Extracts and Premium Ingredients

C&H Pure Cane Sugar: www.chsugar.com

The Stafford County Flour Mills Co.: www.hudsoncream.com

King Arthur Flour: www.kingarthurflour.com

Land O'Lakes: www.landolakes.com

Penzeys Spices: www.penzeys.com

Sarabeth's Kitchen (we adore her preserves): www.sarabeth.com

Library and Archives Canada Cataloguing in Publication

Moore, Kathy, 1954–
　　175 best babycakes cake pops recipes / Kathy Moore, Roxanne Wyss.

Includes index.
ISBN 978-0-7788-0297-6

　　1. Cake. 2. Cookbooks. I. Wyss, Roxanne II. Title.
III. Title: One hundred seventy-five best babycakes cake pops recipes.

TX771.M655 2012　　　　641.86'53　　　C2011-907440-0

Index

Note: "GF" indicates gluten-free recipes; "VG" indicates vegan recipes.

A

almond bark, 18
Almond Cream Cake Pops, 46
  graduation display, 196
Almond Glaze, 78
almond milk. *See also* soy milk
  Almond Cake Pops (GF), 177
  Banana Nut Cake Pops (VG), 184
  Dark Chocolate Brownie Pops (VG), 182
appetizers, 14, 127–39, 149–55
Applejack Glaze, 84
apples and applesauce
  Apple Ebelskivers, 104
  Applejack Cake Pops, 159
  Apple Pie Doughnuts, 93
  Applesauce Spice Cake Pops (VG), 183
  New England Cornbread Bites (VG), 185
  Rise and Shine Muffins, 121

B

Babycakes cake pop maker, 9, 11–12. *See also* cake pops
  cleaning, 15
  filling wells, 11–12, 25
  rotating models, 8–9
baby shower centerpiece/favors, 210
bacon
  Bacon Cheddar Biscuit Bites, 115

Beer, Cheddar and Bacon Fondue, 147
  Pizza Bites (variation), 134
Baked Pizza Dip, 143
Bakerella cake pops, 8
baking (biscuit) mix. *See also* baking mix, gluten-free
  Bacon Cheddar Biscuit Bites, 115
  Cajun Cornbread Pops, 151
  Firecracker Biscuit Bites, 150
baking mix, gluten-free
  Almond Cake Pops, 177
  Berry Tea Cake Bites, 174
  Carrot Coconut Cake Pops, 176
  Harvest Treats, 178
bananas
  Banana Cake Pops, 58
  Banana Nut Cake Pops (VG), 184
  Banana Nut Muffins, 120
  Bananas Foster Ebelskivers with Rum Sauce, 105
  Chocolate Banana Cake Pops (GF), 173
  Mini Banana Splits, 74
beef
  BBQ Cocktail Meatballs, 137
  Mexican Meatballs, 138
  Spicy Buffalo Meatballs, 155
  Swedish Meatballs, 139
  Taco Dip, 146
  Treats for Dogs, 225
beer
  Beer, Cheddar and Bacon Fondue, 147
  Brewmaster's Chocolate Cake Pops, 160
Beignets, 99

berries
  Berry Tea Cake Bites (GF), 174
  Blueberry Doughnuts, 94
  Glazed Strawberry Doughnuts, 96
  Lemon Blueberry Ebelskivers, 106
  Mini Dutch Babies, 124
  Rise and Shine Muffins, 121
  Strawberry Shortcakes, 73
birthday party treats, 199–201
  birthday party gift, 200
biscuit bites, 112–15, 122, 150
Biscuits and Gravy, 113
blueberries. *See* berries
Blue Cheese Dipping Sauce, 141
Bourbon Glaze, Tennessee, 84
Brat Rolls, 135
Brewmaster's Chocolate Cake Pops,
  160
Brownie Cake Pops, 54
  Sweet Thanks gift, 221
Buffalo Chicken Dumplings, 154
butter, 16
buttermilk, 17
  Apple Ebelskivers, 104
  Cajun Cornbread Pops, 151
  Cherry Almond Ebelskivers, 103
  Chocolate Banana Cake Pops (GF),
    173
  Chocolate Cake Pops (GF), 171
  Chocolate Cake Pops, Old-
    Fashioned, 26
  Chocolate Chip Cake Pops, 52
  Cinnamon Candy Cake Pops, 157
  Confetti Doughnuts, 95
  Devil's Food Cake Pops, 53
  Gingerbread Cake Pops, 63
  Hush Puppies, 132
  Lemon Blueberry Ebelskivers, 106
  Lemon Thyme Biscuit Bites, 114
  Maple Nut Doughnuts, 98
  Old-Fashioned Buttermilk
    Doughnuts, 91

Pancake Bites, 123
Red Velvet Cake Pops, Classic, 38
Red Velvet Cake Pops, Easy, 36
Red Velvet Cake Pops, Easy (GF),
  172
Ricotta Herb Ebelskivers, 110
Sour Cream and Buttermilk
  Ebelskivers, 101
Southern Biscuit Bites, 112
Spice Cake Pops, 62

C

Cajun Cornbread Pops, 151
cake mix, 11, 13. *See also specific
  types (below)*
cake mix, chocolate and devil's food
  Chocolate Banana Cake Pops (GF),
    173
  Chocolate Cake Pops (GF), 171
  Cola Cake Pops, 56
  Cream-Filled Chocolate Cake
    Pops, 66
  Easy Red Velvet Cake Pops, 36
cake mix, white and vanilla
  Almond Cream Cake Pops, 46
  Champagne Cake Pops, 161
  Cinnamon Candy Cake Pops, 157
  Confetti Doughnuts, 95
  Glazed Strawberry Doughnuts, 96
  Key Lime Cake Pops, 71
  Princess Cake Pops, 28
  Strawberry Cake Pops, 42
  White Chocolate Cake Pops, 51
  White Velvet Cake Pops, 34
cake mix, yellow
  Coconut Cake Pops, 59
  Easy Red Velvet Cake Pops (GF),
    172
  Easy Yellow Cake Pops (VG), 181
  Everyday Yellow Cake Pops, 32
  Lemon Cake Pops (GF), 175

Orange Cream Cake Pops, 44
Peanut Butter Cake Pops, 60
Rum Cake Pops, 163
cake pops, 8, 13. *See also* Babycakes
    cake pop maker; cake pops,
    decorating
  baking, 12
  chilling, 12–13
  coatings for, 77–84
  displaying, 21–22
  drying, 20–21
  equipment for, 19, 20–21, 229
  filling, 48
  fillings for, 85–86
  glazes for, 77–84
  glazing, 13
  gluten-free, 171–80
  ingredients for, 16–18
  problems with, 226–28
  sticks for, 19, 27, 228
  storing, 14–15
  upside-down, 48
  vegan, 181–85
  wrapping, 22
cake pops, decorating, 20, 41
  coating, 13, 29, 33, 37, 39
  equipment for, 19
  faces and hair, 45, 47
  glitter, 33
  marbleizing, 39
  rose buds, 43
  for special occasions, 187–225
  sprinkles, 18, 31
  sugar-coating, 35, 48
  supplies for, 17–18, 229
  swirls, 33
  tips, 48
Canada Day centerpiece, 198
candies (as ingredient)
  Caramel Cake Pops (variation), 61
  Chocolate Malt Cake Pops, 67
  Cinnamon Candy Glaze, 82

Thin Mint Cake Pops, 68
Treats for Dog Lovers, 222
candy melts, 17–18, 227
Caramel Cake Pops, 61
Caramel Glaze, 84
Carrot Coconut Cake Pops (GF), 176
  Easter centerpiece, 192
Champagne Cake Pops, 161
Champagne Glaze, 83
cheese. *See also* cheese, Cheddar;
    cream cheese
  Baked Pizza Dip, 143
  Blue Cheese Dipping Sauce, 141
  Buffalo Chicken Dumplings, 154
  Creamy Spinach Artichoke Dip,
    144
  Firecracker Biscuit Bites, 150
  Italian Rice Balls (GF), 180
  Mexican Spinach Cheese Dip, 145
  Ricotta Herb Ebelskivers, 110
  Rosemary and Goat Cheese
    Morsels (GF), 179
  Sausage Bites (variation), 135
  Savory Peppered Cheese Muffins,
    117
cheese, Cheddar
  Bacon Cheddar Biscuit Bites, 115
  Beer, Cheddar and Bacon Fondue,
    147
  Cajun Cornbread Pops, 151
  Cheese Bites, 133
  Jalapeño, Corn and Cheese
    Morsels, 152
  Jalapeño Poppers, 150
  Olive Cheese Bites, 134
  Southern Cayenne Cheese Bites,
    149
  Taco Dip, 146
Cheesecake Surprise Cake Pops, 72
cherry. *See also* berries
  Cherry Almond Ebelskivers, 103
  Cherry Cake Pops, 57

cherry (*continued*)
  Chocolate Cherry Cake Pops, 69
  Strawberry Cake Pops (variation),
    42
Chicken Wonton Cups, Pesto, 129
chocolate. *See also* cake mix,
    chocolate and devil's food; cocoa
    powder
  Brownie Cake Pops, 54
  Chocolate Cherry Cake Pops, 69
  Chocolate Chip Cake Pops, 52
  Chocolate Chip Ebelskivers,
    109
  Chocolate Ganache Filling, 86
  Chocolate Malt Cake Pops, 67
  Chocolate Truffle Cake Pops, 70
  Easy Frosting Coating, 77
  Mexican Chocolate Chile Cake
    Pops, 156
  Neapolitan Cake Pops, 65
  Root Beer Cake Pops, 55
  Thin Mint Cake Pops, 68
  White Chocolate Cake Pops, 51
  White Chocolate Glaze, 79
Christmas gift, 195
Cinnamon Candy Cake Pops, 157
Cinnamon Candy Glaze, 82
Classic Red Velvet Cake Pops, 38
cocoa powder. *See also* chocolate
  Brewmaster's Chocolate Cake
    Pops, 160
  Chocolate Cake Pops, Old-
    Fashioned, 26
  Chocolate Doughnuts, 92
  Chocolate Glaze, 78
  Dark Chocolate Brownie Pops
    (VG), 182
  Devil's Food Cake Pops, 53
  Red Velvet Cake Pops, Classic,
    38
  Red Velvet Cake Pops, Easy (GF),
    172

coconut
  Carrot Coconut Cake Pops (GF),
    176
  Coconut Cake Pops, 59
  Piña Colada Cake Pops, 166
coffee
  Chocolate Cake Pops, Old-
    Fashioned, 26
  Chocolate Doughnuts, 92
  Chocolate Truffle Cake Pops, 70
  Dark Chocolate Brownie Pops
    (VG), 182
  Devil's Food Cake Pops, 53
cola
  Cola Cake Pops, 56
  Cola Glaze, 78
  Halloween centerpiece, 202
  Root Beer Glaze (variation), 82
  Rum and Cola Cake Pops, 164
Confetti Doughnuts, 95
congratulations gift, 212
cornmeal
  Cajun Cornbread Pops, 151
  Hush Puppies, 132
  Jalapeño, Corn and Cheese
    Morsels, 152
  New England Cornbread Bites
    (VG), 185
crabmeat
  Crab Cake Bites, 136
  Creamy Crab Wonton Cups, 128
  Thai Crab Bites, 153
cranberries. *See* berries
cream. *See also* cream cheese
  Chocolate Ganache Filling, 86
  Mexican Spinach Cheese Dip,
    145
  Mini Ice Cream Sandwich
    Sundaes, 75
  Mini Scones, 116
  Strawberry Shortcakes, 73
  Tennessee Bourbon Glaze, 84

cream cheese, 17
   Baked Pizza Dip, 143
   Buffalo Chicken Dumplings, 154
   Cream Cheese Filling, 85
   Cream Cheese Glaze, 77
   Creamy Crab Wonton Cups, 128
   Creamy Spinach Artichoke Dip, 144
   Key Lime Dipping Sauce, 85
Cream-Filled Chocolate Cake Pops, 66
Cream Puff Bites, 99

D

Daisy Day gift, 219
Dark Chocolate Brownie Pops (VG), 182
Devil's Food Cake Pops, 53
dinner rolls, frozen (as ingredient)
   Brat Rolls, 135
   Cheese Bites, 133
   Dinner Roll Bites, 127
   Garlic Bread Bites, 133
   Jalapeño Poppers, 150
   Pizza Bites, 134
   Sausage Bites, 135
dips and dipping sauces
   savory, 141–47
   sweet, 85
doughnuts, 14, 15, 89–99

E

Easter centerpiece, 192
Easy Frosting Coating, 77
Easy Red Velvet Cake Pops, 36
Easy Red Velvet Cake Pops (GF), 172
Easy Yellow Cake Pops (VG), 181
ebelskivers, 14, 15, 101–10
eggs, 16
Everyday Yellow Cake Pops, 32

F

Filled Breakfast Bites, 122
Firecracker Biscuit Bites, 150
flour, 16
flour, whole wheat
   Honey Wheat Mini Rolls, 131
   Rise and Shine Muffins, 121
fondant, 48
Fourth of July centerpiece, 198
French Toast Doughnuts, 97
French Toast Glaze, 81
Frosting Coating, Easy, 77

G

Garlic Bread Bites, 133
gifts, 187–88, 195, 200, 212–21
ginger
   Gingerbread Cake Pops, 63
   Thai Crab Bites, 153
   Wasabi Mayo Sauce, 142
Glazed Strawberry Doughnuts, 96
glazes, 77–84
gluten-free recipes
   Almond Cake Pops, 177
   Berry Tea Cake Bites, 174
   Carrot Coconut Cake Pops, 176
   Chocolate Banana Cake Pops, 173
   Chocolate Cake Pops, 171
   Easy Red Velvet Cake Pops, 172
   Harvest Treats, 178
   Italian Rice Balls, 180
   Lemon Cake Pops, 175
   Rosemary and Goat Cheese Morsels, 179
Golden Yellow Cake Pops, 30
   child's birthday party treats, 199
   moving day gift, 218
graduation display, 196

H

Halloween centerpiece, 202
Happy Faces gift, 220
Harvest Treats (GF), 178
herbs
    Homemade Bread Bites (variation),
      130
    Lemon Thyme Biscuit Bites, 114
    Ricotta Herb Ebelskivers, 110
    Rosemary and Goat Cheese
      Morsels (GF), 179
Homemade Bread Bites, 130
Honey Mustard Dipping Sauce,
    141
Honey Wheat Mini Rolls, 131
Hush Puppies, 132

I

Ice Cream Sandwich Sundaes,
    Mini, 75
Italian Rice Balls (GF), 180

J

Jalapeño, Corn and Cheese Morsels,
    152
Jalapeño Poppers, 150
jams and jellies
    Filled Breakfast Bites, 122
    Pancake Bites, 123

K

Kahlúa Cake Pops, 169
Kahlúa Glaze, 78
Key Lime Cake Pops, 71
Key Lime Dipping Sauce, 85

L

lemon. *See also* Lemon Cake Pops
    Lemon Blueberry Ebelskivers, 106

Lemon Glaze, 80
    Lemon Poppy Seed Muffins, 118
    Lemon Thyme Biscuit Bites, 114
    Limoncello Cake Pops, 162
Lemon Cake Pops, 75
    Daisy Days gift, 219
    gluten-free, 175
    Happy Faces gift, 220
    Mini Ice Cream Sandwich Sundaes
      (variation), 75
lime
    Key Lime Cake Pops, 71
    Key Lime Dipping Sauce, 85
    Margarita Cake Pops, 168
    Mojito Cake Pops, 165
    Orange Glaze (variation), 80
    Taco Dip, 146
liqueurs
    Kahlúa Cake Pops, 169
    Kahlúa Glaze, 78
    Limoncello Cake Pops, 162
    Limoncello Glaze, 83
    Orange Glaze (variation), 80

M

Malt Cake Pops, Chocolate, 67
maple
    French Toast Glaze, 81
    Harvest Treats (GF), 178
    Maple Ebelskivers, 108
    Maple Glaze, 81
    Maple Nut Doughnuts, 98
    New England Cornbread Bites
      (VG), 185
    Pancake Bites, 123
Margarita Cake Pops, 168
Margarita Glaze, 80
Marshmallow Cream Filling, 86
mayonnaise
    Creamy Spinach Artichoke Dip,
      144
    Wasabi Mayo Sauce, 142

meatballs, 137–39

Mexican Chocolate Chile Cake Pops, 156

Mexican Meatballs, 138

Mexican Spinach Cheese Dip, 145

Milk and Cinnamon Ebelskivers, 102

  Bananas Foster Ebelskivers with Rum Sauce, 105

Mini Banana Splits, 74

Mini Dutch Babies, 124

Mini Ice Cream Sandwich Sundaes, 75

Mini Scones, 116

Mocha Doughnuts, 92

Mojito Cake Pops, 165

Mojito Glaze, 80

molasses

  Applesauce Spice Cake Pops (VG), 183

  Gingerbread Cake Pops, 63

moving day gift, 218

muffins, 14, 15, 117–21

mustard

  Beer, Cheddar and Bacon Fondue, 147

  Honey Mustard Dipping Sauce, 141

N

Neapolitan Cake Pops, 65

New England Cornbread Bites (VG), 185

nuts. *See also* pecans

  Applejack Cake Pops (variation), 159

  Banana Nut Cake Pops (VG), 184

  Cherry Almond Ebelskivers, 103

  Maple Nut Doughnuts, 98

  Rosemary and Goat Cheese Morsels (GF), 179

O

Old-Fashioned Buttermilk Doughnuts, 91

Old-Fashioned Chocolate Cake Pops, 26

  Kahlúa Cake Pops, 169

  Mini Ice Cream Sandwich Sundaes, 75

Olive Cheese Bites, 134

onions

  Hush Puppies (variation), 132

  Onion Dip, 143

orange juice

  Margarita Cake Pops, 168

  Orange Cream Cake Pops, 44

  Orange Glaze, 80

  teacher gift, 214

P

Pancake Bites, 123

pastry bags, 19

Peanut Butter Cake Pops, 60

pecans

  Banana Nut Muffins, 120

  Carrot Coconut Cake Pops (GF), 176

  Cola Cake Pops, 56

  Maple Ebelskivers (variation), 108

  Rise and Shine Muffins, 121

  Rum Cake Pops, 163

  Southern Cayenne Cheese Bites, 149

peppers

  Bacon Cheddar Biscuit Bites (variation), 115

  Cajun Cornbread Pops, 151

  Jalapeño, Corn and Cheese Morsels, 152

  Jalapeño Poppers, 150

  Mexican Meatballs (variation), 138

peppers (continued)
  Mexican Spinach Cheese Dip, 145
  Savory Peppered Cheese Muffins, 117
Pesto Chicken Wonton Cups, 129
pineapple
  Mini Banana Splits, 74
  Orange Glaze (variation), 80
  Piña Colada Cake Pops, 166
  Piña Colada Glaze, 80
  Tropical Muffins, 119
Pizza Bites, 134
Princess Cake Pops, 28
  baby shower centerpiece/favors, 210
  Easter centerpiece, 192
  Mini Ice Cream Sandwich Sundaes (variation), 75
  Romantic Roses centerpiece, 204
pudding (as ingredient)
  Beignets (variation), 99
  Champagne Cake Pops, 161
  Cola Cake Pops, 56
  Princess Cake Pops, 28
pumpkin purée
  Easy Yellow Cake Pops (VG), 181
  Harvest Treats (GF), 178
  Pumpkin Ebelskivers, 107

R

Raised Glazed Doughnuts, 89
Red Velvet Cake Pops
  Christmas gift, 195
  Classic, 38
  Easy, 36
  Easy (GF), 172
  Fourth of July/Canada Day centerpiece, 198
  Mini Ice Cream Sandwich Sundaes (variation), 75
  Valentine's Day gift, 187

Rice Balls, Italian (GF), 180
Ricotta Herb Ebelskivers, 110
Rise and Shine Muffins, 121
Romantic Roses centerpiece, 204
Root Beer Cake Pops, 55
Root Beer Glaze, 82
Rosemary and Goat Cheese Morsels (GF), 179
rum
  Bananas Foster Ebelskivers with Rum Sauce, 105
  Mojito Cake Pops, 165
  Orange Glaze (variation), 80
  Piña Colada Cake Pops, 166
  Rum and Cola Cake Pops, 164
  Rum Cake Pops, 163
  Rum Glaze, 84

S

sausage
  Biscuits and Gravy, 113
  Brat Rolls, 135
  Pizza Bites, 134
  Sausage Bites, 135
Savory Peppered Cheese Muffins, 117
Scones, Mini, 116
sour cream, 17
  Applejack Cake Pops, 159
  Blue Cheese Dipping Sauce, 141
  Brewmaster's Chocolate Cake Pops, 160
  Buttermilk Doughnuts, Old-Fashioned (variation), 91
  Caramel Cake Pops, 61
  Chocolate Cherry Cake Pops, 69
  Chocolate Chip Ebelskivers, 109
  Chocolate Doughnuts, 92
  Chocolate Truffle Cake Pops, 70
  Creamy Spinach Artichoke Dip, 144
  Firecracker Biscuit Bites, 150

Honey Mustard Dipping Sauce, 141

Lemon Blueberry Ebelskivers, 106

Mexican Chocolate Chile Cake Pops, 156

Neapolitan Cake Pops, 65

Onion Dip, 143

Rosemary and Goat Cheese Morsels (GF), 179

Sour Cream and Buttermilk Ebelskivers, 101

Sour Cream Doughnuts, 90

Swedish Meatballs, 139

Taco Dip, 146

Thin Mint Cake Pops, 68

Tropical Muffins, 119

White Velvet Cake Pops, 34

Southern Biscuit Bites, 112

Biscuits and Gravy, 113

Southern Cayenne Cheese Bites, 149

soy milk. *See also* almond milk

New England Cornbread Bites (VG), 185

Spice Cake Pops, 62

Halloween centerpiece, 202

Mini Ice Cream Sandwich Sundaes (variation), 75

Spicy Buffalo Meatballs, 155

spinach

Creamy Spinach Artichoke Dip, 144

Mexican Spinach Cheese Dip, 145

sprinkles, 18, 31

strawberry

Glazed Strawberry Doughnuts, 96

Mini Banana Splits, 74

Neapolitan Cake Pops, 65

Strawberry Cake Pops, 42

Strawberry Glaze, 79

Strawberry Shortcakes, 73

Sweet Thanks gift, 221

sugar, 16

coating with, 35, 48

sundae syrup

Mini Banana Splits, 74

Mini Ice Cream Sandwich Sundaes, 75

Swedish Meatballs, 139

Sweet Thanks gift, 221

T

Taco Dip, 146

teacher gift, 214

Tennessee Bourbon Glaze, 84

Tex-Mex Rolls, 130

Thai Crab Bites, 153

Thin Mint Cake Pops, 68

tomatoes and tomato sauces

Baked Pizza Dip, 143

BBQ Cocktail Meatballs, 137

Mexican Meatballs, 138

Pizza Bites, 134

Taco Dip, 146

Tooth Sweet gift, 216

Tortilla Scoopers, 127

Treats for Dog Lovers, 222

Treats for Dogs, 225

Tropical Muffins, 119

V

Valentine's Day gift, 187

vanilla, 17

Vanilla Glaze, 78

vegan recipes

Applesauce Spice Cake Pops, 183

Banana Nut Cake Pops, 184

Dark Chocolate Brownies, 182

Easy Yellow Cake Pops, 181

New England Cornbread Bites, 185

vegetables. *See also specific vegetables*
   Creamy Spinach Artichoke Dip,
      144
   Jalapeño, Corn and Cheese
      Morsels, 152
   Pesto Chicken Wonton Cups, 129
   Spicy Buffalo Meatballs, 155
   Taco Dip, 146

W

walnuts
   Banana Nut Cake Pops (VG),
      184
   Maple Nut Doughnuts, 98
   Rosemary and Goat Cheese
      Morsels (GF), 179
Wasabi Mayo Sauce, 142
wedding centerpiece, 208
wedding shower treats, 206
Welcome Spring centerpiece, 190
White Cake Pops, 24
   child's birthday party treats, 199
   Happy Faces gift, 220
   teacher gift, 214
   Tooth Sweet gift, 216
   wedding centerpiece, 208
   wedding shower treats, 206

White Chocolate Cake Pops, 51
   Winter Carnival gift/centerpiece,
      188
White Chocolate Glaze, 79
White Velvet Cake Pops, 34
   Tooth Sweet gift, 216
   wedding centerpiece, 208
   wedding shower treats, 206
   Winter Carnival gift/centerpiece,
      188
wine. *See* Champagne
Winter Carnival gift/centerpiece,
   188
wonton wrappers
   Buffalo Chicken Dumplings,
      154
   Creamy Crab Wonton Cups, 128
   Pesto Chicken Wonton Cups,
      129
   Wonton Cups, 128

Y

Yellow Cake Pops
   Easy (VG), 181
   Everyday, 32
   Golden, 30
   graduation display, 196